No One Ever Asked Me That
Conversations on the Afterlife

No One Ever Asked Me That

Conversations on the Afterlife

Catherine Levison

FOREWORD BY DENNIS OKHOLM

ISBN-13: 978-0692248614
ISBN-10:0692248617

Book design © Pink Fish Press

Printed in the United States of America
Second Edition

10 9 8 7 6 5 4 3 2

For my father, his father and their meaningful conversations.

CONTENTS

Foreword

I teach a course on apologetics at a Christian university. I teach it in a somewhat nontraditional manner—less interested in a semester of arguments and more interested in helping my students understand the modern culture milieu in which we swim. I tell them that the subtitle of the course should be, "Apologetics as if people really mattered." In fact, before we even begin to consider what defending the faith might involve, I assign them the task of just *listening* to a non-Christian with a prescribed list of questions, such as, "Is there one major religious issue that you find very difficult to deal with or answer?" or "What do you think of the Christian church today? Is it a good argument for the truth of Christianity or not?"

Perhaps my approach to this course and its first assignment makes it obvious why I would immediately resonate with Catherine Levison's book. She has modeled for us what it means to truly *listen* as if people matter. Her engagement with the Jewish mystic is about as close as she ever gets to sparring, yet even in that conversation she gains insight into her own commitments and how they could stand a bit of course correction. She models attentiveness to the other in a culture of what one person called "continuous partial attention."

Her opening question about our imagination is clever, though it is obvious that her motivation has nothing to do with being crafty since she is genuinely intrigued about this universal aspect of human life. But it's clever in the sense that, because it *is* a feature of our existence that we all share—whether we're a rocket scientist or a teenage dishwasher—it begins to move her dialogue partners past the banal conversations typical of most network talk shows and the rants of talk radio to consider more important issues in life.

In his book *Making Sense of It All,* Thomas V. Morris considers why people are often reluctant to ask the big questions about topics such as God, death, and the afterlife. He suggests several answers, but among them are what he labels the "folly of indifference" and the "danger of diversion." Years ago I read Gareth B. Matthews' fascinating account of *Philosophy and the Young Child* in which he illustrates with real conversations how the questions of children still celebrating single digit birthdays are the kinds of questions philosophers ask (about time, perception, and the like). Then he inquires why we stop asking those questions. Among the reasons are schools that insist students ask only questions the answers to which can be found in encyclopedias, and parents who tell their children to stop "daydreaming" and start thinking about "practical" concerns that will help them get a job.

What Morris and Matthews speak of provides the backdrop for Levison's book and its significance. Anyone who reads through these conversations will be engaging in a pursuit far more significant than what channel surfing and roaming the media often provide, and more interesting than what most of our nine-to-five busy-ness pursuits involve. In fact, I think many readers will find themselves so engaged by some of these conversations that they will catch themselves entering in as third partners, nodding in agreement, talking back, or astonished because "no one ever asked me that."

A side benefit for most readers of these conversations is that they will learn by example how to engage others in meaningful conversations by asking questions in a manner that Levison models for us. It serves to reconnect us as human beings at a time when ATMs, self-serve checkout stands, texting, and ear buds discourage us from full-bodied interaction with people who might be as close as the next cubicle or the one sitting next to us on the plane.

My suggestion: read just one or two of these conversations at a time, join Levison in her curious exploration of what people from all walks of life think, and find yourself revisiting your own thoughts about some of the most important issues that have to do with being human.

Dennis Okholm
Author of *Monk Habits for Everyday People*
Professor of Theology, Azusa Pacific University

Introduction

Most of us enjoy a good conversation full of meaning and interesting topics. As true as that is, at times we fall into boring small talk—which is not only empty, but also a waste of time.

To help bring out the best in people, I created a short series of questions. They were designed to help anyone to become comfortable diving into life's most vital issues even if we had just met. Using these questions I found it did not take much time or effort to have rewarding talks about even serious topics like life after death.

I was not the only one having fun. I found that those who had answered my questions frequently requested another opportunity to talk with me. They were probably deeply relieved to have had a meaningful conversation, but it went further than that. They wanted to know what the questions were so they could use them with other people. Quite often they would report back to me how much depth this approach had brought to their conversations.

You may want to do the same. The questions are provided here, and if you want to simulate the format I used, ask your friends one question at a time in the order they are given. You do not need to reveal the direction you are going in advance. You will find that anyone can answer these whether they think about a possible afterlife fairly often or almost never. I do believe the meaning of life and what follows intrigues most of us. It is something we all wonder about, but often in our busy society we neglect to talk about it.

I was intrigued by the topic from a very early age. One likely reason is due to my grandfather who died in a hospital in 1924. He was only sixteen years old and, if that were the end of the story, I would not have been born to his only son over 30 years later.

After being pronounced dead, he had the experience of leaving his body and had a very remarkable account of overhearing the conversation that occurred in the hall where his mother was informed of his death. He had all the details of that emotional encounter. According to my grandfather, he next went to a beautiful outdoor place with green rolling hills. After considerable time he returned to his body that was by this point covered with a sheet.

Remarkably, there is more. After this event, my grandfather claimed confidently to know the whereabouts of his soul. This was not one passing comment—quite the opposite. He would recount this annually and he left me with something very important to ponder. He never told anyone the location of his soul but insisted that any of us could know if we would spend time seeking. He did not say how that would be done. It is more mystery than anything else, but quite a lot for a seven-year-old child to think about.

Although this is not intended to be a religious book, the questions I used quickly reveals the spirituality (or lack thereof) in each person. You will see that I asked each one about the location of their soul. It seemed like a good opportunity to find out from others what they had come to believe.

One glance at the table of contents reveals the diversity of those who participated. I wanted to talk with a global cross-section of people from all over the world. I searched for people with vastly different educational levels, backgrounds and religions.

Each interview is unique and you will no doubt find some people here that share your beliefs or scientific theories and those who oppose them. You will have favorites, and if you check with your friends, you will very likely find out that your favorite is not theirs. That is because each one is different and reading these various viewpoints may help you to become more understanding of other people. Like most everyone, I have beliefs, but I had no intention of presenting them during the interviews. Ultimately, it was their beliefs I wanted to unveil, not mine. I have provided more insight into my personal thoughts in the conclusion.

About the Topic

Although the questions used in the interviews begin with the topic of imagination, that is not the true subject of the book nor the only focus. It proved to be a successful ice breaker, and it is clear that the topic of imagination, its location, its role in the human life had staying power in the minds of those who later wanted a second conversation.

I think the topic is easy to discuss because it is a non-stop function in every human being—its use continues whether we are exhausted, excited or even asleep. We come fully equipped, not only with the capability to imagine but the natural urge to use it constantly.

We appear to have a choice to exert our will upon imagination or "let it run wild," as the saying goes. It is always there at our disposal. Some people are labeled with an over-active imagination. Who can say if that is a detrimental condition or a rare gifting? Perhaps we all possess an over-active imagination, but due to our private resistance toward its influence or our silence, nobody knows of it.

We all have the use of imagination and it seems to have the use of us. People have changed the world through their imaginations. Visionaries create music and the musical instruments themselves. Theories, with their ensuing philosophies, develop and medical devices are created. Literally thousands of items or inventions exist that were not previously deemed conceivable. Imagination gives birth to ideas that later become books, religions or governmental policies.

We can all imagine or see nonexistent scenarios. We contemplate imaginary futures with both good and bad outcomes. Pregnant women imagine their unborn baby. People imagine themselves falling down stairs, which may cause them to step more carefully. Regardless of their occupation people use their imagination to create the path to achieving their dreams. Imagination is a huge component in human motivation—it is truly fascinating.

The closing chapter includes the results of my self-interview. I recommend you conduct one yourself before you read what others have shared. Try to view only one question at a time and answer fully before looking at the next one.

The Questions

If possible, view one question at a time. Move on to the next only after answering.

What are the purposes of imagination?

What is the origin of imagination?

Where is it located?

Do you take imagination with you when you die?

Whether you believe you have a soul or not, where do you feel you are within your body? Where do you think the "real you" is located?

Supplementary Questions

What part does imagination play in relation to the ability to remember (memories)?

Do animals have imagination?

Can a person have too much or do we all have various amounts?

What do you think is most important in life?

BUILDING DIRECTOR

"The calm man, having learned how to govern himself, knows how to adapt himself to others; and they, in turn, reverence his spiritual strength, and feel that they can learn of him and rely upon him. The more tranquil a man becomes, the greater is his success, his influence, his power for good."
James Allen, *As a Man Thinketh*

I selected this fifty-eight-year-old building director to represent an average man with an average job. He could easily be cast as a quintessential television father. Even his voice and manner of speaking closely mimic a nice, concerned and caring TV dad. His answers, as you will see, are far from conventional and do not match his outer appearance.

His reply to the first question is very interesting in view of what others have shared about linking or building upon prior experiences rather than relying solely on original thought. He also surprised me with a strong inclination toward artistic pursuits with his wood carving. Then he went on to more than surprise me with very creative answers about the location of imagination.

What are the purposes of imagination?
Wow. Imagination is the portal to possibilities...imagination opens doorways. For me it's the linking together of things that would normally not be related. That's how it would work generally for me. I think I have a good creative sense in linking together things that other people wouldn't see as necessarily being linked. Imagination is words that just tumble and somehow at the end they seem to have linked together without any effort whatsoever. Imagination also, to me, is seeing a line or a curve that fits together—a curving line that moves in balance.

I do woodworking, and I noticed one thing I can do is make a graceful shape from wood. For example, I've carved knives that are just amazing. They feel good and they look good, and they are smooth and tactile. They just kind of came out; that was the shape of the piece, and that was how the line flowed. That was how the balance and the feel of my hand was. I've done other things like clocks and music boxes that had perspective and balance. It was something that just showed up. It was really unasked for. It just popped to me.

I like to shop at thrift stores, and imagination has a lot to do with shopping through other people's clothes. You see some wild shirt or some crazy pants or a coat, and you wonder who would have worn that? What would they have worn that with? What would I wear that with? All those things are just possibilities. That's potential by combining things when you don't know where they came from. They pop up and they are a new entity.

What do you think the origin of imagination is?

I know exactly what it is for me. It's a very heartfelt need to leave behind some unique trace of my existence. Why was I here?

I used to make these little boxes. They looked like a little loaf of bread, and they were all made from one piece of wood. I'd take a single block of wood, and I'd band saw the thing in a special way so that it had a curved lid and the sides were curved. I'd cut it so that I could cut out the middle and I could cut the lid. But when I reassembled it, it was nearly seamless. All the cuts were from the original piece. I loved those things. I made a bunch and I gave them away. I really got into it. They were all different kinds of wood. I had a stamp that had a big tree on it. I'd stamp each one with that tree, and I'd put my initials next to it. It was a need for me to get these things out because I knew they would be hard to throw away. They were cool little things, and I had the feeling if I got these things out then I've somehow put a little mark on the world. There would be something lasting there that wasn't there before. Something tangible.

To me the purpose of imagination is simply that. Lots of little things that were not there before—little seeds planted, little objects, little thoughts, influencing people in some way. That's the "leave behind." That's the gift. That's the thank-you for giving me a shot here.

What do you think the location of imagination is?

It's not within me. I have no sense of it coming from mind or heart or belly. It doesn't feel like that at all. It feels like it comes from without and is location unspecific. But in my case it ends up in my hands. I think I'm simply guided, given something to work with, given some kind of format, some kind of material.

I used to believe in this remote being out there, something a long ways away. I've come to think now that I'm surrounded by some kind of a force that guides me to my better moments—probably doesn't stop me from my worst moments as well, but guides me to doing things in a certain way. I have no idea what that is, and I don't know if I'd want to know what that location was exactly. I have great confidence that it's there and it's always been there for me. Anytime I am willing to be guided and to expend the energy, that force comes to me. So I count on it.

You've experienced that long-term then?
Always.

Do you ever feel like a puppet at all? That sounds negative when I say puppet. It sounds more like a benevolent feeling, a good feeling, for you.
Yeah, it's very benevolent. I don't think puppetry; there might be some negative connotations with the strings and jerking around. But puppetry in the sense of simply being guided to do something—maybe the will of someone else. The puppet has no choice. I like to think I have a choice. I can either say yes or no.

Maybe you need to cooperate at least.
Yeah, I have the choice to cooperate; in that sense it's optional. I'm steered. I also know when I'm on the wrong track because I'm not steered. I'm just sort of doing something, and those are the things I generally end up throwing away or abandoning. They just didn't turn out well. I want to follow that guidance, and it usually works out very well.

Do you think animals have imagination?
[Long pause] The only animals I really know about are dogs and cats. I know the cats I've had do have a curiosity which is probably a part of imagination. My cats have always watched things and investigated things. That's only a part of the imaginary process. I've never seen them follow

anything up. They just act with it until their curiosity is satisfied and boredom sets in and then they leave it go.

Dogs, on the other hand, seem curious too, but they will follow the process further. They don't seem to bore quite as quickly. Dogs follow a little process when they are going to sleep where they find a spot and they circle and circle. They get closer to the ground while they are circling. I think that's like imagination—[like] a dog I'm kind of visualizing the perfect laying down position where I am oriented just right. I can see and I am positioned where I know what's going on, and yet I am going to be very comfortable. In that way I think they do envision what could be.

Do you think you take imagination with you when you die?

[Long pause] Yeah. I think that might be one of the *few* things you take with you when you die. That which is unique about me, as an individual. There's not really too much unique about anything physical about me. There's really not a lot unique about how I think or the facts I know. That's all just information. It's well-known and shared.

The one thing about me that is like no other person is the visions I have had—the combination of experiences into something brand new, that I carry with me. That is the unique aspect. If I am going into a spirit world as a tried human being moving on into something else, yeah I have a feeling that I'll be allowed to take that with me as the part of my little blob of spirit that I have somehow by doing something that has changed others. Yeah, I do think I'll be allowed to carry that with me.

You know that little blob of spirit? Do you know where it is in your body?

Yeah, my gut feeling when I center up and take those deep breaths and so on, I feel that it lies deep in my belly. For me that's the core of me. That's a sensing thing that's pretty strong. I've always gone there. I don't know that I've been instructed to go there.

I used to try to find it in my heart or my chest somewhere. It was never there. My mind sort of drifted downward and I found it much lower. That's where I feel things. That's where I get that commanding presence of what's right and what's wrong, what I should be and what I should not be. I think I feel that down low in my body.

The last question I like to ask is what do you think is the most important thing?

That's the peeling the onion part. You peel the onion and you peel the onion and you ask a question that wasn't the whole question, then you come closer to the question. What's the real question? Then finally you come down to the huge question. I'm just not there yet.

I think the question for me gets closer and closer to the core concept of love. I think love is the purpose, and I think it's the question. Why is there love? Where is that and how can that be? Wherever you are headed down the path, that has to be core. That has to be the purpose, that has to be the reason. It's the only thing that is common, constant, eternal, shared.

This interview is almost like you planned it for the last few months, as though you knew ahead of time what you were going to say to questions one, two, three, four and five. You have an amazing set of answers.

I've had two years of really intense self-examination.

Do you attribute the self-examination to why you can answer a set of questions you had not been thinking about previously and answer them concisely and make sense?

Yeah, very much because I've spent an awful lot of time thinking about what if and why so, and how do I fit in, what is my place? Those kinds of questions that we don't have time for unless a huge stressor hits us. Then suddenly [these topics] become very important.

What I want to be, and there's just no mistake about it, is to become a holy man. I would like so much to be there. I think that it is so possible. It just takes tons of focus, never letting go of that thought.

I spent a fair amount of time wondering what that might look like. It's not the guy in some craggy, little cave in the mountain. It's somebody who is on the street and talking to people and being open and taking in lots of experiences and letting go of things very readily but holding on to the good. To me, it's not so much what I read. It's what I internalize. The more I let things internalize, then when you ask me a question, it's there. I don't have to dredge back in memory and try to link a bunch of stuff together. It's internal. It's already there. That is why I can answer these questions.

I have a question about the holy man aspect. Do you sometimes half expect people to notice that in you? Do you sometimes expect to be recognized for that quality? I don't mean that in an arrogant way, but do you sometimes wonder about that or have you ever had that happen in particular situations?

I think it's a progressive thing for me. I certainly didn't start out at that place. It was very rough. I think people do pick it up in me when my spirit is just extremely pure. People notice that. They gravitate toward that. I'm not projecting something that would put people off. I'm projecting something that pulls people toward me.

I can tell when it is just perfectly right because people around me are perfectly right. I'm manifesting properly in a way that people are pulled toward. In that very moment of time I am behaving like a holy man and people do know, yes.

Now, when you're manifesting this, is this something you can consciously put some awareness to, or are some days just "on" and some days are just "off"? Or is it a process that you go through for that particular day and it all clicks together and you feel it happening better than on other days?

Yeah, some days are better than others. It is a process of sorts. My first waking thought in the morning is of thanks. I just think, "Thanks, this is so great."

As I set up my morning I find myself being aware of everything. I look at how things look from different angles in my house and how the yard might have changed and what the birds are doing, what the sky looks like, and I try to be thankful for everything. I try to let that expand as I go to work. I try to see things in ways I've never seen them before. If I do all that just right, by the time I get to work I feel great. I've got so much going on by that point. During the course of the day, as the world kind of closes in around me, I find my energy shrinking and I contract off. By the time I get home at night, I'm not nearly so big or as expansive or looking at things quite the same way. Now the trick is to start out big and by the end of the day end up just enormous. That would be the real thing, and to not allow myself to be contracted.

What you're saying about how the day goes on happens to me too. I can get more irritable as the day's stresses are beginning to wear away my fascination and my awareness of life around me. I wonder sometimes for me if it's not a protective mechanism, a kind of withdrawing inwardly. It's like the world is kind of beating me up until I become mundane. I don't do it on purpose. It feels like the stress wears away, chips away, and by time I get home I'm the least holy person there is.

I don't feel like a bad person, I just feel like my energy has been pulled off of me. I can't give like I can give at 8:00 in the morning. I don't have anything left.

Almost like it's no fault of your own. You're thinking that maybe with time you can sustain that state on through the day's stresses. That is what some call permanent enlightenment. The kind of holy men that I've never met but have read about who have a twinkle in their eye, that glee at everything around them even when people are being perfectly terrible. They know better. Nothing can bug them anymore. They see another's stupid behavior and they find it kind of amusing. Wouldn't that be a great attitude?

That would be great. I want to experience everything within me that goes on around me. I want to experience people's joy and love and passion. I also want to fully experience their anger and rage. I want to take every piece of that at 100 percent.

Really?

But I don't want to own any of it. I just want to experience it and then let it go right on through. If I could do that—because that's what happens unless I'm cloistered off somewhere—that's what happens, that's the course of the day. Everything comes by. There's the sweet and the sour, the sick and the well. Everything comes by, and it's all good, great stuff to experience as long as I don't particularly own any of it—if I let it come in and go through.

Like if you walk through a formal event, women for some reason, will have on stronger fragrance. As you walk from place to place to place you get fragrance, fragrance, fragrance. You don't have to carry them all with you. You can just pass through and none of them really stick with you. It's not like my lungs are all full of one—I can't let go of that. No. I take another breath and there's another fragrance.

Let's end on a different question. How would you compare intuition with imagination?

Intuition is just observations as to what may be right or wrong for us personally. Observation as to whether we are attracted to a person or shapes or functions. It's just a series of observations. Nothing particularly unique there—unseen but not really unique. Imagination is a whole different thing. It's really not an observation at all. It's the creative force that takes whatever material we have at hand and lets us have the sum total of our unique experiences into a medium and to create something that never was before. I see those topics as being totally different.

Nuclear Scientist

"The fact of evolution is the backbone of biology, and biology is thus in the peculiar position of being science founded on an improved theory, is it then a science or faith?"
Charles Darwin

This nuclear scientist has strong evolutionary beliefs. He is a thirty-nine year old father of two from Phoenix, Arizona.

I could detect no trace of religious beliefs in his answers, however the future generations do evoke meaning for him. He may have had them on his mind as his children were playing in the same area as we were meeting. You can hear their happy voices on the recording.

What are the purposes of imagination?

[Pause] I think it probably ties back to some sort of evolutional point which ended up being a problem-solving tool. As we went through and developed as humans, I think that imagination has to do with going through and doing some of the problem solving. Sometimes the answer would come from a dream. These are all very technical answers but it still takes the imagination to get there. That would probably be the purpose.

What do you think the origin of imagination is? You already somewhat answered that but if you want a chance to restate it...

Yes, as we evolved and worked on evolution and problem solving and developing a little more technology—as humans began applying these things which other species hadn't—it probably developed through that.

What do you think is the location of imagination?

It's somewhere in the brain. Probably because I think the frontal part is more—the reptilian part of the brain is in the back side of the brain—so probably the frontal area which holds some of our less reptilian ideas.

Kind of the higher-thinking area?
  Yes.

Do you think you take imagination with you when you die?
  I guess I'll find out. [Laugh]

You are just not certain of that?
  No, no I never really sorted that out for myself, I'm not really sure how much it matters if when you die the lights just go off and you're kind of done. Or is there something else? I haven't really sorted that out and I don't really think that I will find out until that day comes.

What do you think is the most important thing at the end of a life?
  Well, I think it's passing on—the same way ours was passed on—the learning and what evolved out of imagination, and passing that on to the little ones so that they can start with what we learn and then they can take their imaginations and take it further.

So they don't always have to reinvent the wheel? Or would that being putting words in your mouth?
  Yeah, that's right.

They can pick up where we left off and go from there.
  It kind of reminds me—I don't know how it's working out these days, but that you live a better life than your parents. That progression idea.

The next generation is important to you? All of them? Or just your own particular children?
  All of them of course, but I'm focused on mine.

[Laugh] I can see that. They are pretty cute.
  I'm pretty heavily invested in the little guys, but it just radiates out to everybody.

PHYSICAL THERAPIST

"We were all born for love. It is the principle of existence, and its only end."
Benjamin Disraeli

This was a very pleasant interview situation. We were seated at a picnic table in a lovely park alongside a lake in the summertime. Being able to talk with a former psychiatric nurse was helpful in regard to the question of possibly having too much imagination and how that may play a part in the insanity issue. She is now a practicing physical therapist who was forty-four years old at the time of the interview and she is from Williston, North Dakota.

Like many, she believes that people have a soul, yet her belief in the final destination of that soul may surprise you. I very much like her closing remark because that is exactly what I hope for with every interview.

What are the purposes of imagination?

[Laugh] The purpose of imagination? I guess I would think that it would be to bring joy into your life or to take you out of the mundane.

Can you think of any other purposes?

For me, I think I use my imagination to be more creative. Right now I'm going in different directions creatively. I use it to come up with ideas to help me to go in different directions or see where I want to go. If I see something, I don't want to just copy what somebody else is doing. I want to use my imagination to take it to a step further than what I see.

What do you think the origin of imagination is?

[Long pause] I just think it comes from each person within each person's soul. You might think that somebody is more imaginative or has a better imagination than other people. I think musicians have that talent. People are musicians not just because they can read music. They have that within their soul, not genetically, but just within themselves. I think imagination is within yourself.

That's a lot like the next question. What do you think is the location of imagination?

When you asked me the last question and I felt like it was within me. I gutturally feel like it's in my chest. I feel like it's here. [Indicating chest area with hands] I think it's in my heart, I don't think of it as being in my mind. I think it might be in my mind even though that doesn't feel like that's where it is. It feels like it's more of a guttural feeling.

Do you think some people have more than others?

Definitely. Like I said, just because I had piano lessons, I'm not a musician. Some people have that within themselves. I think everybody has an imagination, and some people might not delve into that or use it. Or they may have it, but it's put back because they are doing their job nine to five. I think everybody has it but some to a larger degree than others, definitely.

Do you think people can have too much?

[Laugh]

Like with insanity?

Well, that's what I was just thinking. That goes back to psych nursing.

Were you in psychiatric nursing?

Well, I was in nursing and yeah. I think you still have to have a reality base to your life to make you tolerable or make you tolerate other people, to function in the world. I don't think you can just live in an imaginary world without being cared for by someone else. You would not function in this world if you just thought it was an imaginary world.

It makes you wonder when people have lost touch with reality and they hear voices and they see things that aren't there.

Right. They can live but that's when somebody else is cooking for them and feeding them and attending to their bodily functions. They can live but that's not necessarily because of their imagination.

Makes you wonder how much imagination could run amok in a mind that is already tormented. Do you think you take imagination with you when you die?

No. [Pause] Because I think that when you die, you die. I don't believe in a heaven.

Biologically...

Biologically, you cease to exist. I think we all have souls or feelings or beings here. I think when people say that somebody's soul is still out there, I think that's from how they have influenced with or interacted with other people. I don't think you take it with you.

Because there's nowhere to go.

Yeah, there's nowhere to go. I think if anything you're leaving it...

In the form of a memory.

Right.

The last question is, what do you think is the most important thing?

[Long pause]

You can think of it as the end of the day or at the end of a life.

What I think about is an exhibit I just saw, "Moments of Intimacy and Love and Kinship," I believe that's the name of it. It's just photographs from around the world. They are incredible. I hate to have the answer be "love" because I don't think that's it.

What I always think is the most important for me as a person, or what I try to tell the kids is, to be a good person. However you define that. I think that being a good person is showing that love to your family and treating the Earth right, being kind. It's how we interact with other people and the world that we're in. I can't just say it's "love" or "family" or something like that. I think it's more than that.

More than just your behavior and your actions? More than just the Beatles song. It's more a way of life?

Yeah, it's who you are and what you show other people you are. That's a tough question. To me right now, what is most important are my kids. I can't imagine a time when they won't be the most important. They are just part of being a good person and having a good life. I have a great life.

That's good. See you didn't die from being interviewed.

[Laugh] No, but I will be thinking about it afterwards.

NATIVE AMERICAN

"*Our departed braves, fond mothers, glad, happy-hearted maidens, and even our little children who lived here and rejoiced here for a brief season, will love these somber solitudes...and when the last red man shall have perished, and the memory of my tribe shall have become a myth among the white men, these shores will swarm with the invisible dead of my tribe...there is no death. Only a change of worlds.*"
Chief Seattle

"*It does not require many words to speak the truth.*"
Chief Joseph

This interview was a beautiful experience, and I sincerely wish you could have seen firsthand how this woman exudes serenity and has a great sense of peace. Her manner of speaking is slow and deliberate. Her accent is one of wisdom and knowledge. When she speaks in her unassuming way you want to listen. It's as if the next word might be so filled with special, one-of-a-kind knowledge, that you would never want to miss anything she might say. Along with her peacefulness comes a candor that is refreshing, as if the listener is allowed into the heart of everything she has to say.

She is a humble woman working in a humbling occupation as a house cleaner. Her unique upbringing includes a childhood lived on the Blackfeet Indian Reservation; her mother was one hundred percent Native American. She was born and raised in Browning, Montana, and she was fifty-one years old when she granted me this interview.

It is worth mentioning that the majority of those interviewed hesitate in answering the first question. I was fascinated by this woman's lack of uncertainty as she confidently answered without pausing.

What are the purposes of imagination?
It helps you to live your life more fully. You can imagine what you can do and what you can't do. It helps me plan things that I can and cannot do.

What do you think the origin of imagination is?

The origin? I think it comes from man wondering, people wondering about life itself and so they give rise to their imagination.

So it's something from within?

Yeah, I think so.

Do you think some people have more and some people have less?

I think some people have a more creative imagination than others.

Where do you think it's located?

I think it's located in the brain.

Do you think that in any way it's linked to a person's personality?

Well, yeah it seems like it would be linked to a person's personality because different people imagine different things and they pursue their imagination, like a painter has a different imagination than somebody else who writes, like you.

So maybe you'd say we all have one, but we use it in different ways. And, if it's in the brain, do you think we're all born with one like we're born with a nose or an eye?

Yeah it seems like it, doesn't it?

I'm wondering where people think it is.

Where have people said that it is? Have they said it's other places?

A lot of people think it's in their brain. Another question is, do you take it with you when you die?

I don't know if it's part of your soul. I mean, to me the soul is different than the brain. So it would be hard to take it with you unless it were in conjunction with your soul. Because you get feelings and inspirations from your soul. It would be nice if you could take it with you.

Like maybe an aspect of the personality?

Yeah. We don't know what we take with us in our soul, when our soul leaves our body. We don't know what goes with us or not. We don't even know what the soul really is. And maybe we don't really know what the imagination really is either.

Where do you think your soul is?

I think it's in my heart.

You think your soul is in your chest area?

Yeah, I think. I never really thought about where my soul is. I just thought of it as being a part of my body. I think that it may be in my heart, when my heart dies my soul leaves. So I don't know.

Let's talk about growing up on the reservation.

I lived there until I was ten years old. This last weekend my sister visited here from the reservation. She lives there and her kids live there and they're growing up there and they all have families now and jobs. Some of them live out in the country and have horses and cows; I thought that was really nice.

I wish I could live back there again. But I'm so far away now that I don't really know the people. In the past, I've gone back and it's so nice just to see people who talk like me and look like me, and it was a real nice feeling. I think that would have made my life entirely different if I would have been able to live there among them. I think I missed out on a lot. So lately I've been wondering what kinds of things I'd have to do to move back there. It would be a big change.

They'd probably accept you because you were from there.

The thing is, I don't know if they would accept me, because I'm an urban Indian and then also I'm a half-breed. The half-breeds and the full bloods don't get along, they have their friction going on between them. So it would be a real challenge to move back there.

I'm going back next summer. Our Indian celebration is in the middle of July. They call it Indian Days and they have a Pow-Wow for four days. People from all over come and camp there and put up their tents and tee-pees.

Sounds like fun. Do you remember living there when you were young?

I remember my grandmother. She was full-blooded Indian and she could talk the language. She used to do bead work and dry meat, and she knew about herbs for healing.

That's going to be a lost art if someone doesn't keep passing it along.

Hopefully they are passing it along to some of their children.

Like the languages.

They're teaching the language in the school there.

Was there a lot of companionship, a lot of family there? A community feeling? It may just be a mystique, but I'm picturing wisdom and people revering their elders. I am picturing older people having something to say.

I think that went on, and I think that still goes on, more on the reservation. Like with my mom and my grandmother. They seem to have a lot of wisdom that I don't find here in the city among people. But I have been doing house cleaning lately for elderly people. They kind of have some of that wisdom, I've noticed. That gives me a little bit of community, just to be around them day after day. I feel their acceptance of me, that they really do accept me genuinely, which is nice.

Maybe all cultures have wise, older people but only some cultures listen to their older people. What brought your family out of the reservation and over here to live?

It was easier to live out here economically and to get jobs and housing. Then relatives starting coming out, like my mom's sister, some cousins, my brothers and sisters that went to Indian school. Now we have a whole extended family out here. Which is nice.

Just recently I've been thinking about the reservation. It would take a lot to go back. I have to think about finding work and housing. It's kind of late in my life to think about going back there.

I face a lot of discrimination and rejection over there. It's easier to stay here where I am getting to know more people. I'm building my own little sense of community.

I go twice a month to a Native American Mass. So I have a little community there that I'm getting used to, that means a lot to me. We've started a Kateri Circle so I'm going to have more community here. That gives me a reason to stay here.

What's a Kateri?

Well see, Kateri Takoweeta was a Native American woman in the 1600s and she died when she was twenty-four. The Pope blessed her, and then in 1980 he beautified her so she's just one step from becoming a saint. She was born to a Mohawk mother and an Algonquin father, and they all got smallpox and she got it too. I think her mother and father died and she lived with her uncle for a while, and they abused her. She got to know Jesus through these Jesuit Priests and she liked their religion, so she ran away and went to live with them at this fort.

She used to help the sick and the poor, and she was really devoted to Jesus, and they say she was a mystic too. She died when she was twenty-four and they're trying to make her the first Indian Saint in North America.

They have what they call a Takoweeta Conference that's named after her. Native American Catholics from all over the country go to this conference and they concentrate on her. All over the country they have what they call Kateri Circles, they're named after her. A lot of them will have fundraisers throughout the year. They do things together, have circles, and talking circles. They just get together.

How does Indian religion correlate, correspond or go along with Christian or Catholic ideals?

Actually, I went through that period in the '80s and it was really difficult, trying to decide whether I wanted to be a Native American with that religion or if I wanted Catholicism, because I used to go to the Sun Dances in the '80s, and I got into Indian religion. Then there was a period of wondering whether to be true to one or the other but then it finally just kind of blended together and I was able to accept parts of both. It was just one God, so I don't feel so bad now. I don't feel like I have to reject one over the other anymore.

Do you have one creator God in both?

Yeah, one creator God in both.

Do you go to an afterlife in both?

Yeah, in both you go to an afterlife.

What would be the biggest difference? What would be contradictory that would be hard to reconcile between the two?

I guess what was hardest for me was to believe in Jesus Christ. It was really, really, hard. For years I wouldn't accept Jesus Christ, but just in the last four years I've been more accepting of it and the church. When you go get the sacraments, the bread and the wine, and just recently I've been more accepting that it really is the body and blood of Jesus Christ. In the past, I wouldn't acknowledge it. I had difficulties with some priests over it, but some were more accepting than others of the different beliefs.

I have one more question. If you had to boil it down to one thing, what matters most? Not what you think you are supposed to say, but right off the top of your head, what matters most?

I think what really matters most is who you are, who you know yourself to be, and what real purpose you think you have in this life. I'm struggling with that right now because I went into teaching, and I spent a lot of time studying for that. Then I only did a little bit of student teaching and I have been away from it for years.

Sometimes I feel like I wasted my life. I go back and think if I had gone into something different maybe it would have been different. At this stage of my life I still want to do something. I want to go back to school maybe and get some more training. I want to feel good, like I have some kind of purpose in this life.

I'm still trying, struggling to do something with my life, even at this age. I don't have that many years left to be doing stuff. I think it's who you really are.

That's what matters most?

Yeah, and your faith. My faith matters to me. Right now it matters a lot to me. It's my faith that keeps me going. A lot of this sounds like philosophy. Is it philosophy that you're doing this for?

Well, you have turned the question on me. I didn't realize it when I started, that it might fall into that category. I really want to know what people think on some topics. I like to have conversations that are deeper, that cause people to think. I've noticed that when I do these interviews, people will talk to me afterward and they'll have thought more and sometimes the topics keep coming back to them...

Where do you think they go when they die?

In my early twenties I became a Christian.

Oh, you did. So you believe in heaven?

I believe in heaven and in hell. One of my relatives is nearing 100 years old and he once said, "Anybody can see there's a God by looking at a tree." That indicates to me that there is a level of obviousness in God's existence and it is apparent in the creation. That gives all of us at least two motivations. One is God's love, including the evidence of organized creation, and if for any reason that is not enough, then there is the motivation of hell, as an eternal destination, that could be a powerful motivation for some people.

I don't believe in hell.

Really, you don't think there is one?

No.

Then what happens to everybody that doesn't go to heaven?

I'm not so sure about heaven either. For a while I had quit believing in heaven. I was practicing the Krishna religion.

Like Hare Krishna?

Then the Buddhist, I was getting into that and into Theosophy. That's the wisdom of religions. They study all kinds of things, the occult, the paranormal, mysticism, New Age, all really different, strange stuff that most Christians would not be getting interested in.

For a while there I didn't believe in heaven. Now, I'm back in the Catholic religion and I hear them talking about heaven. My images are kind of changing. I don't really know exactly what I think heaven is, but I do want to see my family again. I think I'll see them again in spirit, I don't know in what way.

You're not exactly sure, if there is a heaven, if people will be able to recognize one another?

They say that they do. Their spirits recognize each other.

If this world with all its pain and agony has meaning, I would think the next world would have at least as much meaning without as much pain.

That would be good if there wasn't as much pain and suffering as here.

City Planner

"Have mercy on the helpless—
especially when they are to blame for their helplessness."
Abraham Lincoln

"The philosophers have only interpreted the world differently,
what matters is to change it."
Karl Marx

This was an enjoyable interview with a good flow of conversation. Some people are very comfortable with the questions and this man was definitely at ease. He had friendly mannerisms and even a twinkle in his eye. I can easily picture him as a late nineteenth-century confectioner amusing all the young children in his store as each one chooses from his selection of beautiful candy. Quite honestly, he looks very much like Burl Ives or even somewhat like Santa Claus, less the bright red suit.

You will see for yourself that he is a quick thinker and noticed immediately that the question about taking the imagination with you when you die is a mere disguise for what I am truly attempting to discuss.

By occupation he was a city planner, now retired. But he is quick to add that he thinks of himself more as a social planner. He was born in New York City, and he was sixty years old at the time of the interview.

What do you think are the purposes of imagination?
Well, the biggest purpose of imagination, to me, is to pull yourself above the level of which you're going to make most mistakes, the level at which you're going to be able to see beyond the common stuff that's happening to you on a day to day basis. Because if you can't do that you're just pushing the engine—the engine being society.

So, imagination is the thing that gets you above that. It helps you to see what's going on. It's the most critical thing, the ability to be able to imagine beyond. I could go on with that.

Typically with city planning, it's orientated around physical things, parks, streets. But in my world, it was a world of people, the ease of people, the love between people and that kind of stuff. That's what I mean by being able to imagine a world like that rather than just a world with a bunch of streets. It wasn't very well accepted, obviously.

[Laughter] That wasn't the objective?

We built senior centers, and I built a center for the physically challenged. In that sense some of my ideas came out, but not if you're talking about the larger social thing we live in.

Do you think there is too much separation socially?

There's too much separation racially, economically; there's too much separation socially. All of them. We're terrified. If you really look at it, we are terrified. It's horrible. It's incredible. I worked in the inner city for a while and you find out the differences in the perception of the work force. It's a whole different world of people. A whole different way of perceiving the world.

The second question is what do you think the origin of imagination is? Where did it come from?

I would like to say that all people have inherent imagination. I think when people are born, they are told right away what not to say and they tell them they are guessing wrong. Then we start to kind of hem them in. The world starts to hem us in. By the time most of us are ten or eleven years old we pretty much...our world is set.

Now, people do get out of there. Exceptionally great people get out of that. People who have epiphanies, for whatever reason. I think the sad thing is that it's probably there in most people, but it gets molded by society. We really don't want those kind of people. We think we do. We don't. If they're doing something good, if they are doing something economically useful, if they are writing books—the right kind of books. Certain books we don't want, like Henry Miller. So we have this box we put people in.

I think in this society at this time we are seeing a real suppression of imaginary thought. For some reason we not only don't want it, we discourage it. I don't know why that is. I wish it wasn't that way right now. Fear maybe.

I read a science fiction book the other day and it talked about other planets. It's incredible that this man had an imagination like that. He had an imagination to think on those levels. I'm reading another book about the British in the 1700s and 1800s in India, and they were finding out about Buddhism. Then the Buddhism was suppressed. So there are imaginative people who go out and say, I'm going to pursue this stuff. I'm going to do this. Some people imagine doing something out of the box.

What do you think the location of imagination is?

Cerebral cortex. The brain. [Pause] I think other parts of the brain come into play to make it click. Obviously, the visual center, the auditory center. To make it really work they somehow all have to click. You can have a tremendously high IQ and have no visual ability or no auditory ability to put it together. It all has to work. The imagination also has to come from the environment we create.

You can put children in interesting environments where their imagination will soar, or you can put them in sterile little playgrounds. They have all the concrete and asphalt, or you can take them out on nature walks and things like that.

It's a stimulus?

Yeah. It hits the brain and they start to ask where did butterflies come from? Where did frogs come from? What a tadpole is.

What would a flying tadpole be like, for example?

What would a flying tadpole be like? Interesting. You're right. They almost look like they are flying in the water like manta rays.

In my imagination I can see a flying tadpole, even though I've never seen one. I was wondering how you think the vision center is related to or connected to imagination. You brought that up already.

To me it's a recombination of thoughts. I've thought about that a lot. How can you think a certain thing when you've never experienced it? You never have. You're putting together millions of little pieces of things you observed, and depending on what kind of person you are, you might take 50 to 100 pieces of something together and come up with something that is a whole new thought. All my language comes from somewhere.

Even in Jung's psychology system there's a cosmic consciousness. Even if I'm pulling stuff from there, it doesn't make any difference. It's a building of pieces. The idea that Einstein suddenly walked over to the black board one day and started writing down all of these formulas—that's nonsense. There are all kinds of precursors to Einstein's work. There were all kinds of things happening around him.

Original thought is a fascinating topic.

I don't believe that there is any such thing as an original thought. It's a theoretical impossibility to me.

I tend to agree.

What you have are people who have an ability to put together complex pieces of life experiences they have had. That's what Einstein did. There was a lot of different work going on around him—different physicists and mathematicians—and he put it together. The idea that Einstein was born, he grew up, he went to school, he was a mediocre government worker and all of a sudden he started coming up with these formulas—it's nonsense.

We hurt ourselves when we do that because then we kind of shove intellectuals like that off to the side and say they are special people. We can all look around us and put together ideas and thoughts, Einstein was not the only one who had that option.

How do you think imagination and memory connect with each other?

So you're asking how the images are stored, where they are stored?

Let me try again. We just had coffee brought to us and we can "see" that memory because it just happened, right? Let's pretend she brought the coffee into the room, stopped and did a cartwheel and then proceeded to bring us the coffee. Can you see it? We know which happened and which didn't. It feels like the same part of my thinking processes are being used. What do you think about that?

The danger in experimental psychology and all of that stuff is, what are you really seeing? I'll bring you back to your analogy. You say, "Yeah, that woman did this cartwheel." You decided for some reason to bring back that part of the memory even though the other memory was the right memory.

That's why they say it's so unreliable for anybody to recreate the memory. Like when someone tells a story, by the time it gets down to the tenth person it's a completely different story. The same idea; each person in their mind transported that story and manipulated it and changed it around. Either it was an image or an auditory. They changed it around.

[Laugh] Maybe that's why their memories are unreliable, or everybody has a different perspective on the same thing they saw or experienced. It might be because the memory is in, or near, or next to, or adjacent, or even in conjunction with the imagination. You are able to warp it.

You definitely do, yeah. And that's the interesting part. You are taking advantage. You have the ability to recreate an event in your mind. You can change a whole event into a completely different thing. It's amazing. I live in a world of constant imagination. I think of fifty things at once.

Like you brought up before, the way people combine things, to get a possibility out of something?

Well, if you have ever been to New York, for example, September 11 would be a big one. You start to put together all of the images you've ever seen of New York City, and you put together this gestalt, a picture of how the city is. These million little pieces form together into imaginary thought. All the things you saw in pictures or read in a book.

Do you think you take imagination with you when you die?

Do I think there is life after death?

Well, that's of course wrapped up in that question isn't it?

[Laughter] Yeah! That's kind of the question isn't it?

Yes and there is kind of an "A" and a "B" side to it.

My current way of thinking about this is, I've been playing around with Buddhism which has reincarnation. Of course you could be a Christian and say, I'm going to go to heaven and be with God.

It doesn't really matter which way you look at it. I think somehow the thought, the story, the molecules all dissipate when you die. You could argue that they go and reform and regroup until somebody else picks them up, maybe a baby. I don't know. That's the only way I can explain it. Otherwise you need to talk about the brain and the brain cell itself, the thing inside the cell, the molecules. They break apart when you die. They go on.

In a metaphysical way?

Yes, that's the term, metaphysical. They go into the atmosphere and do something. I'm not sure what it is. I'm not very religious. I really don't care. They can go to Catholic heaven, a Jewish heaven, they can go wherever they want as far as I'm concerned. So if I'm told I'm going to be reincarnated, I say, "Terrific. That's great." The Catholics say you're reborn. Oh, great, it doesn't matter.

I just don't care. Whatever happens will happen and there's nothing I can do about it. You see characteristics of people, and they bring previous people back into somebody that exists. That's an argument *for* the idea that you've inherited the molecular structure of some other person. I don't know. I'm open to that. The more important issue is our lives.

We're going to get to that in two questions from now. Where do you think you are in your body? Where is the real you?

Somewhere in the brain—the convoluted areas of my brain. You could say in the muscles and nerves, but I think the lion's share is buried in the brain cells.

Do you think there is a separate "you" from your body?

No, I think that's a complex thing. That's that dualism question. Do I think there's somebody other than me? No, I think it's a complex rearrangement of thoughts. I'd have to say, "Look, there *is* something other than me." No, I have trouble with that one.

So, if I broke it down this way and asked you if you had a soul, you would say that it's something that represents you other than your physical body?

The best way I could answer that is the way I already did answer it. All these little tiny pieces, these molecules in our body, they could live outside of me if I died. I could say that. Do I think there is a separate soul? No, I don't think it's necessary. The brain cells can carry it. That's part of the soul anyway. I'm really saying the same thing. The soul is the composite of all those little molecules. They carry the thoughts.

The last question you'll like. What is the most important thing? At the end of the day, at the end of a lifetime?

The most important thing is to create a place in this world where people can live in harmony and peace where we don't have problems with resources and greed and so forth. I hate to say it because it's so cliché. We want peace in the inner city. People don't want to fight among themselves. People not bickering, not being greedy and trying to get some stuff that's not theirs. People starting to see that there are things that are more important than the things the advertisers are trying to tell us. You can pick up a magazine and see what they are trying to tell us, over and over again. Love, compassion, those kind of things. That's what we should be talking about. That's the end. We need a world like that.

Like in Iraq—that's not love. That's not creating peace by sending soldiers over to blow everybody up. Some of the Special Forces are helping. Somebody the other day rebuilt a school or a fire truck or something like that. That's nice. We think that we want world peace. We have the Peace Corps. We need that kind of thing on a fifty times larger scale. Send people around the world and do mediation, resource development, helping people, loving people. That's what we need to do—not send Special Operations Forces.

We would have a world of Special Ops, the Green Berets, the Black Berets, I mean where we have a problem we send them in to clean out the bad guys. No, you got to send the average person or someone with minimal training. That's what it is about. Not what we're doing. It's not force. That's not the answer. The answer is love and peace. How do you do it? I don't know. Social justice, I wish we had a little more. That's what I think.

We're not here to provide a tax break for big investors. We're here to provide services for people who can't afford it. We're here to take care of the people who can't be taken care of. They are supposed to take care of themselves in this capitalistic system. People who can take care of themselves. Okay. Let's take care of the people who can't. The children, let's give them playgrounds and stuff. I've always believed that since I was in my twenties. The Vietnam War era, I wondered, "What is going on here?" I was asking, "Why are we doing this?" Ever since then, it woke me up. It was an epiphany. That's what I believe.

The thing that you personally think is the most important is something you wound up doing with your life.

Yeah, to a certain extent. I tend to get down on myself a lot. I feel bad about not having done anything. When you get to be 60 you get down and think you haven't accomplished much. It doesn't look so bad when I put it all together, I'm not done yet.

Not dying later today?

No. In this "bubble world" they tried to create for us, I sometimes think they want to keep us in this bubble world, so we don't think too much about things. "Don't get them thinking."

You know what a nightmare it would be if all these people started thinking?

I don't know. I kind of wanted them to. I hadn't thought of it as a nightmare.

Well, think about it. All of a sudden they really start thinking, and they start questioning all of this stuff.

There would be a lot of changes real quick wouldn't there?

Yeah, there would. I'd be interested to see what would happen.

My dream would be that they would simplify a little bit. So they had time to connect, so they had time to have community again instead of the isolation.

Yeah, but you've got to be able to slow down. They have their own mindset. What is your value? If your value is you go to your job and make $85,000 a year, that takes precedence over socialization and getting together with people doesn't it? You've got to change values.

It could create a huge economic devastation. That would cause a social reform that caused people to either possibly be like the Amish, where a community would commit to barn raising together. Or they could be cut-throat, automatic rifles on the street, every man for himself.

You know, that's very interesting because I've been working on a family genealogy. Some of my family all lived in one town. They survived because my grandfather was able to keep working during the war. The Dustbowl had just finished decimating the Midwest and they had the depression. That was hard times for people. They came out of it very stranded, very isolated. People just didn't connect.

So the adversity did not bring them together?

No, not necessarily, it doesn't always do that. When they migrated to California they didn't necessarily form co-ops.

[Laughter] No communes?

They didn't come to form communes. They were tough, little towns. The people from Oklahoma went there. That kind of climate does not necessarily bring out the best in people. It's true. No community is going to be 100% equal. It's always going to spare some and favor others. Are the ones that are spared going to take care of you? Are we taking care of the people now who need to be taken care of?

It doesn't appear to me that we are.

We could change people if we wanted to. We could make the "in thing" to help old people. Why can't you convince people that taking care of children is the most important thing a person could do? Do you understand? We could do that. It's not giving interest rate cuts to people. It's not giving advantages to people who already have advantages. It's getting out there and getting us all convinced that we'd better start helping. If our leadership in this country could get out there and start saying the right things, talking the right talk, start talking like real leaders, we could have some real change. The behavior would change. I believe that. I am a social planner.

Newspaper Editor

"When we think this present as going to be, it exists not yet; and when we think it as existing, it is already past."
H. Bergson

"Religious revelation, philosophical thought, scientific investigation all converge on the problem of time and all come to the same view of it—time does not exist. The world is a world of infinite possibilities. But in fact every moment contains a very large number of possibilities, and all of them are actualized."
Ouspensky

A few of these interviews took place in my car due to the fact that it can be a quiet and uninterrupted place to talk. This is one of those instances. Our interviewee is young, only twenty-two years old, and very articulate. She is a newspaper editor from Boston, Massachusetts.

Most of the interview, in this case, takes place after the interview questions had already been completed. That happens with some people and that is okay for at least one very important reason. The questions themselves help to bring about the conversation and as I stated in the introduction they set the mood for deeper topics and sharing of feelings and thoughts that ordinarily would not come up in daily life.

Another thing I want you to notice is how quickly you can guide someone into opening up about themselves, and in some circumstances, their most frightening experiences. If you ever find yourself wanting to share your beliefs and deeper thoughts with another, try using a few probing questions or even these exact questions in order to help the other person feel safe enough to get to the more meaningful subjects in the quickest amount of time. This young woman certainly shared some very unusual details of her life, as you will see.

What are the purposes of imagination?
Probably to get away from reality, I think. Are there supposed to be more?

[Laughter] There doesn't have to be more than that. I'm giving you leeway to decide.

The only thing I can think of is to have an alternate reality, one that's attainable and believable. Or like a fantasy, unattainable and unbelievable, something you couldn't get from life, from real reality, you could probably get from imagination.

What is the origin of imagination?

What way? Like where did the idea get created?

How did it come to happen or where did it come from?

I can't say the ultimate creation of an idea. I'd have no idea where that would come from. Imagination is something you grow up with, but I wouldn't remember how it would be installed in my brain. I don't know. That's a good question.

I remember as a kid, Halloween was kind of an imagination to dress up in a costume like somebody else. That's not reality. That's like a fantasy. But it wasn't me who came up with the idea of costumes. It was my parents. I probably got it from my parents.

I don't think imagination is installed in you when you're born. I don't know that a newborn or an infant would have it. I don't know what they think or what they already know when they're born, if they know anything at all. I don't think they know anything at all.

Did you use your imagination a lot when you were a kid?

Yes, a lot. Still do. But as you get older, imagination becomes something that you can become. It doesn't have to be just imaginary. To me now imagination is more of a plan. Something you think you'd like to do. It becomes a goal. It's no longer make-believe.

I don't really imagine that I can fly, like I would when I was a kid. I don't imagine I'm a unicorn or anything like that. I imagine myself living in Europe, but that's something I can do. You get older and your imagination becomes more mature and less childish. Things you can actually attain.

When you go to recall a memory it usually comes back in a kind of visual way doesn't it?

Well yeah. Yeah, to have a memory would be visual. I can get memories from smelling things or touching things. To have a memory, you can't smell a memory. You can't hear a memory. You have to see a memory. Yes, it's a visual thing.

Well, that's why I ask because I wonder when I visualize a memory that was real and I visualize something that I imagined it almost feels like the same visualization process. Do you think you take imagination with you when you die?

The thought of something happening after death always seems like a spiritual or religious idea to me. I really never gave it much thought because I'm not religious. To say that anything would be carried after into death, I don't think would be possible. To me, death is the end. There isn't anything after death. You would carry imagination up until your death. After, it would be clean cut, nothing else, so I'd have to say no.

Do you know where you are in your body, where the real you is?

There's a conflict with that question between an area toward the center of my head and the area where we know best to be where the heart is located. It feels like that's where it should be. But that's probably what I was taught to believe and that's why I believe it.

Have you ever thought previously about where you are in there?

Not really. I never gave much deep thought to questions like that because they seemed to be kind of spiritual in a sense—the topic of the soul, to find the unphysical part of who you are. I don't believe there is an unphysical part of the body. I don't believe in souls. I would use the word soul to describe what a person really is but that's just for lack of a better word.

Would an equivalent word be personality?

I don't believe there's this invisible or maybe even visible entity throughout my body that creates my personality or emits ideas or reactions that would be key to my personality. I believe my characteristics are solely in my brain. However, when I think about decisions, or to carry out an action like touching this dashboard, I feel like they're coming from within the center of my chest, not my brain. I can't explain that.

You could still be a biological, physical unit without a soul. I don't think it's contradictory to feel like your essence is down lower. How about when you're emotionally hurt or you know you've wronged somebody, where do you feel that at?

My chest. Everything happens in the chest. Part of me thinks that could be because that's where your heart is pumping so when you get nervous or agitated, sad or happy, or excited—all these different feelings— your blood pressure changes and your heart rate goes faster or slower.

That's why I feel like that's where everything happens and my body is in my heart, but it essentially is. There's a lot of physical reaction, I can actually feel emotion coming from my chest.

The last question is, what is the most important thing?

Your happiness. Without it people don't function normally. Everything from sleep to basic functions of what a body needs to survive, food, nourishment, temperature. When you're very unhappy to the point you can't give yourself those basic needs, you wouldn't survive. That's why happiness is key to survival. I would contradict myself if I said the most important thing was survival, but in order to survive the most important thing would be happiness.

If a person was that unhappy they wouldn't be meeting their basic needs. I hadn't thought about that before.

I've been thinking about that quite a bit. What keeps people functioning? What keeps them going? Because I've had lots of experiences where you become so unhappy that you just don't function normally. Therefore if you were unhappy, life would fall apart. Life wouldn't be very important to live.

It does disrupt sleep and things like that.

Eating, sleeping, feeling, working, tolerating, patience—all that stuff.

I would say it's a very interesting time for you to have interviewed me because around six weeks ago I was supposed to get up in the morning and go to work. My alarm clock did not go off and I forgot. Life before the alarm clock did not go off was normal. Everything was fine. I ate fine, slept fine. Every part of my normal functioning life was normal. Then that morning the alarm didn't go off and I had five minutes to get to the bus. I hadn't showered, eaten, hadn't dressed, the cats were still in the house. Everything was out of order. I had five minutes to get all these things done and catch the bus.

Somehow I caught the bus and went to work. But somehow in that five minutes time stopped and I haven't been able to cope with it since. The idea of time doesn't make sense anymore.

I was really bad the first day. I think my boss wanted to send me home because I was just stupid. Everything was very, very slow the way I functioned. I can remember packing everything in my backpack to run to the bus stop. It was literally like my body was reacting and my brain was too slow. It didn't have time to react and all the things I was doing [were] just automatic.

I was running toward the bus stop and my brain had to stop and ask, "Am I going the right direction?" The body was already going, but I couldn't remember if I was in the right place. When I got there I wondered if I was at the right stop, but it is the only stop, so it had to be right. Then I wondered if the right bus would come. Why would I think these things?

If I could go back and erase that day I would, because now I just can't get things back together again. I don't comprehend anything anymore. The days just roll into one big long day. There is no time, and I can't tell days apart. When I wake up I don't know what day it is. I don't know if I have to go to work when I wake up. Where am I? It's really strange. I can't remember why it was funny that you were interviewing me.

Well, you said that happened about six weeks ago, so it's almost like you were implying that you might have given a completely different interview if it had taken place awhile back than you gave today.

Completely. Reality, that's why I was thinking [about] the difference between imagination and reality after that day. How do I say it without sounding nuts? Reality just doesn't make sense anymore. It's like the unreal world is meshing [with] the real world. The dreams are becoming real, and I can't remember if what I dreamt last night actually happened to me or if it was different.

My dreams are always so emotional. How can you have such a strong emotion and not have it be real? My dreams were about my boyfriend cheating on me or my mother had died with something real serious. I'd wake up and believe it. It would take a couple of hours to become reassured.

In one dream I saw an ex-boyfriend from seven years ago, and he hugged me, and it was as if all the miscellaneous misplaced pieces of my life—like a big puzzle—I saw these pieces come together and make a whole. Everything made perfect sense, almost as if I need that person to make life complete. I don't believe that, but that's what my dream portrayed to me. When I woke up I wondered where he was. Where did he go? Did he go to work today? Things don't make sense anymore.

Well, it seems like you had a "time bend" happen.

Like a warp of some kind. It's like being on drugs or something. Days pass like a blink of an eye. Some days just carry on forever and I can't remember where I'm supposed to go or what I'm supposed to do, but somehow I'm already doing it. My brain never caught up, it's still always a couple of steps behind.

Have you ever wondered, even though you don't believe in a religion, if things are meant to be? As if all things happen as they are supposed to?

Like a fate.

Maybe it's not prescribed out ahead of time like it has to be followed. I know one person who doesn't have religion who always says that everything happens exactly as it's meant to happen. I don't think it has to be the same thing as fate. Do you ever have any thoughts like that at all, or do you think it's wide open, no fate at all?

Wide open from here out, because there's just way too many factors, uncharted factors in the universe that could never be so organized as to prove fate. There's way too many things. Of course I've thought about things like that because movies will bring up stuff like that. I could never believe that to be true, [there would] have to be more organization than I could ever fathom.

Is there a sense of disorganization though? To me if it were so wide open, I'm not saying whether it is or it isn't, but if it were true that it was wide open I would feel a sense of too many options for me because I'm not good at decisions. I would feel like there were too many potentials, like I could move to Europe as you said before. Or I would just feel like it was overwhelming.

It is overwhelming and I've had this discussion with other people. All of the atheists I've ever known are indecisive, not roaming or aimless, not necessarily confused either, but not as relaxed as people of faith. I think that's extremely true because to me everything is up in the air. I don't have answers. I don't know anything. People of faith have answers. They have guidance. They have rules and beliefs of where humans came from and how the world was created.

Topics like fate and destiny...I don't feel lost at all. I'm just kind of one of those people who doesn't really need to be settled to have those kinds of answers. Did I say that right? Did that make sense?

I don't have to have all the answers to feel relaxed. Some questions are unanswerable to me, and I don't lose sleep about how the world was created. I've noticed that people of faith are far more comfortable and at ease with life than everybody else. It's almost as if they are so organized and the rest of the people like me are needing help.

I'm alone. Where's my guidance? Where's my path? They don't have a path, there really isn't any guide.

Do you think there's any path for you at all, I don't mean destiny.

There are many paths for everyone because there are many choices. There are crossroads everywhere you look. Every decision you make, whether it be picking the frayed holes in my pants to going back inside the apartment. There are decisions everywhere. I don't consider those things to be crossroads like that's going to change the rest of my life as I know it. It's not that serious.

Have you ever had those? Have you ever had that moment hit you like a hammer and you know if you turn this way or that way, or you just know this is one of those moments?

Oh yeah! That's probably why I'm such a wreck. I'm so indecisive, and I feel like I run into that crap all the time.

That the decisions will alter your life?

Yeah, that's how I got here. I made a decision to leave my job, my home, my friends, money—everything I had, and one day I left. Now the crossroad is do I stay here or go somewhere else? Do I take a vacation to Greece or buy a house or go to college and get a degree so I can get a job easier? Lots of different things you can do and nobody ever has the answers.

Another weird thing about my time warp is I've become dyslexic. I jumble words. I say things backwards. It got progressively worse. A couple of nights ago I actually started to spell things different. For example, I switched the first two letters of flyer, I switched the "f" and the "l" I spelled "l-f-y-e-r" and thought, "Oh my God, what is wrong with me?"

Things just keep getting worse. I read a menu last night and it said "stone oven pizza" but I read "stove enease pia" or something crazy that didn't make sense. But I read it three times and each time I made up something different, and I couldn't figure out what was wrong with me. It's really hard for me to not be able to find words and to spell because that's what I was just doing for a career before I came here. I worked for a newspaper. I was an editor. I always knew all the words. In fact I had to check those things for other people. Now that's my worst fear.

It's like a painter who goes blind. Can't paint anymore. Or a musician that goes deaf and can't hear his work anymore. When I speak I'm embarrassed, but things get jumbled all the time. Or words come out backwards. It's getting worse and I don't know if it's going to snap back together. It's freaking me out.

It seems like you're concerned about it. Sounds pretty life changing.

I kept trying to tell my boyfriend about it, and a couple of times he looked at me like he was worried. I ask him where I put the phone, but the phone's not cordless. It always goes back to same exact place. Why would I ask that? I know where it is. I suddenly forget where the light switch is. I kept flashing back to my previous apartment and expect the light switch to be located in the wrong place. When it's dark I'm confused. I don't know where I am. I think I'm somewhere else. I never did that before my alarm didn't go off.

It sounds like one day your alarm didn't go off and everything changed.

It was not gradual at all. That bus ride to work was really bizarre. I kept thinking the most absurd things. Thinking about things I already had the answers for but I didn't realize that I did. My body would be reacting and my brain was lost in the dust somewhere behind.

I wondered, "Where do I work? What time is it? What time do I work?"

It was like I'd forgotten everything. I didn't know where I was going. When I got to work I couldn't remember whether to use the front door or back door. Do I answer the phone? Is that my job?

Like a state of amnesia. And you haven't had this happen before?
Never, never.

And so far you don't know what to make of it?
No. When writing a friend about it, all I could say that would make sense was that my body woke up but my mind was asleep. By the time my mind woke up so many things had already happened that it was so behind and it's still behind. I can remember everything but it's kind of like it was an imagination. Like a day dream and it didn't really happen. That doesn't explain why, or maybe it does, why everything meshes together. I can't tell fact from fiction. It's almost like dealing with an alternate reality, like a dimension.

It's funny you would say that, I was going to ask you about alternate realities...
It's kind of like being in the [world] as we know it but jumping ahead of yourself, and it's like seeing two different dimensions at once. I don't know what another dimension would look like. This is the only one I know. I don't want to say alternate reality because, that to me, would be a different life. I'm still leading the same life but seeing more of a picture I shouldn't have seen or shouldn't know as a human or an animal or whatever.

Like living in a dream.
Yes. It's so unclear, it's almost like having "you" as you know yourself, and then having another you, a confused you, going on in the same head. They're living together in the same head like living together in the same place. Trying to figure out what's what and having two separate answers. Not answers but two separate ideas, two separate theories of what's going on and trying to do them both.

It doesn't make sense. I can't figure out what's what. I ask really dumb questions that I already know the answers to. I get lost very easily. I lose track of thought and kind of doze off for a while. Part of me thinks this wouldn't happen if I had a normal 9 to 5 job and the rest of my life was more stable. Maybe it's just stress. My boyfriend thinks it's stress, that the brain can no longer take on that much and is kind of breaking down.

I wondered that myself listening to this if it was a self-protection mechanism.

Some type of break with reality in order to cope with something, but I'm not a psychoanalyst.

That would make sense to me. I've thought about that. If I went to a therapist and he told me that was happening, I'd believe it. I don't have an answer. For me to lose control of myself is a very awkward feeling. You don't feel like you're controlling things. You feel like someone else has taken a hold of you and is forcing you to be dumb, and not allowing you to be at your fullest mental capability. It's not easy. I feel like there's me inside. I'm in there, but everyone else sees someone who is mentally ill or cannot handle themselves. It's like if I was in a mental institution and I acted insane and I looked insane and everything I said was insane. That's not me. "Me" is inside and I can't control what's going on the outside.

This has to do with imagination in the sense that part of the topic is who can tell reality from unreality. Who can tell imagination from non-imaginary things. So your whole experience—maybe that's why you told it to me—it ties in with the topic. Imagination doesn't always have to be a beautiful paradise thing. It can sometimes be upsetting. Like an upsetting dream, as an example. Imagination doesn't always have to be pleasant.

It's not that I'm dumb, I'm disoriented.

Disoriented is a good word, and so is amnesia. Makes you wonder if you'll wake up one morning and it will all be put back right, doesn't it? Is there some uncertainty in that?

That's a creepy thought. I don't want to think that. Sometimes I think beyond my regular theories of life and creation and that sort of stuff. I think, "Is this happening for a reason? Is somebody trying to tell me something?" What if I woke up one day and everything was normal? Is there something I should know or have gained from this that I'm not getting?

It's like somebody putting me through this so I'll get the picture, get a picture that I haven't gotten yet. So when I realize the picture I'll go back to normal. I don't believe that, but I've thought things like that. I'm willing to think about anything. Anything is possible. Not everything is possible, but every idea is possible of thinking of.

It can't hurt to contemplate.

I'll contemplate anything, I just don't believe it all.

The one that makes the most sense is that my mind got too stressed out and it wants to retreat to more basic motor functions. I can't concentrate either. I'm easily distracted. It feels like my brain is breaking down and I feel childish. Someone will ask me a serious question, and I'll just [gibberish] in my head. It's like the body is just a shell, and if you do the things you think of doing, that's when people think you're crazy.

If I jumped out of the car, did a cartwheel, and kicked the tree, that would be kind of weird. That's what separates the people who are normal from the people who are mentally ill. They do the things that they think whereas the rest of the normal world doesn't. I've always had that problem.

When I was younger, I always did everything that I thought. I didn't think about consequences. After awhile I matured and stopped doing the dumb things I wanted to do in my head. Nothing ever got me in trouble, or got me hurt, or nothing really serious. It wasn't like I was really mentally ill. Now that I'm older and more mature and I know that's not normal, I'm holding back from doing it. I find myself holding back from just breaking out. I stutter now too. Part of me wants to hide from people so I can sort it out. It really is embarrassing.

When I talk to people I want to say, don't look at me like that, I'm normal. I know reality, I get the picture, something's just not clicking right. That's it. It's like my brain is a car and things aren't firing right. Everything is fully capable of doing the things it needs but something like a spark plug is missing.

It's very frustrating. I know there's nothing wrong with me. Why can't I just function normally? Is your tape out yet?

Muslim Woman

"To overcome evil with good is good, to resist evil by evil is evil."
Prophet Mohammed

This woman lived most of her life in Baghdad, Iraq. During the war she met an American soldier who converted to the Islamic faith in order to marry her. She has lived in the United States for three years.

I interviewed her because she is Muslim. She is a stranger to me, even though one might think that we knew one another from the way that she presumed to know my religious beliefs. It is possible that she has encountered so many Christians living here that she has come to anticipate that the majority of us are of that faith. She has her degree in software engineering.

The first question is, what do think are the purposes of imagination?
I think that's what keeps you alive. If you don't have it you are going to be nothing. I think it's the whole purpose of life. It's very important to have it.

What do you think the origin of imagination is?
Not sure. I never thought about it. [Laugh] I don't know. I think it's a blessing from God. If we don't have it then every day [would be the same.] Your life would be boring. I think it's a blessing from God.

What do you think the location of imagination is?
Your head. [Laugh]

Do you think that it is in any way a part of your personality?
Yeah, it's basically part of it. If you are not a dreamer you will never, ever have it. You will be in your life and not able to imagine [doing other things]. For me it's a big thing because I moved from the Middle East. In the Middle

East it's hard for a girl to get divorced. I was married for two years. I met my current husband [while married] and we were lovers for one year. Nobody knew about it. I went with him to Turkey and nobody knew about it. One night I knew that I could not do this anymore. This is my life. Nobody is going to help me. None of these people are going to help me with the future.

I think it's part of my dreams. It's part of who I am. I can say "no." There are a lot of other girls in the Middle East that know, "This is my destiny. This is what I am going to do." That's not who I am. I decided to leave everything behind and be here. I think that imagination is a part of your personality. A part of who you are.

Do you think you take imagination with you when you die?

No. I think that's it. This is your destiny. This is what you are going to be doing. Either you are going to hell or you are going to heaven. There is no in-between. So, no. You are going to be in reality. You get to have your imagination here in life. That's what God gives you. That's how he tests you. When you go back, all that is done. No time to play. This is what you are going to be doing.

Evidently, you believe in heaven and hell?

Yes.

What would you say that your religion is?

Our religion is like the other religions. I did read the Bible. The only difference we have is that we don't believe that Jesus is the Son of God. We believe He is a prophet, like Mohammed. Mohammed is a prophet of God. Jesus is a prophet of God. They are prophets. They were here to deliver a message. There is just God. There is nobody else than God. That's the only difference between us and the Christian. We do have the same rules. No drink. Don't have sex without marriage. We have the same thing.

My neighbor is a Protestant and she keeps coming to me. She says, "You need to convert. There is a wall between you and God. Jesus is this wall. If you can believe in Him there will be no wall."

In my religion there is no wall between me and my God. There is just me and God. So if I want to ask something, I cannot use Mohammed or Jesus. I am going to go straight to God because He is my God. He is the one who created me. I think all the religions are the same. [The issue is that] between that time and this time there are a lot of things that were delivered wrong or documented wrong. At this point I think that we all have the same beliefs. We all have to do the same things.

I don't know if it would interest you or not, but at one point Jesus did say don't pray to Me, pray right to God.

That's how I believe. Something touched my head when she told me that there is a wall.

I can see why she said that to you in that way. This is the last question. What do you think is the most important thing?

In life? To me? My kid and my dream. These two things keep me alive. Every day when I wake up and I see that smile. My dreams keep me alive. I know I am going to be successful in my life. I will get there. That keeps me alive too. These are the most important things.

You brought your child from Iraq?

He is American. He was born and raised here. He is my life. He is everything to me. My friend told me to take care of my husband instead of everything revolving around my son. He is the most important thing. At the same time, when you leave, you won't take your kids or your money. You will take whatever you've done in your life. Which is true. That's why I answer my kid and my dreams.

You are confident then that you are going to heaven?

No, no.

Oh, you're not sure? You never get to find out until you find out?

I'm sure that I've done a lot of things like cheating on my husband. That's one of the bad things that I have done. I will never forgive myself. Again, it was something I wanted to do. This is my life. There are other things like leaving my mom in Iraq and coming here. There is nobody to take care of her. That's another bad thing. She doesn't need someone to take care of her. She is a doctor. When I was in Iraq she was like my kid. I give her a bath. I do her massage. I do her feet. Because my dad passed away in 1986. She never got married after that. Her life was me and my brother. My brother is with her now. I feel guilty for not being with her.

Recent Graduate

"I still find each day too short for all the thoughts I want to think, all the walks I want to take, all the books I want to read, and all the friends I want to see."
John Burroughs

"My friends are my estate."
Emily Dickinson

This is a fun interview. The reason is that the young man gave very honest and vibrant answers that match his personality. He was only eighteen and recently graduated from high school. He has since finished his university degree and is living in Asia.

I love his perception of his soul, and I enjoyed going more in-depth on the topic of sleep stages. I ignored the apparent contradiction between having the imagination located in the brain and taking it with oneself upon death. He was a delightful participant.

What do you want to be when you grow up?

[Laughter] Well, I want to be alive. I want to, hopefully, be a man at that point. That's all the ambition I have so far. I want to be something nice, but I have no idea what my career could possibly be.

Okay. The first question is, what are the purposes of imagination?

Purposes of imagination? Imagination breeds creation. Without imagination we would have nothing at all. People often don't understand how important it is. If we didn't have imagination we'd be nothing more than a monkey.

Imagination is like, "Hey, I can use this rock to smash open this shell and eat this animal." Imagination breeds survival. Nowadays it's not so important. Innovation can help create new cures for cancer or whatnot. More or less imagination is housed in the art world. It's really important in that sense, I think. If you were the same as everyone else then you've got nothing. Imagination, even though it's not a tangible thing, it's probably the most important thing when it comes to careers.

What do you think the origin of imagination is?
Probably, personality. It, of course, comes from your mind, but everyone's imagination is different. Everyone has different dreams. They have different ways they see things. I'm assuming that people who have similar mind-sets have similar imaginations. Like an angry person would have a similar imagination to another angry person. It's definitely brought on by personality.

You make it sound like it's pretty individual then?
Imagination? Oh, yeah. You could be talking to someone about an idea of something that you want to create, like a project at school or a piece of art or even a tree house. You could explain it to them in full, and then when you make it, they tell you it's completely different than what I had in my mind. Even though they were there when you were playing with the idea, their image of what they had in their head was completely different. It's built off of life experiences. If I imagine myself living in a house when I'm older, I'm going to imagine it being a lot like the houses I've lived in my whole life. Someone else's thought of a house could be completely different.

It could probably be used in negative ways and positive ways, right?
Oh yeah, you could imagine some pretty horrible things. Think of all the weird forms of torture there are. Sick and twisted imaginations.

What do you think the location of imagination is?
You mean the location, like what part of the brain?

Yes, if you think it is in the brain. That would be an answer in itself, the brain.
I think it's in the brain. Between your brain and your eyes. Not what you see immediately but you visualize things and that is based upon things that you see. But then that's in your brain too. All your memories are there, so yeah, I think the brain.

Do you see any correlation between memories, the visualization and the imagination? Do you think they link together?

I don't know exactly what the correlation would be, but there's definitely a correlation between what you've seen and what you...

What you imagine you saw?
Yeah.

Do you think animals have imagination?
Yeah! You know in Sri Lanka they have elephants that paint?

Really?
Yeah, they have paintbrushes and they sell their art. It sells for a lot of money. They'll have an elephant paint something and they throw away about two-thirds of what the animals paint. Apparently, the animal was not in the right mood.

I don't know how you'd be able to tell if was the right mood or not by the painting, but they pump out a bunch a day and they sell for $3,000 apiece.

I think animals have imagination. They have to do things as much as anyone else. They plan. A cat looks around the room and he wants to get to the fish tank. He has to imagine how he is going to get up. If he's going to jump from that to that to that, you can see it working in their mind. It's not quite the problem solving that human beings have. I was watching my friend's cat yesterday. He was looking at his leg because it wanted to jump to the bed. You have to have imagination for everything.

I was reading about REM sleep and they think they've proven that when a person is in REM and they awaken right then, you're having your most vivid type of dream that you can have. I was reading that they had proven that birds, reptiles and mammals are having REM sleep. Isn't that kind of amazing? They have seen them do the rapid eye movements.

It makes sense because they have memories, too. The thing about REM is that's the time when you can replace all your neurotransmitters. If you don't have REM sleep then you don't have a serotonin release?

It's supposed to be the fourth level of sleep, the most restorative, the most restful. If you only go to stage one, two and stay there, perhaps get into three a little bit but don't ever get down the fourth stage, then you're not rested. You're not okay and can't think as well the next day.

Doesn't alcohol block you from getting past stage two or something like that?

I've heard something similar to that, especially with sleeping pills. I don't know very much about alcohol research but the experts think that with sleeping pills that it's probable that the sleeper does not get to the REM stage. So they've slept for eight hours but they didn't get to that restful point.

I wonder if I have REM sleep because I only sleep four hours a night.

It takes awhile because it's stage four. The first few dreams you might have when you first shut your eyes, they are supposedly taking place in stage one, the more shallow stage. I don't know how many minutes they are apart but they come in intervals. You go through, one, two, three, four and then you go back to one. You do that all night, you [cycle] through one through four all night.

I learned about this in Psych 100, later I'm taking 101 and then I'll know more about REM sleep.

Do you think you take imagination with you when you die?

As in to an afterlife? Your soul? Yeah. I think it's part of your personality. Of course I think that will stick with you past death. I don't know what other people believe, but I've always thought that your mind pretty much stays the same. Your soul, your personality, the way you act, your memories, would stay the same.

I've always hoped that I would take my imagination with me in the afterlife. Because I've been thinking for years that it might work in more tangible ways. I'm only guessing, naturally, since I haven't died. I'm picturing, or I've always thought since my youth that if you imagined a purple tree then you'd get a purple tree. It would be like living in a dream land, in a way, you get what you ask for.

Kind of like *The Cell*. Have you seen that movie?

No.

This lady jumps inside the mind of a serial killer and the landscapes are created. At the end she brings the killer into her mind, she creates this beautiful world. I kind of hope that video games will get to that level eventually.

More of a holograph?

Yeah, like *The Matrix* if it ever gets to that level of skill. Plug yourself into the game.

Connected in the back of your head? Feel it, smell it, taste it—all of your senses could be hooked up to an electrode.

There would be a chance of failure, all kinds of pain. You can't unplug yourself.

*Arnold Schwarzenegger was in a movie [*Total Recall*] where he went to a commercial business and bought a fantasy experience. He wanted to be a spy, an action hero, so he was caught up in his fantasy, got lost in there and thought it was real. But at the end of the movie, if I remember correctly, the audience is allowed to decide for themselves if he really was a spy or not.*

I've seen *Vanilla Sky*.

Yeah, very much like that. Vanilla Sky, *same concept. You don't know that you're dreaming.*

I always have dreams that I realize I'm dreaming. For some reason I'm terrified of the fact that I'm asleep. I try to force myself awake. It's really hard. I have to work my way to awake. It's the most terrifying dream. I don't have nightmares. Being asleep and knowing I'm asleep bothers me.

I have a lot of dreams that I'm aware that I am dreaming. It's a weird mixture of worlds.

You can kind of feel your bed around you and at the same time you're in a room full of people.

I don't even feel my bed around me. I'm gone in the dream but I become aware that these things are so unreal they are not happening.

I had a lot of dreams in Europe, and I would think I was back at home. I'd wake up in Europe disappointed to be there instead of at home. In my dream, I'd be having a good time drinking my Mountain Dew.

You really missed your Mountain Dew.

I missed a lot of things, but Mountain Dew was a focal point for me. It was the last straw.

[Laugh] We'll have to bring Mountain Dew to Europe, turn them on to one of our highly caffeinated drinks. Okay, so there you are. You're in your afterlife. You've taken imagination with you. Where are you? What is your afterlife?
What kind of life do I imagine myself in if I was dead?

Well, yeah, religiously speaking, spiritually speaking, where is it that you're going?
Heaven, I hope.

Heaven?
I hope. I wouldn't like to go to hell.

[Laughter] Given a choice.
[Laugher] Given the choice I'd take the eternal happiness as opposed to the eternal torment.

I guess we all would choose that. So that's where you are going. Do you think you have a soul?
I hope.

Well, that's your basic assumption, that you have one, right? So where is it?
Where's my soul? It's kind of an intangible thing.

Do you have a feeling of where it maybe is?
I've never given much thought to it but in my childhood imagination I always thought your soul is an exact copy of you, only intangible. It's another you.

Maybe kind of more see-through?
Yeah. [Laughter]

I don't know if that came out of cartoons or what, like when the dead soul comes out of the cartoon character and they look just alike.
When you shut your eyes and try to ask yourself where you are in your body, do you feel like you have an awareness of where you are?
I feel like I'm behind my eyes.

Same with me. I narrow it down. I don't feel like I'm in my knee.

Emotions though, like when you have strong emotions, you can feel it in your chest.

Yeah, and what is that? What do you think that is?

I don't know, what is that horrible feeling you get, like when you're being cheated on? Maybe that's just me.

That's why some people feel that their soul is in their chest because they feel their bad feelings there.

Their heart hurts, that kind of thing?

Yeah, that's why so many people think their soul, or their awareness, or their personality or their essence is in their chest area.

I think my lungs are there.

[Laugh] The last question is, what do you think is the most important thing?

The most important thing?

At the end of the day, at the end of a life, besides Mountain Dew. [Laugh]

A couple of things. I remember what my sister said. Right before she goes to sleep, she thinks about what she did that day. She makes lists. If she had a good day, she felt good. If she wasted a day, she felt like crap. If a movie was made about my day and I enjoyed watching it, then it was a good day. If I was able to live my day to the fullest, as much as possible, and fill it with as much fun things as I could.

Really important things to me are friendship, as opposed to anything else. I can go to work for twelve hours in one day and make like $3,000 and all I'd think is, "I made a bunch of money," but my day is wasted, my day is worth nothing. But if hang out with my friends all day and have a great time, constantly smiling and having fun laughing, then I think a day like that was awesome. I wish every day could be like that day. To me that's the most important thing, that giddy happiness. It's not like "love" or being relaxed.

To me, you seem like one of the most alive people. You're always alive. Do you think that's why you sleep less than other people?

Probably. That's what my dad says. He says my body's always up. It doesn't know when to come down.

That seems to match your mental outlook.
    Yeah, I'd like to be able to sleep at night.

I used to have a friend who often said, "I'm going to live while I'm alive and sleep when I'm dead."
    But then you have twenty less years to live.

I guess she didn't care about that part.

College Professor

"I am all in favor of a dialogue between science and religion, but not a constructive dialogue. One of the great achievements of science has been, if not to make it impossible for intelligent people to be religious, then at least to make it possible for them not to be religious. We should not retreat from this accomplishment."
Steven Weinberg, Physicist

This was a delightful interview due to the beautiful outdoor surroundings and the conversational skills of this fifty-year-old professor who teaches in the medical department at a university. He spoke slowly and with much care, and his scientific background influences him at a profound level and even impacts his understanding of spirituality.

Our talk was more reciprocal because he has a thoughtful and curious mind. He asked me some questions which provided more opportunity for me to speak than would normally be prudent. Talkative people interview well and a good conversationalist interviews extremely well.

What are the purposes of imagination?
Purposes of imagination. I'm going to have to get my imagination going.

[Laughter]
[Pause] I think imagination serves many different purposes. It probably springs from your childhood and how you create a sense of reality, whether it's for play or reconstructing your sense of environment—what's around you—to be creative, to be able to tap into something that's inside of you, for fun.

[Pause] I guess what I keep thinking about is coming back to a sense of creativity, a place to start creating other things, other ideas that might just be for fun or play or actually work into something that's a little bit more concrete, useful, constructive. To take people to places that they otherwise haven't experienced or can't practically be at or get at.

The second question is: What is the origin of imagination?

Maybe boredom. [Laughter] That's sometimes where you see it. Or dissatisfaction with what you're dealing with. Or just a sense of play. I guess it can come from a place where people don't want to be, or it can come from a sense of where you want to be. I don't know where it really comes from as far as...I haven't ever thought about that. I think of it through the eyes of my kids, I guess, more than anything.

Kids come by it pretty naturally.

Yeah, and kids don't have responsibilities or a sense of the world. And imagination fills that space for them, where as adults we have other things that fill our space. Unless you're an artist perhaps or you're the kind of person that's engaged in certain activities where the use of imagination becomes much more practicable. Adults have responsibilities and kids probably use it a lot more.

These are good questions. When I'm trying to solve a problem sometimes I'll use my imagination more. I'll try to tap into what is possible. Getting back to your question, what are the origins of it, that's a little bit of a mystery, I think.

Where do you think the location of imagination is?

If my neuroscience friend were here he could probably tell us where in the brain it might be housed. If I was to have to come up with an answer, it might be parts of our imagination probably come from that collective experience that resides in all of us, from the creative force.

Do you think some people have different amounts of imagination?

Yeah, I think people can access it in different ways. I don't know about amounts, I doubt if there's some designated amount that any of us get. It's probably how we can tap into it. Our imagination might be as accessible or available for anybody; it's just how we're put together and our life experiences—what we allow ourselves to be able to think and create.

Yeah, and if you stop allowing yourself—like if you have free reign as a child as you mentioned that you can see it working in your children—then as we grow up we stop or we start to stifle it.

There was a neurobiologist on the radio last night who won the Nobel Prize in the year 2000. He said that the hippocampus actually fills up. Then that information in there has to disperse into other places like long-term storage or become forgotten information. He was saying that we have billions of nerve cells in our brains and he chose to do his work on sea slugs because they only have 20,000 nerves in them. He has come up with this whole hypothesis that we have all of this activity in our hippocampus and it can only store so much.

I'm thinking about that as far as brain biology goes. Many people have said that imagination is in their right brain and that the left brain has to collaborate with your right brain and make connections, but there does not seem to be just one imagination area. Whereas we know we do our thinking in our frontal lobe.

The way we think and how we think is a function of neurons in our brains and in our nervous system. So from a purely biological sense, I would say it's within our nervous system, within our brain. We just barely have understanding of how our brains work, how the nervous system works, how we think, how we take in information, use it and react to our world.

It wouldn't surprise me that in shorter and shorter periods of time that what we know now as we understand it, is not right. From the Earth is flat to it isn't but in a shorter time period and in a more complicated way. I just heard a radio interview about "String Theory." There are different levels of reality, dimensions. They figure it's…have you ever heard anything about this string theory?

Basically, it's the unifying theory. They believe since Einstein they've been trying to develop a mathematical explanation for everything. I'm talking way out of my league here, but the idea is, from what this gentleman was saying, is for string theory to work, mathematical equations to come together, there have to be at least eleven dimensions of reality.

Our visual world and our understanding of three dimensions plus time, the fourth dimension, doesn't even begin to really explain or capture what reality is according to string theory. There are at least seven more dimensions, and what is that? What are those dimensions? For me to just believe that what we think, what we believe to be true is housed just in our brains in some fashion probably is limited. So I don't know where it's housed. How we know, how we operate in four dimensions, in a biological world, physiologically, yeah, that explains it. Our thoughts are created from the interactions and ourselves, but I don't think that begins to really capture the story about imagination and creation.

It seems to me—left brain, right brain aside—it feels like I'm using the same part of my brain when I conjure up, so to speak, or visualize a memory that is real. I'm wondering how imagination and memory are working because they are both based on visualization. What do you think about that?

Yeah, I would agree, there seems to be a connection there. What stimulates those memories? What stimulates what you see in your mind's eye? It could be words, it could be smells, it could be sounds, it could be thoughts. The stimulus that kicks off a picture in our mind can be real varied, which is cool. But for some people, they say smell is one of the strongest stimuli to memory. That has to be a neuro, physiological phenomenon.

Some people, I would imagine, have individual differences with what triggers our ability to have a memory or to have a thought, an imagination, if you will. Some of the brain studies for learning, the more stimulus, the more varied the input you can have—whether it's sound or movement, or touch, or talking—the broader the sensory impact you can have on the ability to make certain connections and the ability to learn is enhanced. Why wouldn't that be true for your imagination? Is it to enhance the sensory stimulus to enhance your ability to imagine and create? Do you equate imagination and creativity?

Personally?
Yeah.

I do. Personally, I think one of its purposes is creativity. When you decide how you are going to design a quilt or create the cure for cancer, whether you are trying to create from what you have or you know or the studies you have been looking at, then you're taking your brain and you are making your links. Even in science they have a term called the intuitive leap, or perhaps it's called the imaginative leap. Even scientists acknowledge this. Sometimes there is not a readily understandable leap.

Mere facts lining up doesn't always give that "aha" moment to a new discovery. I think that creativity and imagination are linked, and I think that imagination has a ton of purposes. That's only one of them. It also helps us not go insane, and I think when we have too much we risk going insane, although that's not the whole story behind insanity. But people do get trapped in an imaginary world that is not real. That would be a really difficult way to live. I think it has all kinds of roles and purposes.

If people are trapped in an imaginary world, the key word there is being trapped. They can't move in and out appropriately. That brings it into your ability to control.

Control is the word. For me, being sane, I can turn it on and turn it off. I can activate imagination at will. I've used it in mundane situations where I was going to be someplace such as a long car trip, I've activated it and used it so that I'm entertained while I'm doing something else that would otherwise just be so tedious.

Where I'm using a certain level of imagination more than I ever had is with the routine and habit of telling my daughters stories at night.

Do you make them up?

We make them up. Sometimes they are just totally from nothing, well, it's probably not from nothing, but a sense of fantasy. Sometimes they springboard from a conversation we're having or an event that has happened. We create some make-believe story. We've done that routinely, and it's been a challenge for me to be able to jump in there and do that. I've found that it was lots of fun to see where it would go. It's a way of being uninhibited, to be able to tap into a place that I can go just anywhere. So that's been kind of fun to do. Probably that's the place where I routinely use my imagination these last few years.

I came up with a story about Jo-Jo the Clown for my children. He was separated from his circus and he came to the door to ask the child how to get back to the circus. That was the basic premise. My kids asked me to tell the same story every time after that. They only wanted Jo-Jo the Clown.

Do you think you take imagination with you when you die?

[Pause followed by laughter] Well, that's kind of a loaded question because how we think about death is all about imagination in some respects.

Isn't that a funny connection?

Do I think that we take imagination with us when we die? Well, I can imagine that we might, but I also can imagine that there's nothing. Something in the back of my head or somewhere in my belief system I hold onto this sense that the essence of us—perhaps it's one of these other dimensions that we were talking about before in String Theory continues to exist. I think our imagination comes from some ability to take in our experience and our collective human experience that seems to be part of who everybody is too. If death is some other dimension, I would say that we would take our imaginations with us.

Do you think you take aspects of your personality with you too?

I would say you would have to on some level if it's that way.

In other words you might just be a little blob of energy or something without personality.

I guess, but who knows? I look forward to finding out, or if I don't find out then I guess this kind of concept...

Won't matter?

It didn't play out and that's just the way it is. Again, I think we really don't know. I see it as a possibility.

You used the word essence during that answer. Do you think you have a soul at all, or would the word essence be your word for soul in your personal beliefs? Is soul a bad word?

I think soul probably is just the term that is used in a certain sense to explain what we are other than this physical thing that we show up in on this Earth.

Do you have one of those, do you know?

A soul?

One of those things that doesn't quite show up, maybe in the eleventh dimension?

My less rational side of me...there's a certain part that says that there is an essence of who we are. It's part of us. It's unique to us, but it's also part of all creation, all experience. I guess that's what people define as a soul, maybe. Soul has religious connotations and I don't necessarily put it in a religious context. It doesn't have to be religious for me.

The essence or the soul or the thing that makes you "you," do you know where that is inside of you? Do you have a feeling of where your awareness is?

No, it doesn't come out of my brain. It doesn't come out of my throat. It doesn't come out of my eyes. [Pause] It's more general for me. Maybe the eyes have something to do with it. [Laugh] If I had to put it in a spot. I've never thought of it as contained somewhere.

The Nobel Prize winner I was talking about before, he was asked about consciousness. He predicted it would take until the next century...

I know they are trying to locate it.

We don't know what consciousness is. We can't define it. We can't study it. The scientific community is infantile on this subject. Even if a person does not talk in spiritual terms but would prefer to use words like consciousness, I'm still curious to know where people think their consciousness is in their bodies or where they feel like it is. Some people have a ready answer.

I guess if I had to isolate it, in the eyes. I have more of a sense that it isn't an isolated thing. It's probably not contained in a physical sense that we have an awareness of. That's why I've got to buy that book on the String Theory.

If we are going to put any stock on the theory, it seems there could be all these potentials around us that are existing, but we're not in a position to observe them.

If your soul or essence were manifesting or exhibiting itself more on this other dimension then you might not really be in touch with, or have much feeling of contact with it. It probably wouldn't matter where it was located?

Right. I wouldn't think so. Again, this is so far beyond me. You look at the subatomic structures, it's all space and movement in an unpredictable pattern. String Theory is saying there are eleven dimensions of reality, that is how we connect everything together.

There could be lots more dimensions. There are mathematical formulas involved. I'm not a mathematician at all, but it takes incredible imagination to think I can create a formula to explain everything.

Basically there's more space there at the subatomic level. We don't operate there, but that doesn't mean that we can't be affected by that in some way we can't ever imagine. Maybe that's where a lot of what you're talking about lives, in those other dimensions.

It may be far more metaphysical than physical. It all depends on who you ask. The funny thing about imagination is, we all have one and we use it all the time.

But we don't think about it. I think my artist friends probably think about it way more than I do. I'm not an artist per se and my work doesn't overtly call for it. I've got to imagine things are going to be okay, right? It affects my life mostly with my kids.

What do you think is the most important thing, at the end of the day, at the end of a life?

I've heard a lot of people say this and I've read it and I believe it to be pretty darn true, it's the relationships you create. The interactions you have with your friends, family and strangers. Those relationships cause people to either change or not. I was having this conversation the other day with volunteers who take our college students. We were talking about teaching and learning, and to end things up I told them that they didn't realize the impact that they have by mentoring these students. It has a ripple effect. It's unpredictable and almost unimaginable how far reaching and significant were their contributions. I think relationships are the most important thing because they affect far beyond our understanding of what happens in the world and beyond it.

It does carry on.

It carries on for the good or the bad. Hopefully, there's more good.

WEST POINT NEUROSURGEON

"Cogito ergo sum: I think, therefore I am."
Rene Descartes

Many interviewees grappled with brain structure terminology as they made efforts to explain the whereabouts of imagination. Who better to ask about these complexities than a neurosurgeon? This is someone we would all expect to know brain anatomy well.

I was able to sit down with this fifty-two-year-old neurosurgeon from Memphis, Tennessee. You will find consistent, straightforward answers.

What do you think are the purposes of imagination?
Well, I think to allow people the opportunity to think about things that haven't been done or things that could be done in a different or a better way. Or to dream about some place or circumstance in their life that's more pleasant than where they are. To help cope with difficulties in their personal lives or their workplace.

You're the first one to bring up coping and that was one of my first ideas when I asked myself these questions. I thought it would help people cope with a mundane job, amongst other things.
What do you think the origin of imagination is?
You mean inside the brain?

We are getting to that next. This question is where did it come from?
Something special about the human brain is that it has so much more capability for the brain to...there are more neurons and they are higher developed than animals. There is lots of brain that is not needed for hunting and fishing and watching out for somebody trying to kill you.

I think as a result of that, it comes along with having a higher intelligence. Part of intelligence is being able to have abstract thought and the imagination fits in with all of that.

Do you think, since you brought up animals and the complexity of brains, do you think animals have imaginations, too?

I don't think so, but I don't really know and certainly haven't read any research data on it, but I would be doubtful that they do.

Okay, now I am asking, where do you think imagination is located in the human being?

To the best of my understanding, most of the problem solving and executive function of the brain is in the frontal lobes, left and little bit more than right maybe. I would think that the conscious imagination is there. Some of the deeper brain structures might respond to things like smell, touch, some of the things we might perceive, not on a strictly conscious or cognitive level.

In what way do you think that imagination might correlate with memory?

Well, I don't think there's a lot of difference necessarily. Memory is if you do something enough times to imprint it in your brain or if you concentrate and you try to imprint it in your brain, that's what memory is. If you have a certain type of imaginary thought that you resort to frequently or you think about frequently then I think that the two can be almost the same thing, because memory can be almost anything that you've imagined more than once.

We know real from what is not real because we are sane, but it almost feels like we are recalling from the same place. How much is memory being worked over in the imagination? Is that why we are so easily able to change our memories about something? For instance, people remembering the same event differently.

Well, I think some of that could be the way they perceived it in the first place. You don't necessarily have to assume that they are changing it if their first impression of what happened wasn't the same. Depending on how long ago it happened, you might remember some parts of something more than another person does. I know if I get together with my brothers we'll bring up some event, and it seems everybody remembers something a little bit differently about what it was and about what one person's reaction was. I think that's normal, but when you add in disease states like head injury, or whatever, your ability to remember short-term things can be hampered. Same thing with dementia.

Do you think, in your opinion, that people would take imagination with them when they die?
    Take it where? [Laugh]

Yeah, [Laugh] that is the question.
    I don't think there is anything. When you die your brain stops working and I haven't really figured out the hereafter very well. From the standpoint of anything physical that goes with you, I'm not convinced that happens.

How about the personality? Or do you not think that people go anywhere at all?
    I don't think they do. That's not to say that there is no heaven or hell or that you don't have a soul. My impression of someone's soul is not that it looks like them or thinks like them. It's an aspect of their being, but not something that you can relate to anything that they do or say when they are here. I think all that pretty much stops when you die and get buried or cremated.

Do you have any concept, in your own opinion, of where your personality is inside your body? Another way to ask this is: Do you know where the real "you" is? If I had to extract the real you, your personality, do you know where I would need to go?
    Well, it's in your brain, mostly in the frontal lobes. I think that because that's where your thoughts, your executive function is. You can see that in people who have frontal lobe injuries and they are still alive, they can eat and everything but they are not who they were in terms of their sense of humor, being able to solve problems with any complexity.

So, if you get an injury in the frontal lobe, the personality is altered. For instance, if they were an outgoing person that aspect might be a little different after a brain injury?
    Yeah, they might be less outgoing or they might be more outgoing to

the point of being totally annoying. Someone who has a severe injury to the brain, especially to the frontal lobes—that's one of the big problems. It doesn't have to be a head injury. It could be from a surgery, or a tumor, or a rupture, an aneurysm, or anything like that. They come back and they are very upset because they are not the same person. There is a capacity for healing over a year or so and recovery, especially in a younger person. I think that's where your personality is.

Interesting. Let's say the person is younger and they started to recuperate; some things began to heal. They could actually regain closer to the personality they had before?
Yes.

Are your patients mainly the brain injured then, or any kind of injury?
Well, brain injury, tumors, ruptured discs in the neck and the back, hemorrhages, strokes—that's kind of what I do.

That has got to be some of the most delicate surgery there would ever be.
A lot of it is, but some of it is less delicate than you might imagine.

That's surprising to me. I studied the nervous system in college, and I have very limited knowledge compared to yours, but I'm picturing this complexity of the nerves and how small they would be.
The last question is: What do you really think is the most important thing? Maybe the way a person lives, what really matters at the end of the day or a life—either one.
The motto of West Point, which is where I went to school, is "Duty, honor, country," and I think that those three things, together. Duty includes doing your job well and carrying out your responsibilities, both personally and professionally. Honor is being someone who is trustworthy, and if someone asks you to do something and you agree then you do it and they don't have to call back and ask why you didn't do it. Being patriotic—loving your country because it's the best. You put all three of those together and it gives you a good core of beliefs and things that you can use to help guide you through your life.

CHRISTIAN PASTOR

"For whatever things were written before were written for our learning, that we through the patience and comfort of the Scriptures might have hope."
Romans 15:4

This interview is with a twenty-three-year-old Christian youth pastor who had only recently graduated from Bible College. If you are preparing yourself for shocking or surprisingly non-conventional answers then you can relax. Everything said here is as exactly as you would expect a Christian to answer.

He preempted the possible chance for a later illogical answer by not claiming to know exactly how the eternal spirit of man works in the physical body. It did not matter as much as he was not very adamant about taking or not taking imagination with you when you die.

What are the purposes of imagination?
The purposes of imagination. [Long pause] God says that He has created us in His image, and one of the things I think we have, like God, is the ability to think and to reason. Imagination is putting together ideas and thoughts and creativity. People are able to put to use those things that He's given us. I think, in some ways, one of the purposes of imagination is that we've been created in the image of God. He is a creator God and He's given us that same capacity to be able, in a limited sense, to create things.

The second question is, where do you think imagination is located?
I know our thoughts and our brains have a huge capacity for that, so probably, in a physical sense, it's located up in the brain. I don't believe that man is restricted to molecular structure. You can dissect a person, and it's just the synapses and things like that. I do believe that man has an eternal spirit. I don't know how that works together in a physical body.

Do you think animals have imagination?

My understanding and basis for what I believe is found in God's word and the truth. Whenever I am asked questions I try to bring it back to my basis for my beliefs. I don't see anything in the Bible that would give an indication that animals have spirits, or that they continue on after death, or that they have an imagination. I know that they can think and they respond.

Do you think imagination plays a role in the ability to remember or to visualize a memory?

I think so. Without memory, imagination would have no meaning. It would have no substance.

Do you think you take imagination with you when you die?

I know that when we die we take some things with us. But there are other things that we don't take because in the Bible it talks about how the former things have passed away, the sorrow and so on. All of those things are gone. If those things are gone, I would think that any memory or thought related to that would have to be gone as well. I think that imagination, as far as our ability to think and reason, will continue after we die, but I think it won't be the same as here.

Minus the negativity maybe?

Yes.

You mentioned before that you think you have an eternal soul or spirit. Which word did you use? Which word do you usually use?

Probably the correct word would be spirit.

Spirit? Do you know where your eternal spirit is located?

No.

Did you ever think about it before?

It's not something, to me, that is dependent upon a location. If something is eternal, I don't know if it necessarily...I know it is connected to me in some way, but I don't know where it is.

If you had to guess if it was outside of you or inside of you?
I would guess it was somewhere inside of me.

Do you think it's tied to your personality?
I see man as a three-fold being. The Bible talks about how we have a body, a soul and a spirit. The body is our physical makeup, soul relates a lot to our mind and our emotions. Then our spirit is that part which is eternal and will continue on after we die. I think our emotions and our mind and our soul is a big part of what we are, but I do see a distinction between that and the spirit. Other people disagree. They only see man as two-fold, the body and the soul or sometimes they'll fuse the soul and the spirit together.

If you have body, soul and spirit and they are interconnected to some point, then do you think the personality is more associated with the soul or the mind or your spirit? Or can we not dissect them?
[Pause] When God first created man, I see Him as creating man as spirit, soul, body in that order. When man fell in the garden, I see that as being reversed, where now man operates first under his body, appetites, then soul and spirit. But when a person gets saved, God reverses that again, in a sense. In my mind it really depends on who you are and what your relationship is with God. What is most influencing your life? If it's those soul-ish things, the emotional—and that dictates what your mind would desire to do, or the will or the spirit—that conscience that God has given you. I think it depends on if you're saved or not.

Let's say a saved person dies and goes to heaven. Do you think there are elements of their personality, minus the negativity, that they would take with them there?
I would think so.

Do you think we'll recognize one another in heaven?
Yes, I don't have any doubt. I don't know how they knew it, but when Jesus was transfigured on the mountain with Moses and Elijah the disciples didn't have to ask Jesus who Elijah was...they just knew who they were.

What do you think, off the top of your head, is the most important thing?
To me, the most important thing is knowing God. That's what Jesus

in John 17:3 said. This is eternal life, this is what life is all about, this is the meaning to life, that they may know You, the only true God and Jesus Christ whom He has sent. The most important thing in life is knowing God.

Some people who don't know God, I would like to be able to get them there. A lot of them will have to face those other questions like where do we come from and why are we here and where are we going? I don't really see any other—at this point in time—philosophy other than what the Bible declares as giving valid answers to those questions. If someone were to ask me, "what is the most important thing," I'd give them one piece of advice, get to know God, from His word and fellowship with other believers and prayer.

Aspiring Rabbi

"Humans inevitably die."
The Terminator

"And I find it kind of funny
I find it kind of sad
The dreams in which I'm dying
Are the best I've ever had."
Tears for Fears, *Mad World*

There is a wide age range represented by these interviews. You are about to spend a few minutes with another bright thinker. This is a fifteen-year-old high school student who considers himself to be a future Rabbi and will pursue a political career as well.

The topic of fate came up, as it often does, and I found myself puzzled by his confidence that all humans have free will and yet are connected. If you have free will most people would conclude that you are independent from other people and even to some degree independent from any deity. I did not ask him about this but it certainly struck me as an issue. Coordinated free will was a new concept for me.

What are the purposes of imagination?

I guess to survive through life. If you didn't have any imagination then you could be controlled by what other people say. That wouldn't work though. You couldn't be controlled because you have no imagination to be controlled. I think imagination is pretty much who you are. That's what makes you different from other people.

If you were to take out physical appearances then that's pretty much all you have left. It's the core of any person, and I think that's how you can tell your true character. Imagination can get you through anything. Without imagination we would pretty much be nothing.

Do you think some people can have too much or too little or different amounts from person to person?

Of course you can have different amounts of imagination, but it's all about how you define imagination to begin with. If you define it as a creative sense, I think that's how most people would define it, like an improvisation, or like writers. It's all about how you define it but I think there is no real way to judge imagination unless you can go inside somebody's thoughts.

The Freudian thing with the id, the ego and the superego, and I think there's different amounts of imagination within those different levels. For example, somebody could have a lot of imagination in their ego but they seem like a very bland person, like the superego might be, they might appear to be bland, but there's no actual way to measure imagination.

What do you think the origin of imagination is?

I guess maybe in the way somebody is raised. Do you mean how do we get imagination? Where imagination starts from?

Starts from, or how maybe did we get it? How did it get into us?

Yeah, I don't know. It seems like animals probably have imagination too. I'm not sure exactly how that would fit in. I don't think the fact that humans have an imagination is an incredible phenomenon. The amount of imagination that humans have—but again if you can't judge imagination.

The origin of imagination, I'm not really sure how, or where it comes from. Maybe it [depends] on how somebody is raised. If they're raised with intolerance and that is ingrained in somebody's mind from the beginning...say with Hitler. Let's say Hitler was raised in a Jewish Orthodox community. Then he'd probably be a lot different depending on his imagination.

So environment could impact it.

Exactly. Environment probably has the biggest impact. Then again, look at genetics and how susceptible somebody is to his or her environment. So if somebody is easily persuaded by his environment, or if somebody has a really strong idea of who they are, then the environment has less of an effect.

Where do you think imagination is located?
Can you define that? Rephrase that?

Well, we know where our foot is, right? That's pretty obvious, so where do you think our imagination is?
Well, I think imagination is in every person. It's within each person. It's how you use imagination. Where it comes from and where it goes basically. I don't know where it can be located, but I think there might be some kind of psychology thing that's not invented yet, a new kind of research that can go into the human mind. They might be able to find where the root of imagination comes from. I don't know. The reason we are here to begin with is because of imagination. That's probably how we got to the point where we are.

You are saying it's that powerful?
Yes.

I ask that question because some people think it's in their brain, some people think it's in their personality. In fact, what do you think about that? Do you think imagination is a part of the personality or would you side more with people who say it's in the gray matter?
I could argue both sides basically. You could say you have no control over your imagination. You could say you have no free will. You are just influenced by everything. Or everything is happening to get to another point. There's a Chinese philosophy about the Yin Yang, how everything is going to equal out. So imagination is going to equal out to another person, back and forth. I think actually neither, brain or personality. The personality is affected by the brain too. I guess it's all like one big circle.

Maybe not so divided but personality and gray matter working off each other?
It kind of builds up, at the end of it you don't really know what the overall objective is.

Do you think people take imagination with them when they die?
If somebody dies and you still have memories of that person, that can definitely influence your imagination and how you think.

People continually die and the memory of the person will grow less and less over every generation. That person will have less of an effect on somebody.

I forget the man's name but there is a quote, "What you do now echoes in eternity." So what somebody does now is going to go on for generation to generation. Eventually that person is going to be lost in history. Forgotten, but echoes and parts of them that will carry on—maybe a vague idea that still influences how people think. Not like they are forgotten. It's not really spiritual.

But if you look at time, it's proven not only theologically but also using time. If you step back and look at one point, you look at time completely differently. We have no actual conception of time, from one time to another time. I can't really imagine what time is like, it's really complicated.

It is. I have a book about it in my office where different philosophers from thousands of years ago until more recently have each written an essay on time. Some believe it exists and some believe it doesn't exist at all and it never did. Some believe there is a past and a present but there is no future. Some people believe there is a future and a present but there is no past. Some have considered Einstein's theories and thought that things are not so much in a line as much as they are hills and valleys.

If you start opening your mind to that idea with time or space, as far as the planets go, then it can change your mind a lot. If you start to see it differently than a flat line, it's very mind opening to look at it like that.

Yeah, for example, if you look at the future itself, its appearance is infinite, the future is infinite. For every tiny thing that could happen—like a fly in California flaps its wings like two times more—that's one different part of the future. For instance, we're like a tree sort of, and it keeps forking out and out with different possibilities to happen.

Do you think there is a fate or a destiny then?

I believe in free will. Yeah, I definitely believe in free will. I think that's pretty much how each person, if you go back to imagination, how each person's free will is going to bring them to a point in the future. For more people in this world, like more variables, more possible outcomes there are for this future to happen. Every single person's free will in the world, it all makes one product. Not one period of time but everybody's will is pretty much put together for each second that we live. Your average person chooses.

So we have free will. Are we connected in any way, one person to another?
Absolutely.

We are connected, we have free will but somehow we coordinate together?
Well, of course. If I went to a baseball game or something and my mom never picked me up, it was her choice. It's her free will never to pick me up. Then obviously my fate is affected by that.

I was told you had a good mind. Back to when an individual person dies. Do they take their imagination with them?
Where?

Well, that depends on any given person I ask.
I think the modern Western or Christian philosophy way of looking at things that there is a higher level. After you die you go to heaven and it's a whole other spiritual situation. I think that would also work if you believed in the Jewish philosophy. They live life as it is. Life is now. They are both connected at that one point. That point can be heaven or it can be life now, it's the same thing. You are looking out at everything. Everything is happening at the same time and therefore nothing happens. I'm not relating this right.

So, in your personal faith, do you have heaven then? Sounds like you do from what you're saying.
It depends what you define as heaven. I don't believe heaven is an area where you resurrect and go to a place with clouds.

A big potluck?
[Laughter] Well yeah, I mean in a spiritual sense of heaven. Everything is like no sin or anything like that. Some people think the physical body goes up into heaven and that doesn't make any sense or the mental [part of a person] or your personality or possibly your imagination going to heaven. I don't know. I'm not sure. I can't talk for all Jews basically.

I know many Jewish people and they vary. They vary a lot.

One saying is: "Two Jews. Three opinions."

[Laughter] Yeah, I've heard that one before. They have told me they like to discuss topics. They like to have a differing opinion. They don't feel as though they have to reach consensus.

Exactly. The more opinions you have and the more disagreement the better it is. The more you get out of it, the more you can enjoy ideas. It's one of the biggest sparks of imagination, without disagreement then human society would probably stop. I think we're built on disagreement with each other. Not harmful (such as disagreements that lead to war). If America was run just by the Republican Party or just by the Democratic Party it would not work. You need to have differing opinions, they are needed to survive.

I can see what you are saying because the power of the debate itself is going to spark new ideas.

That's why imagination is the foundation of society.

It's a pretty important topic. You have a heaven in your opinion but it's not quite the Christian heaven let's say. You talked about a Christian heaven being without sin so your heaven might be more, say human, as we live it here? More an extension...

No, not at all. If you look at time as a graph, this is my view, I'm not speaking for all Jews right now. I think there are different points everywhere [on the graph]. We might be living in heaven now, this might be it. That's why we need to make the most of it and do the best we can do. Look at it as a challenge, heaven is not only a challenge but it's something you need. Heaven means you are always going to be striving to do better because this is all you have.

That's interesting.

By the time you die you know you've fulfilled your life. Instead of being scared of death—I thought about this a long time—instead of fright when you are on your death bed, you can look back and have had a good life. I've helped people. I've been a positive influence on people. That's how you die happy. That's the way to die. If you die like that then you've had a fulfilling life and you lived a good life and you contributed. I think that's the best anybody can do. Instead, if on your deathbed you realize you've slacked off toward society your whole life and you wasted a gift that God has given you. You've wasted it. That's all you have.

You led me right to my customary last question. It sounds a bit corny but what is the most important thing?

Life, of course. Life. In this case, I can probably speak for most Jews. Life is the most important thing. If you don't have life, you don't have thought. Without life there's nothing. Without life there wouldn't be imagination. There wouldn't be the world as we know it now. There would be nothing. That's why you should never waste life. You should never give it up and never let it go.

Bank President

This is a very bright Princeton and Harvard graduate who is employed as a bank president. He was sixty-five years old at the time of the interview. I enjoyed his demeanor and his answers.

His unique contribution to this book lies in his answers about the location of imagination. Also of interest is his final answer in light of what he does for a living. He is from Rochester, Minnesota.

What are the purposes of imagination?

To me, imagination lets you realize new possibilities and it also lets you get outside your hum-drum, ordinary, everyday self. I guess I would include fantasies in that as well as just imagination, because it deals with new possibilities and things that might be beyond reality.

What do you think the origin of imagination is?

I really don't know. I know there are a lot of things that suggest themselves to my mind that sometimes turn out to be true. For some reason, last night I dreamed about a department store that I remember my mother taking me to as a three-year old. When I woke up this morning I read in the paper that chain of stores had been sold. So, I don't know if I imagined it or if there was something psychic that suggested itself to me. I was quite shocked to read about that.

What do you think the location of imagination is?

Physically, I've always assumed that it was in my brain, the center of my brain. I don't know if that's what you mean or not. It certainly has something to do with one's soul, and I do believe we all have a soul.

It is interesting that you answer with both brain and soul. What part do you think personality and soul play off each other, or are they kind of the same thing in your mind? Are they combined, or two separate things?

I think of a soul as on a higher plane than personality. I think personality is probably just a physical manifestation of what your soul is; your store of knowledge and your store of experience. By that I include values.

Do you know where your soul is located?

Physically, no. I think of it as something ephemeral, that it's free floating. It's not like it's in my medulla or cerebral cortex or something like that.

Have you ever had an awareness of where you feel like you are in your body? Have you ever thought about it before?

No, it hasn't really occurred to me. I do think that the hemispheres of the brain are a storage device just like a computer disc or something like that. To me it would be too simplistic to think that the soul is something that you could store there and form electrical impulses.

Some people think that the soul is on a different plane, so to speak. Like on different dimensions, as in one dimensional, two dimensional. It's right here, but it exists on a plane that we don't interact in the same way—a spiritual plane. Do you think that at all?

Yes, that's a much better description of what I had in mind than the way I said it. I just wasn't able to articulate it as well as you did.

[Laughter] Well, thanks. I have the advantage of knowing what the questions are about. Do you think you take imagination with you when you die?

Oh, yes! I do believe that there's some sort of life hereafter. I'm not sure that it's a conventional heaven or hell. I would certainly think that one's imagination, personality, characteristics travel with them.

I think that, in many respects, one is partly the sum of one's experience. You look at somebody by the time they are thirty-five or forty—sometimes I've said to myself that by the time a person is forty they have the face they deserve. I would think by the time someone is sixty or eighty-one they have the sort of soul that they deserve.

Interesting. What do you think the most important thing is? Honestly, if you could leave people with one thought or what you think is the most important thing, what would you say?

I'd be inclined to say love probably. I think without that this life is fairly empty. It would also be an intense belief in something. I contrast that to people who are grasping at materialistic things. They spend their whole life wishing over things.

Hungarian Dancer

"Others are altogether different from us...and it is through but pain and pain again that we come to learn this."
Ferenc Molnar

"It is not enough to be Hungarian; you must have talent as well."
Alexander Korda

It's not every day that I am able to have a conversation with a Hungarian dancer. If you ever attempted to have a meaningful dialogue in a crowded coffee shop with all the sounds of espresso machines and blenders going full speed, then you can picture this thirty-year-old and me seated right in the middle of a busy and noisy situation. Even through the blaring music and ringing telephone, I enjoyed listening to her beautiful accent. Budapest was her hometown.

She answered the questions with full assurance as if she had studied for the examination the night before and knew all of her material well. Self-confidence is a central point for her as you will see when she answers the question about life's most important aspect.

Occupationally, she is a professional dancer, as well as an actress. Like many others in her line of work, she had taken a temporary job as a cashier.

When did you move to the United States?
On the day President Clinton was inaugurated in January. I just came and met people and made some friends and got an apartment and a new job. I could support myself and I went to school. My life was really full. I remember that was the day that I came.

What brought you over here?
So I could dance. I came to New York and I used to work as a professional dancer in Hungary doing theater. I wanted to study more, different kind of stuff like tap and modern and jazz. Classical ballet is very

96

prominent in Hungary. We had some modern, but you have to come to New York. That was a big thing for me.

The first question on the interview is what are the purposes of imagination?

I think imagination is very important. I don't think I would be existing without imagination. For example, if I never imagined that I'm going to come to New York one day, probably I wouldn't be here right now. So I think imagination is very important in achieving your goals. Sometimes it might not turn out exactly the way that you imagined it, but I think it's important to have a goal, a task that you have in your mind.

So it can be a motivating factor or an original idea?

I'm speaking from an actor's point of view. An actor's work is based on imagination. I think imagination can be practical. It can be developed. I was a very imaginative child, so my parents joked about me all the time. I made up tales and stories. I don't think it's a problem for me. [Laughter]

Do you think some people have more than others?

Yeah, I think so. Maybe we all have the ability but some people can shut it down. Or they are not willing to take the extra mile or they are too afraid of something and they don't want to go there. I don't think it's about being able or not able, they just don't use the ability that they have in themselves.

So that would be the down side of not using it enough. Do you think some people have too much imagination?

It's funny you ask me because of where I work there is a lady who is using this far off machine, or whatever it is, if you put your left hand down on these metal buttons it measures the energy waves and it shows what your Chakras are. How many percentage you use [of them]. My upper Chakra, the one connected to the brain and the imagination and the thoughts is very, very high. Mine is 80% out of 100% and my root Chakra which is connected to the earth—that is important as well—that is really low.

She advised me to connect to my root Chakra more. That doesn't mean I have to cut off whatever is in my head. Probably I could use some grounding paths in my life. It is funny that you would say that because this just happened. There probably are some people who are like myself, a little too over-developed in that sense.

What do you think the origin of imagination is?
The desire.

So it starts with a desire or an urge, and that starts the process that results in taking action to make goals come true.
Or not. In the best-case situation, I would say they take actions to make them true.

Where do you think imagination is located?
I would say it comes from the desire of the mind. It might come from the spirit and heart and then it manifests in the brain, in the picture of imagination. It will eventually take form in physical action.

There's a lot of truth to what you said.
I was just trying to think back to how I do things.

Do you believe you have a spirit?
Yeah. Although, I don't know where it goes after we die. That's a question that comes up in my life all the time.

Do you know where your spirit is?
Personally, I think mine is somewhere in my chest because that's where I feel either bad or good things. I know there is a saying that you feel it in your gut. Probably that's true too. I don't know. I feel it in my chest. I feel it there when something is not right.

That feeling you have in your chest, do you think that might be a spirit then?
Yes. Or my guide, or an angel or whatever you want to call it. It's me.

Do you think you could take your imagination with you when you die?
Yes, I would say that would be a logical answer. I don't know if it's right or wrong, but I would say yes. I hope so, yes. I hope it doesn't die, because that's a very human thing, imagination. I hope it carries on.

To clear up your earlier point, you do or do not know where you are going to go when you die?

Physically we know because our body will eventually be gone. Spiritually, I don't know where we go. I would love to hope that it would go somewhere else. I don't even know if it comes back eventually like in reincarnation. But, I definitely think something that is very close to my heart: When we have this life, which is a gift, we can use it to really develop ourselves and I think that's a very important part to realize. We are here. It's a gift. It's not our choice and we need to develop.

I don't know the rest of the story—if we come back in a different form and then we either pay for our sins or we develop more. Hopefully, when I leave this earth I will develop and I will make something better out of myself than when I came to the earth.

I really believe in self-development, here anyhow, regardless of what happens after the fact. I hardly ever find anybody that talks about it or even seemingly thinks about it.

Really? That's interesting because in Hungary, where I am from, this kind of talk, it's not unexpected, I found they did invest time and thought in self-development. It was a really popular thing to talk about there. When I came to the U. S., I found people had different backgrounds but they went toward the same thoughts. I think, "Thank God I can be here." I don't think I would be the same person if I had stayed at home.

The last question is what do you think is the most important thing?

Personally, when it comes down to individuals, I think self-confidence. I think that's the biggest gift that parents can give to their kids. If they deprive the kids from that, that's a big disadvantage in life eventually. I think in life as human beings the most important part is self-development and recognizing how responsible [we need to be] toward the earth, our planet, the environment, each other, toward our kids, toward our future. I think going toward the future is very important. It's very important as well to cherish your roots and where you came from and the past. We could talk about this for a day to go into more details.

Did your parents give you a sense of self-confidence?

No. Probably, that's why I understand the importance of it. That's what I'm going to strive for when I have kids. I think spiritually it's very important to support a child. Sure a nice house and a nice car are important too. But I think the spirituality is important for that child to evolve.

I'm Christian of course—I guess you guessed.

I didn't guess.

But I am, it's important to me to keep Christmas for example and it's a big thing to celebrate it. Sunday should really be for my kids, but I can't stay the whole day with them because I have to shop for the grocery. Eventually, people will lose their own time for themselves, that's why we have more stressed people, that's why we have problems with the teenagers and the school problems.

I'm the kind of person who tends to rush and get caught in the wheel and then I drop exhausted, then I don't know why. I'm that type of person, so I actually have to hold myself back sometimes and sit down and say that's great, but now this is what I'm going to do. Take the time for myself and play with my dogs or doing nothing and be at home.

There is a new topic, a new thing, people are talking a lot now about "being" versus "doing." That people even have to write articles on the topic is amazing, that our culture would need to be reminded and learn how to "be" rather than "do" all the time. I'm like you—instead of falling down dead tired I've learned to pace myself in a different way. I try not to work myself to exhaustion, plus I need time to be alone.

I don't know what's going to happen eventually here. If people will realize it needs to be stopped or what. I don't know how far it can go. Something has to give. When I feel overworked, I feel that spirit of mine, it's almost like gone or it's suffocating or it's dehydrated. It's like it's asking for help and how many times we just don't listen to this. How many times do we just ignore it and we push ourselves.

I think our culture is suffering from stress.

It also scares me how much parents don't spend time with their kids. Kids do need time with their parents and their families. It's how they learn about feelings and relationships. If they don't learn those things they don't know how to act in the world.

Vietnam Veteran

"They say I'm mad, crazed by the war; Have you been there, and if so what for?"
McCollum, of World War I

As I searched for people from varying backgrounds, I knew that I wanted to include a Vietnam veteran. When I saw this fifty-eight-year-old man wearing a tie-dyed shirt and long grey hair, I eagerly approached him. He looked like the quintessential hippy waiting for a Grateful Dead concert.

It's obvious that he struggled with the material. His answers are consistent because he doesn't know the answers and doesn't pretend to know them and he doesn't bluff his way through them with background knowledge that he possesses.

He will probably be the only person that I will ever meet who camps in his driveway so that he can get a vacation from answering his phone. This interview is one of a kind.

What are the purposes of imagination?
The purpose of an imagination. If you don't have an imagination you have nothing. I can't really explain it. I'd have to think a little bit longer on that. The purpose of imagination would be…I'm drawing a blank. Well, if you don't have an imagination you can't do anything as far as I'm concerned. You wouldn't be happy about doing anything. You would have nothing.

What do you think the origin of imagination is?
I really couldn't answer that question, I don't know.

How about the location of the imagination?
I'm not sure.

These are hard questions?

Yeah, I never really thought about stuff like that.

That's why I ask, because some people haven't thought about it yet and then their brains start to work right here, right in front of me.
Imagination, if you want to do anything, you have to have an imagination in order to do something. If you don't have one you just lay around doing nothing. You'd be unhappy. With an imagination you can imagine you are doing things, you have something to look forward to.

Do you think everybody has the same amount?
Absolutely not.

Do you think children have more?
Yes, they do. I'm probably confusing this with dreams. A kid probably has more than a grownup.

When you're asleep your imagination has a chance to really kick in and do what it wants.
Well, mine's kind of dormant right now. I don't really dream about too much of anything.

Maybe you're sleeping too good.
Probably not good enough.

Let's try this one. Do you think when you die you take imagination with you?
You know that's a question I can't answer because I've never died.

Oh, so you're not sure. Nobody ever answered that way before.
Seriously, that is the truth. I don't know of anybody I've talked to even that died and came back so how can you tell? I mean your spirit goes away as far as I know. I don't really know that either. Your spirit might just stay in your body when you die. I don't know.

Do you think animals have imagination?
Yeah, they have to. I think everything has an imagination. Then again, I'm not sure. I've never talked to an animal that told me. When I did have an animal all it did was eat, sleep and play. They do have an

imagination. They get out. Dogs do that. Any animal does that. They want to explore. So evidently they do.

Have you ever thought about this before? If you shut your eyes and ask yourself where you really are at within your body, where do you think you are in there?

[Long pause] That would depend.

Okay, how about right this second?

Right this second. I'm sitting here. I haven't experienced that.

You don't know where you are?

No, I really don't. I don't know where I am in life right now. I kind of wish I did. I have a lot of issues. I'd like to leave this state.

Where would you go?

Anywhere but here. I've lived here too long. I need to experience new places. I went back to Virginia, and I really enjoyed that. I went to the Bahamas. I enjoyed that. I went to Florida. I really enjoyed that.

I just got back from Florida myself.

Cool. You can close your eyes and imagine you are anywhere really. If it's hot out, you can close your eyes and imagine it's cool and you can stay cool.

What do you think the most important thing is, what really matters?

Waking up in the morning. That's the most important thing. Then getting on with what you do the rest of the day. I just do what I do, I don't think. You know what's got to be done, and if you can't do it it's frustrating. If you can it's cool. I can't do a lot of things I used to.

Do you have an illness?

Well, I've had four operations on my neck and that stops me from a lot of things. Plus, I have diabetes. That's why I say waking up in the morning is the most important thing. If you don't [wake up] you don't have anything to worry about then. You don't even have to pay taxes. When I get on my motorcycle I forget about everything in the world.

I can't explain it. The wind hits you in the face and it's just a wonderful feeling. It's something you're doing all by yourself and you're just enjoying the heck out of it. It is nice that way. I love it, but I can't do much of that anymore either.

I rode the other day and had to come back home and get in Blackie (that's my truck) and do the rest of the traveling [that] I had to do in the truck because it's more relaxing.

I go camping. I have a motorhome parked in my driveway. What I do is gather up what I need, take it out to the motorhome and I camp in my driveway. Just to get away from the house. Just to enjoy. Don't have to drive anywhere. I'm out there and don't have to worry about answering the phone. I just go camping, but I can't do any fishing. But I can leave the motorhome and go swimming. I have an above ground swimming pool. It's not very big, but it's enjoyable.

I was in Vietnam in 1965 and '66.

The war wasn't over then.
I don't have anything to say about that.

Not a fun topic I guess.
Not really. I don't talk about it to people.

That's what all the Vietnam veterans tell me. They don't want to open that file.
A lot of things I've blocked out of my mind.

Who could blame you?
That's why I'd like to know what a person from Vietnam would have to say to these questions. I would imagine they would have a lot more to say because they would have a lot more to want. But then they don't ask for much. They are content—at least there they seem to be content.

MEDICAL STUDENT

"There are two facts about the human soul on which depend all things we know of its nature. The first is that it thinks; the second is that it is united to the body and can act and be acted upon."
Descartes

This twenty-two-year-old medical school student is from Saigon, Vietnam. He was raised in the Buddhist faith and you will notice that while many people find the questions to be new and somewhat surprising, this person encountered more difficulties in answering than others I've interviewed. Yet he provides some interesting insight into his faith as he understands it. I think you will notice the large extent of his scientific pursuits have not yet reconciled themselves to his beliefs. It is also noteworthy that he reveals his motivation for becoming a physician: his mother's death.

I will always remember this interview and my own surprise concerning his thoughts on the Christian's destination following death. In addition, some of the teachings on Buddhism included soul transformation, the incarnating from human form to animal form, which are not commonly held by Western Buddhists. I think that he adds greatly to the entire conversation on these weighty topics in spite of the fact that this interview was cumbersome for him.

The first question is, and there are no wrong answers, what are the purposes of imagination?
There's no time limit? Purposes of imagination. I think it's a beautiful thing because, for example, well if you are an architect, if you can imagine how a house is going to be, or a building, in your head before. Of course you can scratch it out first. Usually if you do something you have to imagine it before. Even if you're going to say something, right, the imagination, I think it links to the thought process. You imagine things before you are going to say it, if it's important. I think it's for maturing of mind, the more you do it.

It's like a chess game too, right? You imagine the next play, it just helps your mind and helps you mature. Every child does that growing up and the rest of your life until the day you die. It helps mature, and, I don't know, I guess that's all of it.

So you must think, based on what you are saying there, that everyone is born with some amount of imagination.

Oh yeah, you bet.

Do you think some people have more than other people?

I would say so because not everyone is born to...I think that different people have different levels of imagination. Why do I think that? People are different and they grow up in a different environment. If a person grows up and they don't have a lot of deaths, and the other does, maybe the level of imagination is going to be different. It probably depends on the environment, the culture, the genes. Let's say your dad is creative versus a dad who's not so creative.

You mean if your dad is an artist or something he can pass some of that on.

Yeah, different kinds of creativity, like an artist or creating in any sense, like on the computer, you might see that gene. You might pass on to your child and they may be able to imagine better than those who did not receive the gene. To me that's true.

There's also environment too, that's why it's so important for kids to go to school. They learn to read a book for example, when you read it's not like watching a movie where the pictures are already there, you think. That's why when you read a book you imagine that. It's important.

Well, I can take you to a similar place where you are already going with the next question. What do you think the origin of imagination is?

What do you mean?

Well, the origin of a river is where it starts or where did it come from?

I don't think there is an origin. This is a hard topic, imagination is a hard topic. When you're born with imagination, say for a particular thought, there's an origin in the sense that something triggers it, right? Probably when you were young and use it for the first time and you put it in your memory bank. Later, as you grow up, that becomes more familiar. Like what I'm going say next, it takes something to create it you have to use your imagination. You get more familiar with it, so I guess the origin is when you were little, when you first see it or first use your brain to imagine it.

Where do you think it's located?
Well I can be more specific—I happen to have my book. [He removed a large textbook from his bag.]

Is this class covering the location of imagination?
Definitely in the higher intellect.

More of a frontal lobe area? Have they ever talked in class of the location of imagination in the actual brain? Like we know where the optic nerve is, have they ever talked about where this thinking process takes place in the brain?
Different lobes work together. The frontal one is important because it's involved in reasoning, movement, emotion, problem solving. When you problem solve you use your imagination. You use your memory, you use your experience, what you've learned in your college career, now you're an architect you take all of that together to imagine. So it works together—and vision is important, you have to see it. Touch, pressure, temperature in the temporal lobe on each side.

According to your book, perception, hearing and the memory are located in the Parietal lobe. Now this brings in another question from my list. What part does imagination play in memory? What do you think?
Imagination, again, I just gave an example of how you use your memory and all those senses—your vision, your hearing, your taste, your smell—all pulled together. That's why chemical engineers or chemists recognize the smell of certain chemicals like acetone. They smell, put it in the frontal lobe. They can close their eyes and think of the smell, you can't really imagine smell, but you can recall from the memory bank and think about how it smells.

Like if I ask you what gasoline smells like you would recall from your memory. It plays a very important role in imagination. I can use this later when I am a physician.

Maybe I had a bad experience when I was little. Let's say my mom died—that's true, my mom died. Because in Vietnam, at that time, there was a lack of health care and we were poor. We lacked access to health care and she died. I can imagine myself being a doctor—that's one thing that motivates me to do that. Where you store experience in memory and to review that, to picture that, to recall that, to imagine what you're going to do, or be, or paint.

How do you think imagination and personality correlate with one another?

Imagination and personality. I think it's important, that they do go hand in hand. I see that person acts a certain way. If I didn't like that, I should prevent myself from being like that. I would put that in my memory bank and I would imagine myself, I shouldn't be that person. When you don't like something, or that person for example, then of course you're going to go through that thought process, which is imagination. It's pretty much the same thing.

Pretty much equivalent terms?

Right. Not quite, but let's say for now that they are pretty much the same. If I see someone I like, I can try to be more like them so that people will like me. Usually when you act that way, you like yourself. There probably was a time when people didn't like you, so again that's personality right?

Do you think animals have imagination?

You bet, especially primates, like monkeys. Chimpanzee have a lot of thought process going on, for example, why would in evolution, why would a female choose a bigger male? Because she wants to be protected. Like the bigger one the alpha male he can protect her and her children later on. A lot of imagination too, see? Yes to a certain degree, like a fish, less imagination the lower the animal.

Less brain capacity?

I guess so. When we go down the animal tree...

Probably wouldn't have as much parietal lobe in the smaller animals.

I think this type of question would be great for a psychologist, psychiatrist or a physiologist, or a marine biologist or a zoologist. Also ask evolution professors who are in anthropology.

I think I might already know how you're going to answer this next question because for you the imagination is a part of the gray matter in the brain. In other words, we're born with it and we have it somewhere in here to use as we would any other part of the brain. Do you think people take imagination with them when they die?

To me that's sort of related to religion. I'm Buddhist. I don't know about Catholicism, when you die you turn into ash and you die basically, right?

I think Catholics believe they go to purgatory and then go on to heaven. I'm not Catholic.

I meant Christianity in general, not Catholicism. In Buddhism, we believe that [Buddha] is not quite a God, he is a teacher. He is there to teach you.

Do you have reincarnation when you die?

Yes, reincarnation if you have good karma, basically a good person. If you did more bad than good, there are eighteen levels of hell. When you die and you're a bad person, you go to the second level and there you get punishment and later you reincarnate into another person or to a pig or an animal. If you were a monk you might reach heaven, you might be with Buddha.

If the monk was really good, would he take his imagination with him?

That would be answered differently by different Buddhists.

I'm asking you.

Before you reincarnate they wipe out all of your memories.

They block them out?

You drink this cup of soup, or something, and everything kind of blanks out and you start as another person or an animal.

Would you start with a different personality? Maybe you'd be more outgoing or lots of different things.

Right, if you were bad, like a murderer or whatever, you'd probably be a pig or a bull so that you have to work hard. Like a horse, somebody will ride you. Or after level eighteen you can never go up again.

Ever?
Ever, but again that's Buddhism, I do believe in some of that but I believe in the teaching like being good and stuff like that.

As a way of life maybe?
Yeah, as a way of life.

Are you pretty sure of where you are going when you die? Or do you think you are going someplace when you die?
I never thought about it. Truly, I do believe that when you die that's it. But because to encourage people to be good, that's why we have teaching.

To give meaning or guidance?
Right, if you throw rice away then later you go down and eat worms or other bad things.

It's a motivation?
A motivation to be good, to be a good person, to stay away from evil, etc.

But you personally, you're not so sure that you go anywhere when you die or you are real sure?
I never thought about that, but I believe in Buddhism and all the generations before me did and I will carry on that. I just try to be a good person.

Every medical student is asked why they want to be a doctor. I want to help people, of course, right? It's serious to me. You are helping people. It's a good feeling to help people. You don't have to be acknowledged for it. You don't have to brag about it. It's a good thing inside you, that you get a feeling. I don't think we carry on to a next life. They are supposed to stay away from sexuality and killings.

Okay, I have one more question before we stop. If you shut your eyes and think hard about where you are inside your body. Where is it that you think you are inside your body?

Inside my body, what do you mean inside my body? A certain organ?

Where do you think you are? Like inside your toe? You probably don't [think that]. So where is it that you think that you are?

At first I want to say in my heart. Every organ system whether it's your skin or your bones, every area is incorporated. The heart is also an amazing organ. So I would say the heart. It just came to my mind, I don't know why, it's the first thing I thought of. Where do I see myself as a person?

There's a real you, right? There is a real "you" someplace or a consciousness or whatever word you want to use.

I would say the kidney, it's an amazing organ. I would say the brain too. The brain controls everything—that's why you're not pronounced dead until your brain waves shut down. Without your heart, well your heart can stop beating and you can still be alive. Heart and brain because it controls who you are, it's the most important. Of course the kidney is an organ. The cardio-vascular system—that's a phenomenal system.

ZOOLOGY STUDENT

"The greatest mistake in the treatment of diseases is that there are physicians for the body and physicians for the soul, although the two cannot be separated."
Plato

While selecting potential people to interview, I knew I had to include several university-trained professionals with science degrees. I wanted at least one doctor because so many people want to place the location of imagination within the right side of the brain or squarely in the left. I also wanted to speak with a zoologist in order to get some basic answers regarding animals and their capacity for imagination. I found two for the price of one with this interview. He had completed a zoology degree at a major university and was applying at medical schools to achieve his goal of becoming a physician.

Even more significant than his scientific training is that he is one of the people who firmly places the imagination in the brain, and also with great certainty takes it with him when he dies. Amazingly, he explains to us how that works.

He was a twenty-four-year-old man from Seattle, Washington, at the time of this interview.

What are the purposes of imagination?
The purposes of imagination. I think that God gives everyone certain talents and certain gifts. I think everyone has at least one special gift that they excel at, you might say they do better at it than the average person. I think intelligence comes in a lot of different flavors, and I've always thought of imagination as sort of the universal intelligence. Because people used their imagination differently. For some people imagination, like Einstein, his imagination brought about some of the most wonderful physical theories. He changed the world with what he

did with his imagination. Other people, like Monet, his imagination, he painted landscapes didn't he?

Yes, but they were imaginative.

Great artists like Picasso and Monet and those people, their imaginations brought about beautiful paintings for us to look at. I think that imagination is the universal intelligence. I think the person born without a high IQ is still able to imagine what they might want to do with their lives.

So it's pertinent to the creative process?

Yeah. I think without imagination a lot of the discoveries, the medical breakthroughs that we've done, would not be here without imagination. Broad intelligence only gets you so far. The great portion of intelligence is imagination and the purpose is...there are many purposes. The power of imagination is very great because you can change the world with it. Maybe not necessarily the big world, but just your own world. Maybe you live a terrible, awful life and your powers of imagination, at any moment, can take yourself out of it. You can imagine yourself in a different place, doing different things. Maybe after a long enough time, that could motivate you to actually make your life that way.

Like a coping mechanism, it can actually cause a change and serve as a motivation. Change your reality.

Yeah, even people who have low IQ have imagination. It gives anybody the power to be the best they can be whether they are smart or not.

Speaking of that, do you think people have varying amounts?

Of imagination? [Pause] Yeah, I think that the power to imagine is something innate. It's inherent among everybody. I think some people choose to use it more than others. There is an innate quantity that people are born with. That's the same among everybody. Certain people, for whatever reason—like having a hard home life, their parents don't give them enough attention—so they might use their imagination on a constant basis to try to remove themselves from that.

Maybe other people use their imagination differently. In the sciences you have to use your imagination a lot to think of experiments, to try to learn about new things and prove theories. Then again, maybe someone sitting at a desk, pumping out math problems for eight hours a day, I don't know how much imagination they might need to have. Probably some. Some problems might require more imagination than others. They might not have to use as much as another person. I think the quantity is the same but how you use it varies.

Do you think it might be similar to a muscle, as in if you use a muscle quite frequently it will build to be a bigger, better one?

Yeah, I would say that. I think everyone does start out with a certain level. The more you use it...there are certain parts of the brain that are linked to imagination. The more you imagine, the more you are using those nerve centers in your brain, and they can multiply and become sharper.

Maybe the saying, "practice makes perfect" in a sense, too. Not just the nerves but maybe someone who has had that success using their imagination would be more inclined to go out on a limb and try it on something new.

I've never really believed in "practice makes perfect," because I don't think there is such a thing as perfection. I think practice makes better. I don't know if there is a quantity called perfect for imagination. There's no limit to a person's imagination. We don't even know the limits to what one's own mind can process.

Where do you think imagination is located?

I'd have to go back to my science book. There are centers in the brain that are involved with creative thinking. That creative thinking can be positive or negative, and a lot of that is influenced by the behavioral parts of the brain. For instance, Ted Bundy's version, his idea of having an imagination and being creative, is probably related to how he can murder a person and not get caught. There you have behavioral tendencies that are influencing the creative centers.

I'm sorry, did you ask where was it in the brain or where was it period?

Where is it period.

I think it definitely comes from the brain. There are centers there related to creative thinking. I think that creative thinking is influenced by other parts of the brain like behavioral centers.

That makes sense. I saw a documentary, and I may have the facts wrong, but some frontal lobe damage had occurred or they were at least measuring that area where people do not have as much impulse control as you and I would have. They've lost their ability to control their impulses. If that were the case they could still be using their power of imagination, wherever it may be located, but their ability to control their impulses would be inhibited, like a serial killer.

Yeah, a lot of people say that if a person is extremely creative, they are called "right brain" thinkers. The right side of the brain is influenced by the left side of the brain. One side can imagine something, but I have to carry it out. Maybe when I do carry it out, maybe it doesn't go exactly as I thought it would go. Then I have to adjust on the spot. That involves left and right brain.

Do you think animals have imagination?

Gosh. [Pause] That's a great question. I don't know if they have imagination or not. I think that animals have feelings. I think most people would agree that having feelings is definitely a predictor of some sort of higher cerebral cortex activity.

Do you mean like emotional responses versus sensory feelings?

Yeah, that's what I mean. Emotional responses versus sensory feelings, that's exactly what it is. I think that animals do have that, and I think that is an example of an organism that has a higher order of thinking. One could put emotional feelings on the same plane as imagination. Obviously, imagination and experiencing emotion, those things are clearly on a higher order of thinking. If I had to guess, I would say that animals probably do have imagination. If you're going with the logic that they have emotions, then I would definitely think they do.

It appears as though you can hurt the feelings of a dog. I've seen how they look when they are in trouble.

Yeah. You yell at your dog, it runs off and cowers. Then they forget about it soon. They don't have the short-term or long-term memory that humans do.

If you're going along that line of thinking, is their imagination really that complex? That would be the best question. I don't think it would be real complex, but I'm sure they would imagine things. It's kind of like asking if they dream. I think they probably do dream. You were probably going to ask me that.

[Laughter] They look like they are dreaming when they're asleep.
We know nothing about dreams, absolutely nothing. I think [dogs] are able to process that sort of thing. I think they do have dreams and imagine. I think those are all hallmarks of higher-level thinking and higher-level cerebral processing.

So, I think you would agree then that dreams and imagination are highly linked together?
I think so, definitely. I think they are very intimately involved. A large part of imagination is built off of things that are not happening but may happen—things that you want to happen, or not want to happen. They are events that you envision happening. When you think about something, you're thinking about an action happening in reality. You think about how you wish you were walking down the beach, the sand, the ocean, the palm trees.

An educator who I've studied, Charlotte Mason, said whenever you make an emotional connection with anything, you'll remember your facts better. It also reminds me of when I took Medical Terminology in college they showed us a film to help make connections for our memories. I remember "benign," they showed a bee sitting on the number nine to help us remember and then we were told the meaning of the word. They were using visualization tactics and trying to make a little bit of an emotional connection in order to have us remember Latin terms. People do tricks like that when they are studying for an exam too. I would think that you had done that a lot.
Oh yeah. I've used that a lot.

Association, I guess it would be called.
And that's a perfect example, I can imagine a bee sitting on a nine and that would help me remember. It's more a word connection. It just shows you how diverse imagination is. You can use imagination as a tool to remember. It doesn't necessarily have to be connected with an emotion or trauma, or high and low magnitude doesn't matter.

116

Do you think you take imagination with you when you die?

Do you mean when my soul goes to wherever it goes? Would I take imagination? Absolutely. I do because I believe that imagination is a neural impulse. It's like asking, do I have a consciousness? Do I have thoughts after I die? If a person believes, like I do, that after you die you go to either heaven or hell—and I do believe that your soul takes on all the biological capabilities of your body and carries that on in heaven or in hell—the imagination goes along with that.

With some people the interview goes a little differently. They may answer that the imagination is clearly in their brain and then they know, for a fact, that they are going to take it with them when they die. My question would naturally be, yeah but, you just left it behind within the cranium. But you explained it. That would be like saying I'm going to take my eyeball with me or my left kneecap.

Same thing, absolutely. It's like asking if you can "see" in heaven? Can you touch? These are all characteristics of a biological organism. Yes, you do leave that biological shell behind when you die. If you think you experience all of these things in heaven or in hell, I think you do experience all of these things. So naturally the question is how can you disappear and go into some magical place? You can go around in circles all day on that. I do believe you do go there and I believe you do live, you see, you touch, you feel, you experience all the human qualities that you do on earth. I think that your soul takes on all the biological activity even though you leave your body down here. I think it takes it all on. Of course that includes imagination.

So, could you call it a metamorphosis? Or would I be putting words in your mouth if I called it that?

No, you can use that. Sure. That's exactly what it is. Imagination itself goes through a metamorphosis. What I imagine at the age of five is much different than I would now as an adult.

That would be another influence on it then, maturity itself.

Sure, maturity. That goes along with somebody's upbringing and morals and level of ability. A person dying and leaving the biological shell and going off to either heaven or hell as basically an entity.

Personality and soul, how connected are they? Are they completely different things? Are you taking your personality too? I'd imagine you'd say yes because you said you're taking your imagination with you.

[Pause] I think when most people think of a soul they talk about feeling things in their soul. If I were to take this ball [holding an imaginary ball] and I put everything that is in myself and say this is me. My intellectual life, ability, what I look like, my favorite color, my imagination, my hopes and dreams, my personality, what I want to be when I grow up, my morals and beliefs. I put it all in this container, this magic, glowing ball—that's my soul, that's what I think a soul is. A lot of those things are not biologically related at all, but most of them are. When you die, you're just leaving a shell behind. All these other things, that's what goes with you. That's why when you go to heaven or hell you are still yourself. The soul is all those things. A lot of these things are driven by your mind, which is biologically driven.

I think the personality is a subgroup of soul. Personality is included with what a soul is.

So, if you are an outgoing, easily amused person, which is how I describe myself, then I would take that element of my personality with me perhaps?

Oh, you'd take all of it. I think in order to get into heaven, if you get in, you get in on the merits of what you are on Earth.

Are you getting in to heaven?

I think so. I believe that you are taken based on what kind of person you are on Earth. Since I believe the soul is all those things, you take all those things with you and they either let you in or they send you downstairs. Once you're inside, I would think that you'd be the same person. You would have the same personality. You would have the same morals. You'd have the same favorite color. I have no idea what it would be like to live up there, but if it is anything like people theorize heaven is like, then I would think you'd go through another metamorphosis up there. Personality may be completely different because you'd be surrounded by a much different world.

Do you think we'd be able to recognize one another? Say if we were both there later this afternoon, do you think we'd know one another then?

Oh yeah. Your soul will manifest, it will take on the biological responsibilities that you have here on Earth to run your body. The soul takes all that on, even physical characteristics. So I think we would definitely recognize one another. I would recognize my great-grandfather that's been up there for twenty years.

Is it a Christian kind of heaven or a Catholic kind of heaven? What are you?

I was baptized Catholic, and I believe in a lot of the Catholic interpretation of the Bible. I hear a lot of people say that Christianity embodies everyone who believes in God. I don't really know. I'm not an expert on religion. I don't know a lot of the differences between Christian and Catholic. It basically comes down to how you interpret the Bible. I believe the interpretations of the Catholic religion. I do know that if in a person's faith that they believe in God and that there is a heaven, a place where people go that have been good in life, then it's not a Christian or Catholic heaven. It's for whoever believes in God and believes in heaven, and they have faith and they try to do their best to be a good person. I think there are more religions out there that do believe that there is a God and a heaven.

Definitely, you have the American Indians for instance. They may not have a Catholic Priesthood or Jesus Christ for that matter, but they believe they have an afterlife of some kind and they have a God. I wonder if they'd be let in then, in your estimation.

I think so. I don't know who has been let in and who hasn't been let in. I think it all comes down to this: You have to have faith in God and believe in Him and be a good person and give to others and be kind and be unselfish. Those basic qualities. I think that is what gets you in. Yeah, if a Native American believes in God and he is a good person, I think sure, he'll be there. If he believes in Jesus and God, tries to do right, yeah, definitely.

One of the last questions I ask is something people really struggle to answer. The way you held your hands out a while ago and your everything was in that ball, this question might be easier for you than other people. Let's imagine that is your essence, your very "you"—everything that is you, your favorite everything, your personality is all there. Where is it inside of you?

Oh, you can't. You can't reach anywhere and get it.

Where is it at though?
Well, because it's all different things, like I said, this globe...

Is the whole globe inside of your body then?
It's my whole body.

It's the whole you? So your soul is body size?
Yes. It's whatever physical size I am. Because a lot of the things you can't touch are within my mind. Because my mind is in my body that basically takes care of it all.

When you feel your awareness then, where does that feel like it is at?
What do you mean by where do I feel it?

Where do you feel a bad feeling?
A bad feeling?

Where do you feel that?
[Pause] Again, I feel it in my mind. There are sensory things I feel in my heart or my gut. The fact that I'm even feeling those things, it comes from my mind. There are sensory things that I feel that come from a bad feeling, so to speak. Or a bad thought, but those are from my mind. I may feel them in my chest, but it's all processed in my mind.

Personally, I think because thoughts are cognitive, you think about it in your brain and then perhaps your stomach gets sour, or you get that beating heart. First you thought about it and then it manifests as a physical symptom.
Exactly. That's exactly what it is. The reason I focus on it being in my mind is because even though I may be feeling something in my heart, it's my mind wondering why I don't feel right about something. What do I need to do now to not get myself in a bad situation, or how do I fix this? Even though I feel it here, the feelings there are not going to do anything for me. In terms of fixing the problem, it's not going to do anything. That's going to rely on what is going on in my brain.

The brain is thinking of ways to get me out of this situation, and it's also sending another type of signal that manifests itself in a physical way, like you said.

Just in case you are ignoring the thought then the body will take over and let you know more action is needed. The last question sounds a bit corny but I mean it. What do you think is the most important thing?

Most important thing?

What holds the most importance? That might be a more eloquent way of asking. Some people have a ready answer.

I don't have one ready, but I think everyone is given one or more gifts that they can use to make the best out of their life. Probably the most important thing is to take care of that gift. Use those things to do good for other people, not just for yourself. I might go further and say that the most important thing is to be kind to other people and not always think of yourself. Be unselfish. Give to other people. Use these gifts that you are lucky enough to have for the good of other people and for yourself too. Yourself is very important too. It's important to know the balance.

Makes sense because if you don't take care of yourself you can't be much use. Do you plan on using whatever your gift is when you later begin to practice medicine?

I do. I do. I don't want to sound like a big-headed person, but I've always been a person of reasonable intelligence. I think that is one of the biggest gifts that God has given me. I feel it would be foolish not to use it to the best of my ability. If I were to just pump gas the rest of my life...it would just be a waste. Instead of that, I want to become a physician. If you want to help society, I think that is one of the best things you could possibly do.

Unfortunately, it takes quite a bit of smarts, creativity, imagination, social skills. I feel like I've been blessed with all these things, to a fair amount at least. That's why I want to use them to do those things, to give back to other people. I think that's the best thing.

Young Girl

"Fair are grown-up people's trees,
But the fairest woods are these;
Where, if I were not so tall,
I should live for good and all."
Robert Louis Stevenson

My goal when setting out to interview people was to get a sampling from all walks of life in terms of economic and educational level. I wanted to draw from various religions, backgrounds, geographical locations, as well as a wide age range.

This girl was only eight years old at the time of the interview. She was chosen due to her precociousness. She is fearless and outgoing to an extreme degree. I love this interview. It is short and to the point, and she answers some of the most difficult questions with intelligent simplicity. When she does not know the answer she lets you know that without all of the bluffing and sidestepping that some older people tend to do. She answered slowly and deliberately. I could see in her face and hear it in her voice; she was thinking very carefully and thoroughly.

She is one of several who answered that imagination is located in the brain, but that we do take it with us when we die. Because she was young, I allowed that contradiction without further clarification. Having a child answer in this manner makes it more apparent that it is very natural to answer with that particular combination. In some interviews I delve into the problem of having imagination in our physical brain and yet taking it with us into the afterlife. This was not the time for that persistent line of questioning.

Why do you think people have an imagination?
[Pause] So they can think of things. I guess, maybe, so they can have a creative life. I don't know how to put it. So they can think of things...I guess if they didn't have an imagination they wouldn't be as happy.

That's a good reason. Creativity and happiness. Does it ever help you to think of a new game to play or anything like that?

Yeah, because you can get creative with your imagination and you make fun games, activities, art and stuff.

Do you know where imagination came from?

No.

You're not sure. Have you ever thought about where it came from?

No.

Do you know where it is?

In your mind, your brain.

Do you think you use it when you are sewing?

Yeah, because you need to think of creative ideas to make it and it wouldn't be as cool if you didn't use your imagination.

It might come out kind of boring looking?

Yeah.

Do you think you use it when you are sleeping?

Yeah, because in your dreams you use your imagination to make these dreams.

Do you think you use your imagination when you are remembering things?

I'm pretty sure you use it but I don't know how to say.

Do you think some people have more imagination than other people have?

Yeah.

Do you think children have more than big people do?

Not always.

Really? Do you think different people have different amounts?

Yes.

Have you ever thought about imagination before?

Yeah, I think about it, one of the questions you asked me, do you think and use your imagination when you're sleeping. I've thought about that because you dream.

Sometimes when a dog is sleeping they look like they are having a dream because it looks like they are running in their sleep.

Yeah.

Have you ever seen a dog do that?

Yeah.

So if they are dreaming I wonder if they have an imagination?

Yeah, that makes sense.

Do you think you would take imagination with you when you die?

Yeah.

So you plan on living after you die? Or being somewhere else?

Your spirit would still be there. Your body may not, but your spirit would.

Your spirit would have imagination still?

Yeah.

And probably, maybe, your personality?

Yes.

Do you ever wonder or know or thought about…let me put it this way. Do you know where your spirit is?

Yeah, I think.

Where do you think the real "you" is inside of you? Where do feel like you really are?

In your heart.

Think so? What do you think is the most important thing?

The most important thing? To me it's my family and friends.

ADOLESCENT BOY

"When I approach a child, he inspires in me two sentiments; tenderness for what he is, and respect for what he may become."
Louis Pasteur

"A child of five would understand this. Send someone to fetch a child of five."
Groucho Marx

This twelve-year-old does not mince words. Many of his answers surpass people who are three times his age. His rapid responses were free of hesitation.

What are the purposes of imagination?
To think of life, and what to do with it and to make your ideas flow. To invent things like when Thomas Edison invented things or when Benjamin Franklin discovered electricity. The next question?

[Laugh] What is the origin of imagination?
Imagination came from God so that it could flow through our heads to make us think practically. I'm talking right now, imagining what I'm going to say. It's made by our own head.

The next question is, what is the location of imagination?
Imagination can be anywhere. It could be in the chair. It could be outside. It could be in your pocket, anywhere.

If I asked you where it was in the human body what would you say?
I would say it would be mostly in your mind and the intelligence of your brain and how it functions.

Do you think some people have more imagination and some people have less?
It depends. If a person thinks they have more imagination they

would prove it by imagining something they could make up that would be better than another person.

Do you think animals have imagination?

Yes, because apes can make tools out of ordinary things, and they use their heads to make these things.

Do you think you take imagination with you when you die?

Possibly, yes. If you took imagination with you when you die, you would go to heaven and do anything you want. You just have to think of what you want to do.

Is it possible then that imagination is located in the brain and yet you still take it with you when you die? Or is it more likely that it's located in your soul?

Like I said, imagination could be located anywhere. It's obviously in people's bodies so no matter what, the imagination will be with them because without imagination you can't think.

That's a good point. When you die, and you go to heaven, and you don't have your body anymore would you still have your imagination?

Yeah, because you can still think.

Good point. You can think and yet you don't have your human brain anymore, but you are still able to think. Do you know where your soul is located?

Every soul needs to be in something until death. If they don't have a purpose then they can't exist and they would be in heaven anyway. The soul wouldn't be in your body any more once you go to heaven. It's only in your body while you are still alive.

Do you know where, inside your body, your soul might be at?

Everywhere, you can't point to a place in your body where your soul is.

The last question I ask is, what do you think is the most important thing?

Life itself. It's very important. Once your life ends then you have a life in heaven. Life is the most important thing because it holds everything like your purpose.

Do you know what I've noticed about that question?
    What?

Some of the most intelligent people say that life is the most important thing. Do you know what that makes you?
    What?

One of the intelligent ones.
    [Laugh] Okay.

I skipped over a question earlier. What part do you think imagination plays in people's ability to remember things?
    Imagination holds all of your memories, but if you forget your memories, then your imagination still has it. Imagination helps every moment of your life. Like if you are in a play you improvise if you forgot your line. Sometimes it turns out better than it was supposed to be.

You know how it feels when you are remembering something. Do you see it in your mind? Do you think you are using your imagination to see that? Even when the action you are remembering was real?
    It was real, but imagination can be fantasy or it could be real. If you don't remember something, like I said, then your imagination is weak.

MARINE BIOLOGIST

"The calm sea shines, loose hang the vessel's sails;
before us are the sweet green fields of Wales."
Matthew Arnold

"Can di bennill mwyn I'th nain, fe gan dy nain I tithau.
Sing your grandmother a sweet song, and she will sing to you."
Welsh Proverb

As you might have noticed, the question of whether animals possess imagination surfaced in some of the interviews. That caused me to seek out animal experts. The issue of higher order animals versus less advanced organisms has been discussed, and any time I think of intelligent animals I think of whales and dolphins. I was very pleased to spend time with a Marine Biologist, and I received an added bonus, her lovely accent. She is a thirty-year-old Welsh woman from Cardiff.

What are the purposes of imagination?

[Pause] I haven't thought about the purposes before. Maybe to take yourself outside what is the real tangible stuff around you. Sometimes the solid stuff around us can make us forget that there are other dimensions to life as well. Imagination can go anywhere. It's unlimited. That can open you up to that.

What do you think is the origin of imagination?

My granny who died when I was quite young was really imaginative. I used to really love going over to her house because she always was really good at making up games about princesses and castles and just really cool little stories. I think of her as being someone with a really good imagination. She's probably someone who encouraged me to develop my imagination as well. The origin, in that respect, would be passed on. Kind of a legacy from parents and grandparents.

What do you think the location of imagination is?

Like in our bodies? Head, my brain.

That's where it feels like it is?

It could be heart or spirit or something, but to be honest, if I really think about it, I'd say my brain.

Do you think that's possible because it's a visual function like memories are? Because you see memories in your head and not in your knee cap?

[Laugh] Exactly, that's a good way to put it.

Do you think animals have imagination? That question would include marine life. [Laugh]

This is the thing. I know that fish don't dream. You kind of think of dreaming and imagination being linked with each other. I don't know if they do. That's a tricky one. I'm kind of running through lots of animals in my head.

Run through some of the higher order ones for us who don't know as much as you might know. For example, the whales and the dolphins and the big...

Right. I was just thinking of elephants, actually, funny enough, because I have read that they did a study and they found out that elephants mourn their dead young and their dead relatives. So that anything that gives animals a kind of human emotion like that always gives it the possibility that they are going to have things like imagination.

If you think about it, sea otters and dolphins appear to play. I don't think you can play if you haven't got imagination.

They do appear to play.

Definitely playing, right. That's something that's so necessary in a lot of ways.

Yes. Playing doesn't feed you.

Maybe I'll revise my answer to that and say yes.

Maybe we can't really know. Do you think we take imagination with us when we die?

No. there's no need to. Because once you're in heaven...I think a lot of imagination is wondering what things are like and imagining what things could be like and thinking about these fantastical places. I think that once we are in heaven all that stuff is going to be irrelevant.

Would it be fair to say that it served a purpose here, and when we are dead there is not a purpose for it?
Yeah, that's a good way of putting it.

The last question isn't about imagination, what do you think is the most important thing?
[Laugh] That's where the question ends. What is the most important thing? Man. If you can call God a thing, then God.

Going back to something you said before, it sounds like you believe that you're going to heaven and you believe in God and so that must mean that you have a soul or a spirit. Where do you think your soul or spirit is located at?
I don't think it's located. It is something. It's a part of me, but I don't think you take a part of the body and say there is where the soul is.

But, it is within you someplace?
Yes, correct. But it's not a thing, it's not a physical, tangible thing, it could be anywhere. It's like an essence of me rather than being a physical part of me.

Did you ever think about the location or size or shape of it before?
No, not like where it is or what it looks like.

PROFESSIONAL PHOTOGRAPHER

"...your religion is something you not only think about but also sing, dance, eat, paint and sculpt. To find your religion you must engage all of your senses."
Rev. Scotty McLennan, Unitarian

"Photography records the gamut of feelings written on the human face."
Edward Steichen

In my search for interviewees, I looked for people with scientific backgrounds and some with artistic abilities and everything in between. I was certain that a professional photographer would be of the category of occupations that would rely heavily on the use of imagination.

This is a sixty-year-old former school teacher turned photographer. She was born in Cleveland, Ohio. If you could hear her speak you would notice that she alters the volume of her voice significantly as she moves from sentence to sentence. I do not know if this is intentional, a teacher's trick, or an old family trait but it makes the conversation interesting.

She is a lovely and kind woman, very easy to talk with, and she made the jump on her own accord to spiritual topics as soon as I asked her about the origin of imagination. She not only jumped to that deep topic but also to the location of imagination without having to be asked. Also worth noting is how easily she breaks into laughter.

She does not reveal much in the way of inconsistencies due to lack of definitive answers on the afterlife. She calls herself a fallen-away Unitarian. That is original.

What are the purposes of imagination?
[Long pause] The purposes of imagination. Creative work. Anything creative starts from imagining conditions or something beyond the reality, the literal reality, around you. I think having imagination really enhances a person's life tremendously. Because it's an escape too, an escape

from reality which can sometimes be hum-drum or routine. It lets you soar beyond.

There are a lot of purposes. Some people only have one answer. That's one thing I thought of early on was the coping mechanism of the humdrum life. I thought of a farmer out on a tractor all day, at least he'd have imagination to distract him.

Exactly. There's the story, *The Secret Life of Walter Mitty*, the story that everybody reads in high school. That's the whole point, he was a nobody, but in his imagination he had an incredible strategic role to play. He'd get totally lost in his daydreams. It gave him so much relief, but I think he got totally carried away.

Do you think people can have too much imagination?

Yes. So that they can no longer relate to real people and their whole life around them. It takes the mental energies away from coping.

Did you say that you used to teach school?

Yes.

I bet you had to use your imagination teaching people.

Actually, I felt less drained, in using imagination, when I was working at the college. The people wanted to be there. High school kids don't. It takes up too much of your imagination trying to motivate people who don't want to be in your class. Given the choice, they wouldn't have been there. That's pretty clear, except for drama.

The adults wanted to learn—the same people ten years earlier would have probably been the troublemakers or the restless ones in the classroom. They didn't want to know what I was teaching. I'd trick them into maybe wanting to get involved, but as adults, ten years older, they wanted to know how to write better. They want to be able to express what they want to say so they would ask questions about sentence structure. What a concept! They wanted to know. [Laughter] All I had to do was make comparisons to something in their own lives. They thought I was the most fantastic teacher they ever had. But if they'd had me ten years before they would have hated English.

I divide people into two groups, the teachable and the un-teachable. Almost everybody I meet, given any time at all, I can see which group they fall into. Do you ever divide people into two groups like that?

No. I know there are some people who don't listen to anybody else. If they won't listen they can't take in concepts. ADD keeps getting more common and it explains the squirming, and inability to focus. Maybe it's television.

Let's move into your work now as a photographer. How do you think you use your imagination with photography?

I try to work with lighting and posing in a different way each time. I try not to do the same poses, particularly if it has some room for creativity. Sometimes there is no room for that. A business portrait is not supposed to be moody looking and it's not supposed to have an atmosphere. Its range is limited. It becomes more about lighting and how the person feels about smiling, and that's more based on experience. That's a more cognitive thing. I think in personal portraits I try to think of something different. No formulas. That's where the imagination comes in.

I don't say I am an artist and I work with a camera, like others like to do, because I don't think that's true. I run a business; I'm in a business to make money and to please the client. If I tried to use my imagination in every setting, that would be foolish. I'm not keeping in mind what my client wants. They want to be happily surprised at how good they look. Most people think they are not good-looking or they can't take a good picture. My job is to make them feel better about that than they did when they came in. You do try to make it interesting to yourself.

I can understand that. You need some private amusement now and then or it would be the same thing and it would lose its creativity.

Sure, and there is an opportunity to do that in this work and it makes it a better job to me than jobs where you don't use imagination.

What do you think the origin of imagination is?

That's a good question. There are parts of the brain that are more developed for intuitive things and imagination and things that are not organized. If you ask me, I'd say right brain. There's a lot of things I don't understand. I guess I'm the kind of person that doesn't have to know. I can think it's wonderful. A lot of things about life are wonderful, but the imagination, the spiritual dimension, is what makes living sort of a game.

I was raised in a strict religion in which they had all the answers. I don't know where they got them. Somebody received a vision or a prophecy. I fell away from that, definitely fell away pretty far. I'm a fallen-away Unitarian.

[Laughter] I didn't know that was possible.

Well, I don't have to answer to my mom anymore.

That's the good thing about growing older.

I believe we can be in awe and appreciate a spiritual dimension without being committed to one particular explanation. It doesn't drive me crazy. It would drive my sister crazy. How can you wake up in the morning and not follow your purpose that you were put into this world for? I know people are different.

You sound like you've become okay with not having to know.

Not having to have an answer.

Where is the location of imagination?

In the body and the brain. I wouldn't know where in the brain.

Maybe it's like having an eyeball. You get to use it—it's there for everybody to use.

Oh yes. Depending on the environmental situation, some people are totally discouraged from using the right brain. My father told me a story about his father. He was out in the yard collecting bugs for biology class and his father came home from work and asked him about this. My father explained and his father said, "That's crazy. You're not going to spend your time doing that kind of silly stuff."

Talk about stifling. What did he think learning was? Just enough to get you into a job, a paycheck? Some people are not encouraged to be creative as children. Things changed. We started putting everything your child did up on the refrigerator. I still have things in my drawers from my daughter's precious imagination. Our job is to nurture that. Art for art's sake.

Compare that to where I grew up. We didn't have our drawings on the refrigerator. Art was something you did but you didn't parade it up on your walls and cherish. Some people just don't appreciate it. I could give so many examples of that. Some people really have talent. I know a talented illustrator whose father was a banker and he did not encourage him to follow that.

So he didn't grow up to be an illustrator then?

Oh, no! He hasn't drawn in years. I don't think he respects it anymore. How many people go around and wonder what their special talent is their whole lives? People want to discover it, and this guy had it. I think it's an important thing to help children to reach that.

You're causing me to think that if imagination is like a human eyeball and your parents trained you not to gaze about the room, not to look up, not to look down but to keep your gaze always straight ahead. Maybe after a time, a child would get into the habit of keeping their eyes straight and have decided it was wrong to use their eyes to their full capacity. Maybe it's similar. The imagination may be in the gray matter of the brain, but it's not always encouraged to develop like a muscle, for example.

This next question I could probably answer for you based on what you've said. Do you think you would take imagination with you when you die?

[Exceedingly long pause] Do you take consciousness with you when you die? I don't know. I have experienced a near-death experience. A few years ago I was in a car accident on the freeway. I thought, "This is the end. This is it." That's what I was wondering during the impact, but I didn't lose consciousness. I didn't have a vision. Well I did think I was in a white tunnel but those turned out to be the airbags. [Laughter]

You were expecting a white tunnel or white clouds at least.

So I don't know. There have been several deaths in my family. There is a spiritual presence, but they are gone physically. I read a book that made me think about the possibility of consciousness after death. Maybe there are spirits of the dead. We're just not open to it. Maybe like some people's imagination are stifled. I suppose ours are numbed as a culture. Don't you think?

I'm not sure. Maybe in certain professions, like the movie industry, that would be the big thing to have, the imagination. But I'm wondering about the everyday person who goes to school and gets a job. It seems to be fostered in writing by creative writing teachers. To write a story you have to dig deep into your own imagination.

You're right. Writers create imaginary worlds. Special effects people are creative.

I just re-read the whole Tolkien series including a biography of his life. I wonder now, who is the more imaginative person? The person who created the world out of his head and put it to paper or the guy, in our time, who has to read it from the paper and then makes characters like Gollum appear on a screen. Who had to work harder? My hunch it was Tolkien.

Both of them would be very creative. The originator did conceive it out of nothing.

That's a good point. When I read the series as a child, long before there was a movie, I created my own characters. Years later, I saw the movie and then re-read the books. Then I had new characters, the Hollywood actors appearing in my imagination.

That's right. Movies try to tell you that this is how you are supposed to think of these characters for now on.

Another question, where do you think the real you is inside your body? Where do you really think you are? If I had to perform an operation and remove your personality?

My brain.

Does it feel big or little? Does it have a sense of size?

[Long pause] I don't know. Physically, I'm a relatively big person at least compared with most women. I could say that it's big, but I'm only saying that because I'm tall.

Do you feel like your personality or your "real you" is separate from your physical body?

We're trapped in a body. I can say that, literally, my mental process is happening in here. That's not real. The real thing seems to be out there. It's like dreaming at night, it's big. It's really big. It's not just this head on the pillow. There's a world out there. My dreams are really interesting. I don't know how it is for other people but I won't remember any dreams for weeks on end and suddenly I'll have one that's really real. There are people who really learned from their dreams. They catch them before they get forgotten.

What really matters most? What's the most important thing?

It's connections. Connecting to other people and enjoying their ideas. As you get older it's to forget material things and concentrate more on friendships. It's true of me, I get more a feeling of connectedness. It's the most important thing. You have these moments of what you feel to be intimacy with people and then they are gone.

People—when they come to my photography studio—tell me things they would never tell other people. "I have one eye bigger than the other and I want you to do something to make them more the same size." Or they talk about something they perceive to be a problem. I'm glad they tell me because then I'll get better pictures being tuned in to what they want. It's amazing what people will tell you.

Classically gorgeous people are insecure. People will say things that are probably the fourth layer of revelation of who they are even though we just met. I feel we have a rapport due to the type of job that it is. It's more satisfying than teaching. Isn't that awful?

On a scale of worthwhileness and social purpose and social utility, teaching is pretty up there compared with what I do now. You have to get your reinforcement internally when you're teaching. Thirty-five kids is too many to teach, yet it's built into the system and you can't do anything about that, so you do the best you can. You are always compressing. It's not good enough. The education in this country is really in trouble. The trends are threatening to our culture. I try not to think about it too much.

JEWISH MYSTIC

"One common effect of the truly Existentialist writer is to provoke in his readers the exasperated desire to rewrite what he says in plain language, and to show that it doesn't after all amount to more than a platitude."
Warnock

"Shema Yisrael Adonai eloheinu Adonai ehad.
Hear O Israel the Lord our God, the Lord is one."
The Shema, Deuteronomy 6:4

You have arrived at a long and extremely interesting interview. This forty-eight-year-old college administrator and I had both presented speeches at the same educational conference. He is the Math, Science & Engineering Division Chair at a college and holds a Ph. D. He is from Newark, New Jersey.

Our interview began with a mishap at the table that caused considerable laughter. That was the best thing that could have launched our conversation. I say that because he and I are very different from one another and, had I been more dogmatically inclined, this could easily have been a hostile exchange rather than a fast moving intelligent conversation.

It probably goes without saying that I have not met many Jewish mystics who primarily consider themselves to be Buddhist. But do not worry; I have not given away the punch line. There is much, much more about this gentleman that is intriguing.

I appreciate his constant admission to not knowing the answers to the questions, some people hide behind their academia to conceal the fact that they cannot know the answers. This man freely admits that he does not know, yet shared what is important to him. He does this in a bright and amusing way.

This is yet again, an excellent example of how much more meaningful a deep conversation can be as compared to barely getting past dull greetings and empty well wishes.

What are the purposes of imagination?

What are the purposes of imagination? Well, that's interesting, I never thought about that. Well, that's not true. I thought about it in a very restrictive sense in terms of the issues of wonder and curiosity and learning. So imagination comes into play in terms of creativity and learning. The purposes of imagination I would have trouble defining. How would we know? How could we possibly know that?

We don't, unless you have an opinion.

I have no idea what the purpose is.

Okay.

It sounds like an existentialism trap, you know, what's the purpose of this? But, it does concern me that we've often put restrictions on imagination with our kids. For example, in all kinds of ways either by having media do their thinking for them or having schools do their thinking for them or in other areas, taboos against their thinking certain things or carrying out certain kinds of creativity.

You're interested in people not being restricted in their imagination, and the opposite of that is letting their imagination be enhanced and developed. Okay, well, if you thought that was hard [laughter] they are not going to get easier.

What do you think the origin of imagination is? Speaking of things we can't really know, this will definitely be your opinion.

I have no idea and how would we know? I mean these are really epistemological conundrums. Right?

I don't know, what is epistemological? I know what a conundrum is.

Well, it's an epistemological one. Epistemology is the study of knowledge, right? So how could I know what the origin is? The other way we could know is actually, ironically through an imaginative leap.

Interesting, isn't it?

How could you possibly know that? You can't possibly prove that. It's interesting because it gets to an interesting question in terms of the evolution of the brain. You get into Freud and Pearce and all those guys. Right? Do dogs have imagination?

That question is coming up, but go ahead.

Oh, the answer is no.

[Laughter]

Once again, how would we possibly know? It's very imaginative how we think of speaking for animals for example.

In my opinion, we think we know because we observe dogs and they are supposedly dreaming.

Okay, that's it. We project on to them what we think is going on. But that's an interesting question. This gets back to your first question, "What's the purpose?" If you look at it from an evolutionary prospective, why would that have happened? What's the adaptive reason? I don't know.

The whole issue of creativity has interested thinkers for so many years. Freud wrote a lot about this, the relationship between creativity and neurosis—poets and day dreamers all the stuff that today's ADD kids would be given prescription drugs for. Freud would have investigated that very, very differently.

What is the relationship between the poet and the day dreamer, for example? He wrote a piece on that. That's an interesting question from the psychological angle in terms of evolutionary psychology as to why something like that would happen. Does imagination have a role to play in rational thought? Because rational thought, presumably, has something to do with adaptation. To what extent is that necessarily true? To what extent do we need the creative as part of the survival of the species?

It's interesting because people who are creative—this is probably going to sound egotistical, but I have a part of that also. I played music for many years, and I picked it up very, very easily. It wasn't difficult. Although I had to work at it to get better at it, there is absolutely no question it came to me easily.

At four I learned piano. I won a competition, it wasn't difficult. Then I wanted to learn drums, so at five I learned drums. I played for many years. It came to me naturally. Where did that come from? Why is that? *Yes, why is that?*

I don't know, that's a long-winded answer there. I want to answer long because you gave me a short time on the first question. Go on, you're stalling.

No, you wouldn't let me finish. [Laugh] Do you think some people have too much imagination?

Too much, what does that mean?

Can some people have more than other people? Do people have varying amounts? Can someone have more than I do? Is that possible?

I couldn't possibly know that in any kind of epistemologically, sound way. Let's use an imaginative metaphor. This is sometimes used in Buddhism. Right? Which is: The seed you water that's going to determine...

That's the one that's going to grow?

Exactly. If you watered the seeds of imagination, if you allowed that to really develop, you're going to have somebody who has developed it more...maybe has more confidence or something like that. Whereas, if you've not watered those seeds, and you've stifled it, the person's potential is probably still there. Aversive conditioning. That's very powerful—if somebody has gotten the clear message not to think a certain way. Some people work in undoing aversive conditioning with families. School certainly does not encourage imaginative thinking. It's just the opposite.

Would you like some more wine?

I haven't had any wine.

Another bottle for Catherine.

I don't drink, I get migraines.

Sure.

This is all not making it in the book. You know that? [Laughter]

This is the stuff that should be in the book.

I think the next question to skip on to, in your case, would be where is imagination located? I know what you're going to say now, we can't know that. But if you had an opinion or a guess as to where it's located what would you say?

You know, the truth is, I really don't know. My guess, if I had to make a guess, it would be that it's got something to do with right brain. I also think there's a lot of imaginative work that goes on analytically. But I would be curious to know if they could locate where that kind of activity is.

If they know, maybe you can tell me, I honestly don't know. I'm actually quite serious. They are able to locate centers in the brain that control certain activities. I would imagine, no pun intended, that they have a sense of that. Is it right brain?

Most people say right brain, but some people don't even say brain. Some people say in their soul or in their spirit. They are sure of that, and yet other people immediately want it to be in their brain and they want to be specific on where in their brain it is.

That's an interesting point. There's been some interesting research done on the brain and spirituality anyway. Why are you doing all this? Can I ask that now or do I have to wait?

Why am I interviewing people?
Yeah.

Because, for one thing I like deeper conversations. People make a lot of small talk, and that's fine. I don't enjoy it as much as I enjoy talking about something else. I wanted the people who ultimately read the book to think in a way or in an area that maybe they haven't thought about lately. All I want to do is cause some stirring. It doesn't have to be the intellectually profound reader. I want the average, everyday person to think. And then I want them to go have deeper conversations with their own peers and friends. That's all I really want.

Back to the questions: Do you think—in your opinion because I know we can't know—do you think that you would take imagination with you when you die?

When I die? What do you mean by that? [Laughter] I don't want to say something that's going to offend somebody.

It doesn't matter whether you offend or not, it's just your opinion.

Are you saying my opinion is not strong enough to offend somebody?

[Laughter]

Because you're right. I just want to be clear. I don't necessarily see the next manifestation of being in that way, the human form in a more ethereal sense.

I'm kind of drawn to the Buddhist concept of no birth, no death.

There's no absolute birth. You'd have to be there already in order to be born or otherwise how can you be born? Nothing comes out of nothing, and nothing goes into nothing. It's just manifestation, transformation of manifestation and cessation of manifestation.

Now what does that mean in a spiritual sense in terms of when the present life form ceases to manifest? I don't really know. I do believe in a soul, but I think the soul is a complicated concept. I don't think there's one concept of the soul. In Judaism, in Jewish mystical thinking, which is really where I'm attracted, there are different kinds of souls.

Really?

Yeah, and there's even the belief some teachers taught that everything has a soul. One famous Rabbi taught that even a blade of grass has a soul and a death and a song.

That reminds me of Buddhism.

Actually, Jewish mysticism and Buddhism are very close, very close. So is Christian mysticism. At those levels they all get along. They are all speaking the same thing.

I've been researching Christian mysticism recently, and I've seen the similarities with the Buddhist ideas.

You're a Christian, right? You identify yourself as Christian.

As you know, the head of this convention went out of her way [laugh] in her introduction of me [to the keynote audience] to make my faith very clear to all of the attendees. I am a Christian who can see a few aspects of Buddhism that correlate with my personal faith.

It's interesting. If you look at the literature out there now on Buddhism and how it lines up with the other religions, there's a little bit on Judaism. There's a lot on Christianity, and for a number of years I wondered why that was. I came up with an answer that might be in the ballpark of somewhat accurate, although how accurate I don't know. Roughly a third of American Buddhists have Jewish roots.

Interesting, I didn't know that.

Yeah, if you look at the last names you'll see that a lot of them are Jewish. It hit me, of course there won't be that many books because we don't need convincing. We're already there. We already feel an affinity. Whereas the community that has needed a dialogue in terms of, "Don't be afraid of us. We really have a lot in common," or "We have differences but that's okay," is really the Christian community and the Buddhists. I think at the highest spiritual levels the truths are the same. One of my teachers taught me something very important—that religion is associated with ego and spirit is associated with soul.

That seems pretty accurate.

Yeah, I always thought that was pretty accurate too. At the ego level we fight, "My God can beat up Your God." That's where the ego thing comes out. At the spirit level the differences are not that important. Objectively, the truths are the same. Subjectively, different paths work better for different people. What's interesting is that I used to do a fair amount of work in the area of Jewish/Christian dialogue and I stopped. I couldn't deal with it any more.

Was it negative?

Yeah. It was almost always the case that the Jews came to the table with the attitude that we can be different and that's okay, and your path is just as good as ours, but it isn't ours. There was always an agenda on the other end of the table. The discussion always turned on Jesus and we would say, "That's your thing. He's a good Jewish boy and we have no problems with him. There are other things we want to talk about," and it never went anywhere. I stopped. I didn't want to fight. I didn't want to get any bad feelings. I thought the better thing to do was to pull the people out. I'm going to say something that's going to sound really weird, but what the hell, I might as well. I'm going to steal a line. Freud's work is too precious to be left in the hands of psychoanalysts.

I've heard that one.

I would say in many ways Christianity is too precious to be left in the hands of the Christians, I don't mean that to be offensive. I want to say that I haven't read the whole Christian New Testament, but I've read a fair amount.

Where does Jesus preach hate? Where does he say to kill as many people as possible in his name? I must have missed that. I grew up as a Jew, and I was very defensive around Christians. There was always an agenda.

Really?

Yeah, and if it wasn't anti-Semitism it was always this sense that I needed what you had, what I had wasn't good enough. What we had was old, the Old Testament. I'll tell you what a number of Jews say among themselves, they won't say it publicly, there's a sense that our stuff has been stolen.

Like plagiarism of the Old Testament.

Exactly, this is our stuff. Don't tell us how to read our stuff. Now if you want to borrow it and build upon it, go ahead. But don't tell us how to read our text. A number of Jews who don't want to talk to Christians, they're position is to the extent of, "You've stolen our God. You've stolen one of our concepts on the Messiah. It's only one of several we have. You've stolen our text. You kicked us out of countries. I'll tell you what: I think if you want dialogue, you've got a lot of explaining to do."

I tried to bridge the gap with the dialogue. There's a lot of sensitivity to that. I talked to a man years ago who studied with a number of Native American Elders who was the only non-Native American in the community. He grew up with them and was actually the pipe holder for one of the tribes—a very honored role. He said the elders taught him the same thing about Native American spirituality— some of the books were not what the tribes believed. He said that you've stolen everything else from us. You're not getting this too. I wish you luck in your common ground search there, I think you'll find a lot of common ground. Jesus was a good Jewish, Buddhist mystic.

Really.

There's a lot of what he says at a more profound level, for example, his teaching in Matthew 25, you know, what you do to the least of my brethren you do to me, good or bad. That's interdependence. That's "no self." That's a very high level of teaching.

That's why when somebody professes to be a Christian and is in favor of the death penalty, I'd ask them what do you do with Matthew 25 then? If you take that teaching seriously, and you advocate someone's death, then you advocate Jesus' death.

They are going back to an eye-for-an-eye without knowing much about it, or maybe they do know about it, I don't know which one.
Here's another thing that bothers most of us.

Quoting? [Laugh] Quoting the Bible? I'm sorry. I'm just saying that people may be going to that teaching.
Not that you are making this move, but in Judaism we don't just point to a passage. There's a lot that goes on in a Jewish text. Don't forget most of us read a translation. I'm in a study group with a Rabbi.

I've studied Hebrew just a little, I couldn't hold a candle to what you've probably been doing but I see that the translation that we are dealing with, especially in what we would call—a Gentile like myself—would call the Old Testament. The translation. Oh my, what leniency did we have.
Isn't it amazing?

Some Christian tenets are built on that too. You need to go back to the original languages, and I always have.
My Rabbi says if you read through Christian texts of the story of Genesis, a central theme is the issue of sin, original sin. The Rabbi says the word for sin never appears. In fact, in Hebrew there are twenty different words for sin, and one of the most common definitions means to miss the mark.

Oh, there's a Greek word that has that meaning. It comes right from target practice and every imperfection is a sin and you counted your score by how many sins you had.
There you go, but none of this is in Genesis, the opening of Genesis.

You mean with the fall of Adam and Eve?
That's all Christianity. That's who invented the concept of original sin there. It's just presented as though this is what the text is about. Of

course you're going to get Jews who say this is our text, and if you'd like to be respectful and read it in the way that it's supposed to be read, which has multiple meanings. But don't start inventing things and putting it in there and then telling us this is how we have to read it.

One of my Jewish friends doesn't like it when I use the words "Old Testament."
That's a Christian term. You know what the Jews call it?

The Torah?
It's called the Bible. The Torah is literally the first five books.

I probably answered that way because my friend only believes in the first five books of the Bible.
Really? Why is that?

That is the only part he believes. Nothing else.
Is he inspired by God or something like that?

He's a Sadducee. He doesn't believe in heaven or hell. He doesn't believe he has a soul or a spirit.
Actually, the opening of the Bible is very interesting. In mystical Judaism, when you read text, and I have a long way to go myself, you read on several different levels at once. The literal level is one, but then it gets progressively more interpretive. The opening of the Bible, if you translated it literally, it would go something like this. The first words are already difficult to translate into English. It would be something along the lines of "with beginning" or in a "beginningness" state. Then there's a third-person verb and it can either be masculine or neutral because of the way verbs get conjugated in Hebrew, past tense, third-person singular.

Third-person, past tense, either neutral or male singular.
Like he or it, it's the verb to create. It's either he created or it created, then the next word is Elohim.

God, one of the God words.
Well, that's an interesting word. That's a plural word.

Yes, that's one place that we Christians get the Godhead from, the trinity belief.

Okay, I didn't know that. But it's a plural. It's a generic word for God or the gods. The English translation is always, "In the beginning God created." Elohim cannot be the subject of the verb because the verb is singular.

I see, you have a plural word and a singular word and they don't grammatically go together.

It's called subject-verb disagreement. The great mystical question is: What does this mean? One response is, is there an implied subject in that verb so that Elohim becomes a direct object. The mystics often talk about something called the Ayn Sof, which means without end.

Like infinity.

Well, without end.

Isn't that infinite rather than finite?

It means without end. This Ayn Sof is like the ultimate creator, the ultimate giver. One of the things it created was Elohim. Which is to say that the concept of God, or gods, where you go with that is very difficult terrain. Knowing that literal level puts a whole different spin on things.

What I used to tell my students is if you look at this really carefully, what it's telling you is similar to what the scientists say about the universe contracting. They've now discovered that it's infinitely expanding. This is exactly the mystical teaching. It's always interesting and pleasing to me when science catches up to mysticism.

The mystical teaching is that the Ayn Sof is infinitely creating and giving. The moment you attach anything personal to it—human characteristic, emotion, judgment, morality—you are no longer talking about it.

If Ayn Sof created Elohim possibly, then you could have an Elohim who is a jealous God? A so-called human emotion. Remember when it goes on to say, "Let's create man in our image" or whatever the exact words may be in the original text. Because then, in Elohim you have that plural type of meaning to the Hebrew, right?

Right.

So if the Ayn Sof created the Elohim, but the Elohim was a jealous God, that demanded no graven images could come before Me, that God, the "in My image God" plural God, then that would change everything wouldn't it? It would change quite a few things because you'd still have the Elohim God then, who has the Ten Commandments, and all...

There's 613.

But you know what I'm alluding to. If there is a precursor, so to speak, a creator of the Elohim one, or ones I guess you should say because you need a plural there?

You're on to something here. I would have to look to see what the other words were there, because the English translates them all to God. That's unfortunate because as you might remember, when Abraham enters the picture, a new concept of God and a new word forms, Andonai, that's the personal God of Abraham. That becomes fascinating in Genesis Fourteen, which Christianity has always mistranslated as the sacrifice of Isaac. There is no sacrifice. It's an anti-sacrificial story. In Hebrew it's called the binding of Isaac.

Well, literally all that he does have happen to him is the binding.

Exactly. When Isaac asks where is the ram and so on? He says that God will provide. That's also what happens. The story is clear. There is no sacrifice. The God that calls Abraham to begin with is Elohim.

Elohim, but then Andonai shows up later?

That's the one, the angel of God. It's not really Lord, that's a Greek translation.

I understand. I studied Greek.

It's Andonai. It's a personal God. That's the term that is used for Jews because the central prayer in all of Judaism is called the Shema. The prayer means, "listen people of Israel" hear, listen. It's a command. Andonai is one. Our Rabbi taught us that before the year 900...

You mean AD or BC?

Well, those are Christian terms.

I know but which one? If you use my term then I'll know.

I think he meant CE in ours and AD in yours. Up until that time one of the words in the prayer was always understood as one with everything, not the only one. That was a later concept.

"One with everything" is one of the most Buddhist teachings there is.

Exactly.

"Namaste," the God in me sees the God in you.

That's what I mean. These are all the same teachings. That's why I say, why argue? There's no point. People should help each other out here, because at these higher levels, it's the same stuff. It's just talked about differently. There was an eighteenth century Rabbi who defined holy and pious as a people who promptly pay the butcher. I loved this line. How do you treat a waitress or a maid or a cashier? To me these are the questions for your spiritual practice.

Well, good, with those questions I am doing really well.

In Judaism, we don't believe anybody can run spiritual interference for you. You can't be saved automatically. There's no such thing in Judaism. In fact in Yom Kipper, the holiest day of the year, the Day of Atonement, there's this central part of the liturgy that says, "For sins committed against God,"—those would presumably be breaking the commandments— the Day of Atonement atones. "But sins committed against your fellow human being, the Day of Atonement does not atone until you have made amends to that human being."

Interesting.

No one runs spiritual interference for you.

I see what you mean. You don't have a savior for your sins. That would then obliterate that. We'd have to go make our own amends in that case.

Karma. Same concept. If I harm somebody then I need to try to fix that. If I can't, I'm stuck with that karma. Even the whole concept of forgiveness is very tricky in Judaism. Like in a homicide trial, a parent may forgive the killer for killing their child. In Judaism she can't do that.

Why?

She can forgive him for whatever harm has come her way, only the victim can do the forgiving.

She can forgive for her feelings and her loss, but she can't forgive on the behalf of the pain her child suffered as the murder victim.

There you go. So the question is, what can be done about the dead? The answer [itself] is a good reason not to commit homicide.

Because you can't make amends. What happens if you can't make amends because you don't have a...

You're stuck with that karma.

Do you have a hell or something?

Judaism doesn't really believe in that. In the mystical sense there are some images of that, but it's not the same. There is a concept of rebirth in Judaism, of reincarnation in mystical Judaism. Your Karmic issues are dealt with in that way. I think honestly, Buddhism has a much more sophisticated way of understanding karma. I lean more toward Buddhism in that regard. But if nothing else, the time you are alive you are stuck with that.

With your karma?

Yeah.

Some believe that if you reach enlightenment through meditation in either the Hindu or Buddhist belief or even something in-between those systems, such as some of the Yogic teachings, when you hit enlightenment and your meditation becomes effective enough, then eventually your mind can be stilled. That will bring the cause and effect to the point of cessation. It can happen after years of practice, or by being one of those people who lives off water and milk and exists in a cave, or some people have it happen instantaneously with very little effort on their part.

But ultimately, when it happens (this is a teaching, I'm not saying it's true), the person wipes out their cause and effect. Their karma stops. Therefore you can quit reincarnating back in too. That's one reason the Buddha did not have to come back. He was not a God, he was like you and I, and he became so enlightened that he didn't have to come back.

He awakened. That's interesting. I'm interested in what you said about Yoga. I've done a little bit of Yoga, not too much. When I started doing Yoga myself, I was ignorant. I didn't know this. In the West we've kind of turned it into...

Fitness?
Yeah. I don't want to be offensive.

Go ahead, I'm not easily offended.
From what I understand it's a very powerful spiritual thing.

I have studied Yoga so I know what you are saying.
Is that correct?

Yes, that is correct. The public doesn't always know it. Teachers vary a lot. Are people coming to it for the physical reasons or are they coming to it for the spiritual reasons? I believe the average American is coming to it for the physical reasons. They are trying it out. Maybe it's a good fitness thing. They don't know. They feel incredibly better the first time. The next time they try it, they keep on feeling better and the improvements come. The backaches stop or whatever problem they possibly suffer with, but they get this physical release. Then they can get hooked on it for physical reasons. A lot of times a person will start eating in a more healthy way and they won't even know why. They have a saying in Yoga and some other beliefs: "the body never lies."
Interesting, I like that.

I like it too. Some of what it seems to try to tell us is that we are under stress. The body may be telling any given person to take it easy, take a nap, cancel some plans. Let's go back to the question we're on. Do you take imagination with you when you die? You've talked some about the afterlife as you see it. I'm not sure you've told me exactly where you think you are going to go when you die, and I won't know your exact thoughts unless you tell me. I also won't know if you think you'll take imagination with you when you die unless you tell me.
I don't have a clue. I really don't.

Okay, why don't you just tell us where you are going when you die then?

I have no idea. The only thing I feel a little bit confident about is this form of being will cease to manifest. I will continue on being in the earth, the trees, and the air.

But you have a soul, right?
Yeah.

So, is your soul going to disperse? You're not sure?
I don't know. I don't even know how to define what the soul is. In Jewish mysticism there are different levels of souls. It is very complicated. The work on the soul is very important. The whole obligation for the Jews is that you are supposed to help repair the world. There's another one not very well known that you are supposed to repair the soul. That's a meditative mindfulness.

There's a great Zen teaching: "Don't get hung up on the finger pointing to the moon. You're supposed to look at the moon." Don't get caught in the language.

That's a good saying.
I don't know how to define soul. There's something very deep within us that's beyond the rational. The integrative psychology people have a great point. We're used to a Freudian concept of rationality and psychology. To Freud there are only two realms. There's the rational and the pre-rational. Since the infantile is not rational it has to be pre-rational. Therefore religious thinking, which is not rational, has to fall into the infantile category.

That happens every time you put things into two categories. Once you've done that, you've eliminated every other possibility.
Exactly. Of course Freud was sort of right, there is a lot of infantile in religion. People act like children. The spiritual, Freud never really got to. This integrative psychology is talking about a trans-rational realm as well.

The physical is very much caught up in the experiential present. Right? In Buddhism, they explain it this way: If I want to explain what this cup of tea tastes like, I could use all the words in the dictionary but, finally, you need to taste it.

Patanjali taught in the Yoga Sutras that you have to taste a lemon. Talking about it and describing it to someone else only gets you so far.

That's a mystical experience. How can you talk about it?

You can't but you can try.

That's the finger pointing to the moon. Some people have a defense mechanism to prevent them from going there. They are very stuck and find ways to explain it away.

I don't usually ask this, but what do you think about telepathy?

In my family it doesn't even phase us anymore that we'll have the same dream. We will clearly influence each other's dreams. I wish I had a dollar for every time my dad and I said to each other when the phone rang, "I was just going to call you." We don't even bat an eye on this stuff, if that's what telepathy is, then sure, I believe in that.

A psychologist I was talking to the other day said that telepathy can only happen human to human. Even long distance, like telephone, means "far away sound" in Latin. Telepathy is a far away passion. So it can happen across the country, but it still occurs person to person. My kids and I always say, "That's my brain. Get out of it."

My wife and I say that. Get out of my thoughts.

[Laughter] Part of that is knowing each other, but knowing who is on the other side of the phone which happens so frequently...

A number of years ago I did some past-life, age-regression therapy. I went to someone a friend of mine had been to. I went and did this because ever since I was a kid I had a real draw to the Holocaust... When I talk about the Holocaust publicly, people come up and talk to me afterwards and there is stuff they needed to work on. They told me things they've never told anyone else. I don't know if it's the telepathy. I don't know what it is at the level it is working. One of the things I learned during the past-life regression...

You weren't on the opposing side were you?

I don't want to talk about that. [The woman I went to] was very intuitive, she was in her eighties and she had been doing this a very long time. She interviewed me before she would work with me. I didn't want to tell her my predisposed ideas, and she asked me if I get really frustrated with people because they just don't get it and it's so obvious to you. I agreed and asked how she knew that. She told me I was a teacher.

I also had a reading done by the Native American man I told you about before. My power animal was a wolf. I asked, "what is the wolf" and he said that it is a teacher. Interestingly enough, I've always loved wolves, they come into my meditation

Wolves came into my past-life regression work but in a very good, powerful way. One time I just got out of a car, and I just had to get out and see this dog. It turned out to be a wolf.

You felt compelled?

I had to get out and go up to the wolf, and I'm not that kind of person, I'm not making this up. I'm not some New Age kook, I really felt this.

The past life woman told me I was a teacher and I'm supposed to be patient with people when I teach them. Later, I had a different teacher and I was complaining about students that did not seem to understand the course I was teaching, and I wish they would drop my class. He told me I had no right to think like that. These people have come to you in this lifetime. They might get only one thing, and you have no right *not* to teach them. That was one of the best things anyone ever told me. I didn't feel offended. I felt it was part of the path I was learning as a teacher. In mysticism humans are vessels through which the Divine or the Divine mystery operates.

Do you know where your soul is?

That's interesting. I feel something very deep internally. It's beyond rational. I don't know if I can point to it. I don't know if it's the heart, the brain, sometimes beyond or something within and beyond at the same time. I don't know. Whatever that thing is, it's part of everything that is reunited with everything in the world. To get back the shards from the breaking of the vessel when everything was created, if you will. It's a unification. It's the soul that unites you with everybody else. Everybody has a soul. Not everyone possesses rationality.

Do you know where your awareness is? You mentioned that you meditate. Has that ever brought about a sense of where you are in your body?

It's very complicated. It shifts and changes. Sometimes I can get out of myself and see myself, and sometimes I feel myself go very deeply inward. One time when I was facing a lot of uncertainty—because that's all there is, uncertainty—my ancestry, my spiritual ancestors came in and surrounded me in a circle and basically let me know that I'm protected and I'm going to be okay.

I didn't ask for this. I wasn't trying for this. I got a feeling inside and the room got a certain glow. I even opened my eyes to see if the light had changed in the room. The room was just as it was. I remember having done some acupuncture, feeling the same shift happen because I had meditated through that. The light took on a different hue. There was a different temperature.

I just accept these experiences. I don't question the mystical experiences. I don't see this as anything weird. I think everybody has the potential to awaken the Buddha within, to awaken these experiences. It's just a matter of working at it, being aware of it, being willing to see where it goes. I'm not afraid of this. I don't believe there is a Satan at the end of the line waiting to get me.

How about the serpent who came to the Garden of Eden?

It's a snake. Christianity takes on Satan. Satan in Hebrew just means adversary.

Like Angel means messenger. You've got the accuser in Job?

That's interesting. There is a Satan concept there in some of the interpretations as the adversary. I've heard that term used, but it's very different than the Christian concept. I'm not here to knock the Christian way of dealing with that. I just don't have any of those fears. I will go where my meditation has taken me. I feel it is getting me somewhere deeper.

The Dali Lama was asked if he remembered his past lives, and he answered that he did but that was not what mattered. It was how you are living now that mattered. Understanding your past lives should help you with now. Meditation is taking me somewhere. I go with that. All that is me anyway, in a sense.

Like when people dream? That's all your own mind too? It looks like there are other characters there...

But they are all your own projections. Where is it taking you? What is it teaching you?

AUSTRIAN SECRETARY

"Public displays of hatred commenced across [Vienna...ultimately] more than 65,000 Viennese Jews were deported to concentration camps."
Rebecca Weiner

"I was born an only child in Vienna, Austria. My father found hours to sit by me by the library fire and tell fairy stories."
Hedy Lamarr

This pleasant little interview is like a short detour from some of the more academically-based ones. I was invited into the home of a fifty-nine-year-old from Vienna, Austria. Her native tongue is German and her accent is strong and beautiful.

While her small dogs played with squeaky toys in the nicely decorated living room, we talked about the post-World War II education she received as a child. She was formerly an executive secretary. Not many people linked the origin of imagination to religion. She did immediately.

You were born during the war?
Well, the war ended in 1945, and I was born in 1944, so I was young.

Just a tiny baby.
Yeah, and the interesting part was when I grew up we had to take history in school—that was mandatory—we never learned anything about Hitler. That was too short after the war. There was no "why" given. I heard it from my parents. They filled me in, but nothing at school.

It's interesting that they'd leave that out.
[Laugh] I don't know how it is now. I would assume they tell the kids now. It's been so many years. I'm sure they learn about Hitler and the wonderful Second World War.

They couldn't keep it secret. How old were you when you learned English?

We had to take [it] in school, English. That was about ten years old. It was mandatory. You had a choice of learning either French or English, and I decided to take English. It was a main subject, too, like math and German and geography.

The first interview question is, what do you think are the purposes of imagination?

The purposes of imagination. That's a tough one. To think you live in a better world. You think of something more wonderful.

So it's helpful to people...

Yeah, I would assume it is helpful to imagine things. On the other hand if you imagine too much, and you wake up one day and the reality is completely different, what are you going to do then?

That's a good point. I often ask people if they think you can have too much imagination.

Yes, I think that some people do. They see everything as a wonderful world. I like to be more realistic.

What do you think the origin of imagination is? Where do you think it came from?

I want to think some of them through religion. People believe in things. I'm a Catholic, I believe, but I don't believe everything. I think that some people, when they really believe religion, maybe it comes from imagination or old ancient history.

You're not the only one to say that religion has a...

It has an influence in it. I remember how when I was a kid, that the angels are watching over you, and God is looking down. If you are a bad girl, He'll punish you. Imagine then, He's really watching me. Is it true? These are questions.

Yes, you'd wind up picturing this unseen world. Do you think that now that you are older?

To a certain point, yes. I don't know why. Maybe because I was brought up in the belief. I have no idea.

Where do you think imagination is located?

I think more in your heart than in your brain. It comes more from what you want to believe when you have a happy feeling, and from there it goes to your brain, of course. I think it's that way rather than the other way around—from the brain to the heart.

Do you think imagination plays a part in memory?

To a certain point, yeah. I would say so. Sometimes you think about things, and you tell them, and another person who was there says it was completely different. That's what you imagined it was like.

I'm thinking that it does. I know the truth from my imagination but it feels like I'm using the same part of my brain. I can visualize it either way. I'm wondering about the connection.

I remember my mother telling a story and it didn't happen quite as she said it. I never corrected her. It could be that she wanted to have it different than it really was.

It could be that when they get older, they want to see it in a different light. They want to see it nicer than it really was.

Do you think people take imagination with them when they die?

No. No, I don't think so.

So you would go more with it having an Earthly use with no need for it...

No. That's another thing with the Catholic Church. They say when you die your body stays here and your soul goes to heaven, if you're a good person, of course. The world there would be so wonderful that you wouldn't need imagination anymore.

Some people think imagination itself is a gift of God here. Do you think that's a possibility?

[Pause] I don't think it's a gift from God.

If I asked you where is the real you, where are you in your body? Do you know where you are in there?

The real me, I would say, is in my heart, because if I like somebody or love somebody I try to show them. If I dislike somebody I show them too, so it comes really from the heart. That's what I would say.

That leads right into the last question. What do you think is the most important thing, what really matters the very most?

To be a good and honest person. Don't hurt anybody. I would say if I hurt somebody I would say I'm sorry about it. To be a good person.

That answer would probably count for the end of the day or the end of a lifetime?

Yes. To try to make the people around me happy and to not hurt them. That is important to me. I had a wonderful childhood, wonderful parents, especially my father. I was a spoiled little monster. I'm honest. My father passed away a long time ago. I told myself for the longest time when I would visit the cemetery, he's just on vacation. I'm going home soon and I'll make myself visit the cemetery.

Do you notice a difference in the way of life in Austria as compared with the States?

That's a good question. Everything over there is more relaxed, we take it more easy. We make the same amount of money, like the Americans, but it's a completely different lifestyle.

Less stress maybe?

Less stress, especially the Viennese, we enjoy life really a lot. It is nice. My husband fell in love with the city of Vienna. He says he'd move there in a minute. He thinks the people are so friendly, more polite, and the city is clean.

Speech Pathologist

"Dreams full oft are found of real events. The forms and the shadows."
J. Baillie

This is a bright thirty-four-year-old speech pathologist originally from Akron, Ohio. You know that I frequently do ask the person if they think animals have imagination whereas here her thoughts go to that topic right away without any prompting from me.

Asking about the potential for animals' imagination, along with one or two other questions, is not considered a mandatory or core question but rather a secondary issue that sometimes helps to foster better communication with the person as they begin to feel more comfortable with the interview process.

Perhaps her thoughts were prompted by the beautiful outdoor setting in which we were seated. Chirping and singing of birds accompanies the entire interview. It was truly a lovely environment in which to have a good conversation.

You will also be struck by her scientific background and how that permeates so many of her answers. And yet I will vouch for her that her answers were very genuine. She was answering the questions, not avoiding the questions. There are times when an interviewee will resort to the base of their knowledge, their field of expertise, and they hide behind that. They are comfortable with what they do know, and when they are facing questions that they feel they cannot know the answer to, they resort to that base knowledge. I firmly believe our speech pathologist is not dodging questions through diversion techniques. I believe she is honestly answering them and she simply cannot hide or ignore her scientific education.

What are the purposes of imagination?

The purposes of imagination. I don't know, to help you create? To help you dream. So that people can develop new things. It's like a higher level brain process, but at the same time it is kind of a primitive thing too—in terms of dreaming or incorporating some of the things you're thinking about into dreams. You know how things get reflected at night?

It is almost like we're working out our problems at night.

Yeah, and I think that's shown scientifically in terms that the brain has to do a lot of work at night to take care of all the stuff your brain has been processing. So that's a really helpful thing. I heard that from a doctor and I thought that it was pretty cool.

It does seem like whatever we have on our minds comes out at that time. The second question is, what is the origin of imagination?

The origin of imagination. I don't know. I wonder, can animals imagine, like the higher-level animals, like the apes? We can teach them signs but do they create a new word with the signs that they have? It's cortical, higher level. I don't know though. A lot of emotions are limbic, I just don't know, I'd have to look it up. Does anybody know?

Everybody has a different opinion.

The imagination, to me that would be the brain combining with your experiences and your environment and what you're exposed to, what you've been told you could do. Like if you have a lot of limits set around you as a kid then maybe you would act out your imagination just to get beyond those limits. You would have a big imaginary life if you had a lot of limits and were real confined. But I also think if you had a lot of limits as a kid maybe you would think you couldn't do things so maybe you wouldn't try to explore and create and all that.

The way you answered that you almost answered the next question. Where do you think imagination is located?

The brain, I think so, because it's a higher-level thought process. It's like object permanence. Let's say there's a teddy bear on that chair, and I take that teddy bear and put it here or behind the chair. A little baby goes through a stage where they think the bear is completely gone or they know it's just hidden. The ability to know you're in reality but you're thinking about things that are not.

Knowing the difference.
Yeah. Kind of like knowing the difference that something is gone forever or it's just hidden.

What role does imagination play in memory?
I don't know. That's a good question. I think that probably, because there are so many neural networks, I don't really think that we process serially. I think we process in a parallel fashion. I think that we're probably accessing similar neural networks in our brain. They might not be exactly the same but I would imagine that they are connected somewhere along the way. I think we're probably drawing many different networks simultaneously.

But we know which one is real?
Yeah.

What are your thoughts about children and imaginary friends or the huge capacity they seem to have to use their imaginations?
You know I wonder if it's a mental muscle thing. Their brains are so plastic and they're just massively developing all these neural networks. I wonder if that's part of the process of developing their nervous system. I don't know much about child psychology because this [material] is a lot of child psych with memory, attention, I don't know much about kiddos. I've never had kids, I don't even work with kids. The kids I worked with in school were all cleft palette. Something close to memory would be language, again, to have language you have to have certain concepts down like object permanence. We talk about things in past tense and that's represented in language so you have to know that the ball went down the street but the ball didn't disappear completely.

I don't know about the child psych stuff. I imagine you know about that though maybe at least from raising kids. Have you studied that?

No. I read a lot but I didn't study it formally, that's the way that I am though, a self-taught person. Another question I have is, do you think you can take imagination with you when you die?

Oh yeah, that's a pretty cool idea. When you die...you mean in a spiritual sense or just in any sense?

Any sense you want it to be, I don't want to give you ideas on how to answer.

Let's see, Catherine. I don't know what happens when you die. My tradition is Catholic so I guess I thought I kind of just...everything is supposed to be good if you make it to heaven. So I would imagine you get your imagination with you there. But, if you have everything there why would you need to think about things that weren't there? But maybe you need to create or problem solve but then you wouldn't have problems to solve.

These are really good questions, they're pretty cool. I'm not a very abstract thinker. Language is very abstract but that I've had training in, for speech, things that are more concrete. The brain's pretty wild, totally cool.

Sounds like you studied it plenty, probably in college.

Yeah, and I don't have it all down. I don't think anybody does. I work with a lot of people with head injuries. But the concept of imagination and brain damage, that has never occurred to me.

How do the brain-damaged act? Do they act like they still have their imagination?

No. But we're not thinking about that. It's all about...they act disoriented and uninhibited. They act extremely impulsive. They can't inhibit behavior. They'll stand up every second even if you keep telling them to sit down. Their brain can't process that information or utilize it and integrate it in such a way that they can inhibit their behavior. They can't plan and direct and initiate activities like washing the dishes. Where do you start, what do you do? Things that we take for granted we have to re-teach. They have no judgment in terms of safety. They can't walk. They'll get out of bed and fall down. So those are the ways I'm used to thinking about it. Not in terms of imagination. But I would bet it's still there.

I've asked people if they think some people have more imagination than others, if you can have different amounts.

Yeah I think so. I think there are certain brain differences. I'm not strong [in the area of the] abstract, visual, spatial, but I'm very strong in terms of semantics and language and lexical things. They have done studies on that. Have you seen the things on brain sex differences between male and female?

I've watched a lot of documentaries.
You might have seen that one. It is so cool because they are showing the differences between male and female brains. Starting at six months they teach a male and female baby to pull a string and a light comes on. They take away the light and the girl instantly gets up and communicates. She starts screaming. She stops [trying]. The male baby is stubborn and he pulls harder, harder and harder.

No, I didn't see that. It is interesting.
Women, anthropologically, we're supposed to be good at communicating. We're supposed to be facilitating harmony in our family structures. The guys are not supposed to be giving up.

Let's say they're hunting in the old days and there's a bear you can't [give up]. You have to get your food.

There's also a test to see if men and women would change their opinion under pressure. They have these set-ups where they would ask how high do you think that wall is? Then they would either agree or disagree. If they disagreed with the woman she would give up her opinion and say, "Yeah, I guess you're right." The guys didn't give up their opinion. It was so interesting, it was just wild. [Women] have the greater connections between the hemispheres.

The guy's brain mass is larger over all but [females] have greater connectivity so we're utilizing [more]. The part of the brain that's used to pick up on facial expression, that's in the right side of the brain. We studied facial expression matching language because if you have a stroke in the right side of their brain they'll tell a joke without any intonation in their speech and their affect is flat. That's really hard to treat. But it's that part of their brain that's damaged.

I think that women's intuition is that they are picking up on those signals. Sometimes men don't perceive the same as women do. I think it's because of those greater connections that we have. I do believe there are female and male brain differences and I don't feel that means I'm less than. I imagine that there are imagination differences.

I watch as many documentaries as I can. I studied the brain a long time ago in college, but they've changed their minds about so many things that most of things I was taught have become obsolete or they realize now it's not true.

Yeah they really screwed up a lot. I think it's because psych is young. Psych is probably where antiseptic technique was when they weren't even sterilizing things in the old days for surgery. I think that's where psych is. It's only a hundred years old. We just don't know anything. I think they used to think that schizophrenia was caused by bad moms or something. What a joke. How can anything that complicated as a disease process be caused by [parenting]. I just don't buy that.

They spent the early twentieth century thinking that moms caused Autism too.

What a crock. Yeah, that's some damn powerful moms. I'm sorry but...[laughter]. There are speech paths. who work with kids with Autism. I don't have any experience with that either but that's a big area. They're doing a lot of work in that area. So when they figure that one out that will be pretty cool.

There's a genetic disorder where girls get no male hormone at all and their visual, spatial skills are horrible, such that they can't path-find to drive. They can't find their way. I don't buy into that thing that women are not given the opportunities in science and stuff. I think our brains are different. There's probably a large percentage of girls that don't really have an affinity mentally for that kind of stuff. Then there's those lucky girls that do and they make more money [laughter]. I wish I was good at math and engineering.

The last question is, where do you think the real you is, inside of your body?

Oh, I don't know, I'd say inside my brain. Yeah, definitely my brain. Because you see people—their personality, everything—changes with brain damage. Theoretically, when you're brain dead, that's what dead is. You don't die, well you die in your heart, but the reason you die is because your heart stops pumping blood with oxygen to your brain. It's your brain that's dying. Theoretically, you're alive as long as you're conscious. Well, I mean you can be unconscious and alive but...does that make sense?

Yes.

I think it's the brain even though there's that whole soul concept. That's big in the Catholic tradition, the whole soul concept.

So you're not positive that you have a soul?

I don't know and my brother's a priest. I came from a really Catholic family. He was ordained a year ago.

You see brain damaged people more often than others typically do. Is it your opinion that you see a personality loss, so to speak?

Oh yeah.

If they were really outgoing, or bubbly before...

It can go really the opposite way or really amplify.

Because they don't control their own impulses, as you said before.

No, it's the saddest thing, brain damage. That's something I would say. Get some helmets on those kids.

I tell my kids all the time, they don't bring you back from a brain injury.

They don't, you can't. There's nothing you can do. They will never be the same. Usually, we take into account our listener's perspective; do they have enough background or do I have to give them more information. If I told you about James, and I didn't give you the details about him first, you'd be wondering what I'm talking about. Well, some of these people are like that. They have a really hard time stopping the speed when presenting concepts. A brain tumor can do that too.

Maybe it's not personality though, Catherine. Maybe it's behavior. Because our personality is reflected in our behavior.

That's another thing right brain injuries will do, they don't have a sense of proximity, so they'll sit right next to you. See, there's a social kind of thing. We don't do that. See I'm doing it too. I'm hopping really quick from one thing to another which I do. They won't code switch. Like talk different to their mom than their kids, and then to their boss, and then to the President. Like, I don't swear [when talking to my mom] but I might when talking to my girlfriend. They don't have that sense. The adults are set, but if you get a kid early enough, while the brain is still growing, you can do some pretty good stuff.

What are people with left-brain injuries like?

Some of it's the same for all traumatic brain injuries, but left-brain you see more speech and language, if they're right-handed. Language is represented everywhere, that is the understanding now. The old understanding is that a lot of the nuts and bolts of speech and language of right-handed people are represented in the left side of the brain, so are your dictionary and your grammar. It's all over, the social structure of knowing what to say to whom and how close to get, and to put facial expression on it, and [they have problems with] intonation, right rhythm, stress—that's on the right and you might be pulling some words up from the left, but you're outputting them with a certain rate in-between words from the thalamus, so it's all over.

When someone can't find words, that's really obvious, an obvious deficit, and that's what you'll see. People can't name something. That's what you see with classic left-brain, or else they can't produce speech sounds because of the part of their brain that programs the motor movements. So they couldn't say tor-na-do, because they couldn't do tongue up and round your lips. They got the word, they can name a butterfly, but they can't make their muscle move to produce the sounds that represent that.

I used to work at a trauma center. I had a burn patient who pulled herself out of a car. A drunk driver hit her. She was just covered in burns and she would cry. She wanted to know what she did to deserve this. It was this huge loss. We would stretch her skin grafts. It makes you count your blessings, let me tell you, Catherine. I wonder why did it happen to that person and not me?

ENGLISH TEACHER

"Thinking: The talking of the soul with itself."
Plato

This is a forty-eight-year-old private school teacher who specializes in English and journalism. He is from Portland, Oregon. You will witness his ability to weave together aspects of literature, philosophy, and other ancient knowledge with the well-known topic of transcendentalism.

We are afforded very little insight to what he truly thinks in terms of personal answers but we are given much to consider. It is constantly amazing to me how different minds respond differently to these questions. One might think that the answers would be far more redundant than they proved to be. This teacher bounces ideas quickly like a ping-pong ball in play. His paddle is his vast expertise in the Romantics and other heady matters.

He informed me mere seconds before taping that he teaches journalism and interviewing skills.

[Him] First, you're supposed to tell your interviewee your name and the purpose of the interview, I mean, it's just not fair to the interviewee if they don't know the purpose. Young news reporters, for example, always want to trap someone. I say that's unethical. You have to say what it is.

Now, if there's something that you're really trying to uncover you don't have to tell them exactly everything you're after, but you need to give them the topic and the purpose. So anyway, I am delighted to talk to you.

Our first question is, what are the purposes of imagination?
[Long pause] I think people have purposes, I'm not sure imagination has a purpose. When people imagine, if they are doing it purposefully or if it's some part of them taking over, I'm not sure.

I'm a bicycle racer. I have a big race this weekend, so I've been imagining myself on the bicycle at various points of the race, kilometer by kilometer. I guess that's a purposeful type of imagining, which people call visualizing too.

What most people think of the word imagination is a little more creative—whether that has purpose or that just comes, whether that's an aspect of the unconscious, the part of our minds that is going to work on things that interest us, or that we have compelling reasons to worry about. But it just happens? I'm not sure.

I think artists are struck by imagination. That doesn't imply purposefulness because if they're struck by it then it's just sort of coming out. Where does that kind of thing come from? It's like where does creativity come from?

I guess the short answer to that ramble would be...I think sometimes you can imagine purposefully and sometimes you imagine serendipitously and it kind of depends on which kind of imagination you need or which kind of imagining. More might come to me later, but what's your next question?

What do you think the origin of imagination is?

Well, that goes back to the first two things I said. In the first case, like my imagining the race, that's very conscious and deliberate and it comes by feeding my mind with data. Is that imagining when I visualize and recreate? What do you think?

If you're doing it in your head and you're not on your bike, yes.

Then so would be the planned or deliberate or the conscious kind of imagining. Where does it come from? Is that what you asked?

The origin.

As I was suggesting in the previous answer, the other kind of imagination may come from things that are below our conscious awareness, the Jungian or the Freudian or things that are in our minds. They are not coming from outside. It's in us, but it's not the things that we are aware of.

I guess dreaming is that way when our conscious mind is relaxed and that which is below or submerged during the day is out. I guess imagination could be like a waking dream, in that respect, that it's coming from the same source as the unconscious. It could be like that.

Of course the Greeks thought that the imagination came from a muse, who would touch you. The writers would pray for that to happen.

Homer would begin the Odyssey with, "O, Spirit of Muse, invoke in me." So address the muse and you call and invoke. Invoke means "call in." You are calling something in that is outside, that you're hoping comes to you sort of like a spirit or a gift or a wind or a breath.

Inspire is a breath, you know; to breath in. I don't think it is that. I think it is inside you. The outward forms that we take to nurture it, maybe with time like the Greeks have taken the form of a prayer. Calling for imagination, you're really not calling for something outside yourself. I think, so much as a way of ritual, of opening a door and looking in. We don't do that all the time. We are obsessed with schedules and details and all of the other things. We sort of have to create a mechanism for looking inside.

Maybe when the Greeks say, "O, Spirit of the Muse," they are just sort of putting everything else at abeyance and saying this is the time I'm going to try to mine or nurture or dig down and find these interesting thoughts that I don't take time to figure out day to day.

Do you think some people have too much or more than others or less than others?
Too much?

Too much imagination?
"More than" would mean someone who is in touch with his way of thinking really, more often. Some people don't imagine very much, they are more into the material world or their conscious thought of the day to day. Some people do that more. I guess artists do that more. I think there are just dreamy people who do it and maybe their lives are enriched by it in ways that other people don't recognize. "Too much" implies something negative. I'm just trying to refine the question before I answer it, someone looks within or looks beyond the here or now of the material so much that it interferes with their life and it has negative effects on their life. That's how I'm going to interpret what you said by "too much."

I suppose that could happen. Who are we to say that the person who doesn't succeed in the material world but is dreamy, is having a worse life than someone else who may not be as dreamy but who succeeds.

There's a tradition there in history. I'm going to jump to an exaggeration of maybe too much imagination, too little in contact with "real, unreal" world. That would be people who would be considered insane. Where they say in England, if you read Shakespeare's plays about

Bedlam and the houses, they had to separate people who were not sane. That's probably such a general word that it's not worth using, but that's the word they used. Society was pretty cruel in its treatment of such people that they deemed out of touch or sick or whatever.

At the same time there was a double standard. There was another attitude running parallel with that attitude of bigotry, prejudices, and cruelty. They were also lucky in that there is divine madness. Sometimes the very same people who wouldn't want to be that way and would put them aside, they would say they have divine madness, they are touched by something special.

Other people, who would be more caring, would really truly value them. They would articulate that value more. They would say maybe this is rational in a higher way. We just don't understand. Maybe this overly imaginative person has something we should all have.

Back to your question. I guess you could be so imaginative that it could foul you up from day to day and cause you hardship. I don't know how you could say for another person that this is bad or good. In history people have done both.

I've been waiting for someone to make that link, on their own, to insanity.

Artists are sometimes considered mad. They sometimes have difficulty in the everyday world. Those are people who are active in what we are calling imagination—active at looking at things in a special way. The romantic poets of the late eighteenth or early nineteenth century priced imagination above all things. Coleridge and Wordsworth were neo-Platonists.

Plato told a story to one of his followers, actually Socrates tells the story and Plato writes it down. Someone goes into a cave because they are punished and they fail to see the world as it really is anymore. They are chained at the back of the cave and a jailer keeps them alive by bringing them food and keeping a fire going. The fire is behind them and they are chained to the terminus of the cave looking at a blank wall. The light source is behind them and all they ever see for years is shadows dancing on the wall. Their own shadows and the shadows of their jailers but they never see things as they truly are, as they used to when they were out in the daylight.

Eventually, this person's confinement is over and they come back into the world. The first thing is blindness. It's so dazzling they can't see. The story has a happy ending. The person adjusts to the light and they see and they find it wonderful to see things as they really are.

He asks his master what is the point of the story? He told him that we live in a cave and all we see of life, as it truly is, is shadows. We're condemned to not see things as they truly are. We did once. Before we were born we lived in realm of perfect existence. Of course, Christianity borrowed that and called it heaven. [Earlier] the Greeks had it described a different way.

A pre-life heaven?

Yeah, everybody existed there, and by definition there was no matter. It was all essence or soul. Everything was an idea. A circle isn't really an object, it's an idea. You can draw a circle but it's always going to be imperfect. The same relation exists between everything that you might think of and then things in the world.

We live life on Earth as if in the shadows—we get good at it, the older we get the better we get at discerning the shadows from one another.

That's Plato. Wordsworth, Coleridge and the neo-Platonists, they were influenced by a guy named Swendenborg, a German philosopher—they changed Plato's ideas and came up with these romantic ideas. Yes indeed, we live our lives in shadows and get to see through the shadows to the perfect forms that we once knew. Children do it the easiest because they are closer to having been born. The older we get the farther we get away from the shadows. Wordsworth writes, "Shadows of the prison door close upon the growing boy." As we grow older we are more trapped by the shadows of the material world. We get farther and farther away. Wordsworth writes sonnet after sonnet about children and how innately they see the good and the true. That's what he describes as innocence.

This is all leading up to imagination. Wordsworth poses a question: Well, then are we lost? We adults, can we never regain this innocence, this ability to not be touched and ruined and spoiled and made bitter by all that goes on around the material world? He demonstrates that no, that is not the case. Philosophy and the imagination is what saves us. It's through a mental act which as an adult we have to do more deliberately.

The child does it naturally. That's the attitude he gives children in his poems. The adult is on the outside and never the less gets into the inside through an act of the imagination. Through the act of what he calls, a philosophical mind. But it's an imaginative mind is what he is talking about.

He uses the word imagination too in other poems and contexts. He also links it with nature. He says it's nature and the imagination that saves us. The romantic poets would say that life is all about nature and imagination.

Are there people who imagine more or too much? Well, there's a huge tradition in literature and philosophy that says that's what we ought to be doing. That's what saves us. Whether you do it too much or not, I suppose if you go into some sort of trance and can't deal with anything around you it might impair your body. But then again, with divine madness, maybe your soul is just having a great time and we all should be doing the same thing. Who knows?

Do you think you take imagination with you when you die?

I'm glad I told the story because now it has purpose. The allegory with the cave has to do with dying—it is simply returning to that realm of perfect forms.

The pre-life heaven is where you go to as a post-life heaven?

Yes. Socrates and Plato did not get into that. The Greeks were not into heaven and afterlife.

If I understand correctly, there was a pre-life heaven but no post-life heaven?

Well, with Socrates and Plato. The neo-Platonist, the English Romantics, they were all coming from a Christian background. It was very easy for them to say if there is a pre-life there's also this return. That's the whole goal, to return. It wasn't to return to God the Father, the Son and the Holy Ghost. That's part of the Christian Church. These poets and philosophers thought it was a return to the connectedness of all things.

Like a big consciousness?

Well, like Ralph Waldo Emerson, the American Romantic philosopher said, "I go into the woods and I am nothing. I see all. I am a transparent eyeball." Which is a grotesque image. He has reduced his entire being to perception and consciousness. There's no body. He is now just connected with all of nature, like a Steven Spielberg ET. To try to liven up life in the classroom, when I tell this story to students, when I talk about poetry, I try also to appeal to pop culture [which is] rife with these images. John Lennon and Paul McCartney: "Get back, get back to where you once belonged." Do you know that song?

Yup.

The whole idea of the force in Star Wars as being something that permeates all of life. Obi-Wan Kenobi and Luke Skywalker have higher imaginative powers, you might say. The ability to connect with...

The force?

The force and those things.

Back to the Romantics. You ask, "Can you take it with you?" I mean the whole point of some ways of thinking is that you leave this life, the material world passes away, and this is some kind of stopping off point. It's where we don't want to be. Where we want to be is...you don't take imagination with you. You don't need imagination because you're seeing things as they truly are.

Like the guy that gets out of the cave, the allegory of the cave, by Plato. He needed imagination to distinguish one shadow from another. Oh, that's Bob, jailer Bob. He's big and fat. Now the shadow is twisting and distorting just like life in the material world. It's never quite perfect. I'm pretty good at reading shadows, and that's Bob. I'm using my imagination to take in the twisting distorted data of the material world, and I'm getting to Bob. He will not use his imagination when he is out...

He will see Bob.

He will see Bob as he truly is. Looking at it that way, imagination is just truly seeing. Without any impediment, it's just simply the right perception as opposed to...we are filled with wrong perceptions now in the material world, and we just have to get beyond that. It's a good thing that the poets and philosophers helped us conclude that we are not doomed in the material world. [Laughing]

We don't even have to postpone it like some Christianity does, until later when we can see things as they truly are. If we work at it, sit in the backyard enough, we can do it now.

I haven't seen the movie, but I understand that David Bowie's movie, *The Man Who Fell to Earth*, is sort of a rock and roll, pop version of basically the same story. He falls to Earth and he is an alien, I guess. He falls from a place that was really good. No?

His place had no water, there was a big drought. So it was really bad and he came to a water-filled land. He has a reason to go back, and he wants to do that because his wife is there and he is deeply in love with her. His children are there. He is without them. There is a sense of loss that he has left his family there.

Where do you think you are in your body? Your real self, your real personality?

Where am I? Do you want me to connect this to what we've been talking about in terms of where am I in my ability to imagine?

You don't have to. Your real essence, who you think you really are—where do you think you are in there? In your body?

I'll redefine the question as that. I think, ironically, an activity that's very physical, biking.

It's material. There's a bike, a road, a pedal, there's exertion. That's my way, not necessarily the only way, that I have increased my contact with things that are important. Nature.

I don't know if you've ever been an athlete, but Joseph Campbell wrote four huge books. His thesis of his fourth book is that all the great religions, the Witch Doctors, the Pantheistic religions of the Greeks or whatever, have all served as ways to make easier for the common person, spiritually—a way to touch or see God.

A simplification.

Yeah, the ritual is all outward but it's all designed to move you inward to some understanding.

What role does imagination play with memory?

Memory and imagination are closely linked because memory...well, I guess from a chemical point of view it's going back to traces that have been laid in your brain. They touch, something happens chemically and you recall an experience. The more you rehearse that the more deeply the paths in your brain are lined. Whether we described it chemically, medically or just in terms of something like magic, it's kind of going outside the "here and now" to some other time or place. It certainly has a place in this conversation I would think.

I can simply remember a moment with my kids. Sometimes I worry about traffic, about getting hit or doing something in a race and hurting myself. I'll have these transcendental moments where I value them so much, and my wife, because of the danger I'm in. That's a combination of my physical experience of the moment and memory of other experiences not in the moment, and they produce, I don't know, I haven't really named them before. I value them. Are those transcendental moments? I don't know.

I certainly come beyond myself to something high, something important. I think reading can do that for me. I think for some people, not me, a painting can. It doesn't do it for me. Music can do that for some people. I enjoy music but it doesn't have that same power as say an athletic moment or with someone I love.

Moments in nature can. I used to be a lot more active as a hiker. Up until I was in my thirties and I got really into my job, journalism, teaching. I sort of broke away. I didn't break away from that because I'm still doing all that. I refocused somewhere around forty-three years old. I got more into cycling which got me back outside and back into physical experiences that to me are powerful. I can't remember your original question.

I think we want to get back to, where are you in your body?

I guess, where I am in my development, if I change the question that way, then I think Wordsworth's idea of growing, I think that happened to me. I think for seven to ten years that was true. I like to think of these last five or six years as progressively getting more open to imagination, to these transcendental moments, to the important things other than just work. Everything has a trap and a double edge. I could get so focused on my cycling that I could ignore my family or other responsibilities. In which case my methods for transporting myself could become a new prison or a new set of chains or a new confinement. Try to keep balance in your life.

Well, that's a good one to end on.

Educational Psychologist

"There is, then, nothing mysterious or mystical in the discovery made by Plato and remade by Froebel that play is the chief, almost the only, mode of education for the child in the years of later infancy...the playful attitude is one of freedom."
John Dewey, *How We Think*

I think of psychologists as experts on the mind itself. To catch up with one of these busy professionals proved to be difficult. Due to our time restrictions I limited the questions to only the most crucial.

Our sixty-five-year-old educational psychologist answered the first question rapidly and precisely. She claimed to not have thought about the purposes of imagination much. Many people say that. Yet she quickly proceeded to give a very thoughtful answer.

Her certainty on life after death is interesting as is her brief reference to reincarnation. She placed the location of imagination in the mind with a new twist to that answer. We might have expected some very specific and scientific answers from a psychologist, a mind expert, but at this point we have seen repeatedly that a person's profession will not always determine predictable answers.

What are the purposes of imagination?
I would say the value of imagination, the purpose, the cause, the effect would probably be several fold, not having thought a great deal about it. But certainly to release us from stress, to give us a chance—rather than get angry, rather than become more confused—to take a breath and relax. Let the mind free. That would be one thing, depending on our age.

Imagination as a child would seem to be the free state of the human child's mind which is not filled with all kinds of facts and tools for finding reasons and causes and effects. So that ability to open the mind and play, I would think, would be the child's zone for imagination—basically a playground. For me it's a playground, imagination, because I enjoy it. It's a fun place to go.

179

Imagination for an artist could be a crossover for perhaps a scientist, someone whose mind is extremely focused in a direction, let's say professionally or psychically. Their intuition is a skill they have that they can reach for, so is, again, the release of tension but more with the direction they ask themselves what's possible. Their imagination could fall into place and help them give up all of the, again, fixed ideas, the directions they travel to get new clear moments. In so doing that imagination is to get away from the fixed mind. That would certainly be the adult way.

Often times, I do know, when they release themselves the imagination, of course intuition is right there, so it does assist. What you do when you are focusing as per an artist might, or a scientist might or a mathematician might—because I know them very well—they might be asking, "What else do I know?" In that asking, what they might know, that question "what" triggers one's own intuitive process to set off and give them information from their search. It's perhaps a causeway on the way to the ocean of the mind we call intuitive. That would be my first reactions, my first impressions.

Where is it located?

The imagination? I'm sure it is psychical. There would be no question in my mind that if we could put an electrode to the brain, there would be a zone in the brain—or a region in the brain to use a more correct term—where there is certain brain activity going on. Where do we go for our imagination? We go to questions, releasing our other mental activities, our other psychical functions, that otherwise direct us. You use your memory, your reasoning—it's a tool—one that we use as a nondirective route. But it's still a tool. In some sense in psychical, but the actual zone where we get the information is universal, I've no doubt.

Do you think it plays a role in memories?

Not specifically, no. I'm of the mind that memory—let me use the word without implying that it's absolute—it's an encapsulated zone that we have in our region of our being which locks in our experiences and staying—limiting myself in my conversation with you, if we are not discussing reincarnation or life after life, life before life or afterlife, if we are not discussing that it seems to me that memory has a very specific task, like your fingers have a very specific task, to contribute to your ability to learn and to make your way psychically through the world at large.

Because we have limited time we are heading straight to the chase.
Okay. [Laughter]

Do you take imagination with you when you die?
That, I don't know.

You don't know? Any thoughts? Any inclinations?
Take imagination with us when we die? [Pause] Let me put it this way. It's not well thought out but perhaps it's useful. It's part of a human being human to have imagination. Experience has given me two slight, bright lights through death's door to know that there is afterlife to the extent that I know it, which is limited. But I can articulate some of that. In that—when there is communication across what we call the life and death line—my experience has been that there's a communication that would not be related to imagination. But that's a communication back to the likes of me, the likes of you.

Does that individual still have the capacity to be free of mind? I would think it would be unnecessary in the scheme of things, because that is a freedom. In our wildest dreams, our freedom to imagine is very human, very much a requirement for us to make it through this life. I would say I don't know the answer, but I would in rapid-fire response suggest that we don't need it there. Does that give you an insight to the way I think?

STOCK ANALYST

"Your soul is the closest to you, but it is not you yourself."
Goethe

There were absolutely no hesitations answering any of the questions for this fifty-seven-year-old stock analyst. You will see right away that he has a certain brilliancy of mind as he gave a rapid list of purposes rather than naming one or two as many others have done. He has an Ivy League education and was born in Atlanta, Georgia. He is active in more than one demanding profession.

This interview occurred in late 2001 as made obvious by the mention of the September 11th attacks on the World Trade Center in New York City. In all honesty, I had never heard the word transponder at the time of this interview. In following years, I have not only heard the word, it has become very common now that freeways and bridges use them to communicate with automobiles while they travel on roadways.

This interview will wake you up from any drowsy state you may have fallen into. Our white-haired, older, established stock analyst confidently answers the location of imagination as having "plasticized metallic elements that pick up microwave electromagnetic energy." That answer in itself is imaginative.

What are the purposes of imagination?
The purposes of imagination, I'd say, are to keep human beings evolving into something better than they are. Without imagination we'd all follow each other down the path to oblivion.

Imagination is what differentiates people from each other. Something that brings pleasure to our lives. Without it we're not a lot different from the crustaceans, I don't think. It allows us to grow into fully functioning adults when we start out knowing nothing as little babies. The imagination really starts from the moment our eyes open. You start taking in information, I don't think it ever stops until we die. Imagination is particularly good when you're dreaming because you get such nice restful sleep when you're doing it. It's not good to use too much when you're driving down the road because you might get into trouble that way. Imagination is something that everybody enjoys, don't they?

Probably, that's another question I have. Can you have too much of it?

Sure. I mean the [band] Jefferson Airplane had this song about this mentally retarded boy named Lather, that was from the psychedelic era, and all he would do is play word games in his mind and fantasize about sexual things without anything coming to fruition. It wasn't really connected with reality.

So people have different amounts of imagination?

Sure. Some people don't choose to utilize their imagination very much, they have it, it's innate in probably all people but their circumstances, maybe it's poor nutrition or lack of exercise, they just don't have their brain going on all sixteen cylinders. I think obviously some people have lots of imagination and they write books, like you for instance. Other people with limited imagination might work for the post office.

I'm sure they've got imaginative people there, but probably not as many as they do at Microsoft where they're busy thinking of new software programs and so forth that haven't been written yet. It all comes down to imagination being a binary code whipping around in our brain.

There's a new book out called, *The New Science*—it's physics, I think. This renegade physicist shows that all of nature's complex processes, such as a running ripple through a stream, you could recreate that exactly if you put enough binary bits together in a computer program. That program would have the end result of that rippling stream looking exactly as it looks in nature. It's kind of an interesting thing to look at it that way.

I'll say. The next question is, what is the origin of imagination?

I certainly believe it's God, a lot of people don't believe in God. I believe in science too. I know science can't be compared with God. I think that science can say that the universe started with a particle smaller than a grain of sand and blew into a flat-ish, infinitely expanding universe that is so big we can't comprehend it.

With that is many different parallel universes simultaneously expanding in different directions, many of which are identical to the one we're living in now.

If that is true then I don't know why God wouldn't be the source of that. We don't know what God is, but we can only have our primitive religious theories to guide us somewhat. I just don't think things like that happen by accident. Because if it did, why aren't there many other grains of sand out there expanding equally into infinite universes? There may be.

Maybe they're expanding outwardly, maybe they are expanding inwardly, or imploding. Maybe inside of us we have many trillions of rapidly expanding universes and we're not even aware of it. Maybe there are no real time/space limitations. I think that there is some creative force out there that is the source of that and it becomes more than just particles expanding.

You can't scientifically measure a soul which is the source of imagination. You have to give it a name. That soul came from somewhere and the closest I can come up with is a god or gods, collectively they would be gods to us. That's where I believe it comes from. I could go like this for a long time.

What do you think the location of this imagination is?

I think we have plasticized, metallic elements that pick up microwave electromagnetic energy that results in sending a signal that broadcasts from a distant area. It comes out through a transistor and a transponder and out through a transducer to create sound that we listen to. That is someone's imagination that is condensed and expanded again so we can hear it. Or encoded and decoded.

I think something similar may be happening in the sense that God or other humans out there are putting out information that is then somehow condensed and transmitted to some kind of pipelines, decoded and expanded again. That's why I think there may be some truth that there are some paranormal elements out there. Some people are maybe able to sense a poltergeist or a ghost, or some kind of presence, or actually feel a connection with their former relative or husband or wife through a séance or right receiving state.

Why some people can be hypnotized and why some can't; they have to have their crystals aligned properly in affect to receive the signal. Some of the signals are unconscious, and I think there's a lot of energy flying around, and some of it maybe just kind of collides and somehow it creates a signal that we convert into a different electrical process in our brain. It varies and that's why our thoughts vary from time to time.

Obviously we take in things through our eyes and ears that are processed in our computer-like brain that are constantly taken apart and rearranged by our brain when we're asleep. Most creative things are done supposedly when you're asleep anyway. Through the process of writing or preparing for a speech, or whatever, you then try to tune into that somehow. You're not aware you are doing it. You think you're doing it right from that moment, but it probably was already stored there.

Do you think animals have imagination?

Yes, I do. I think they have to have imagination to stalk a prey. There may be a lot of other examples. I'm sure a lot of imagination is pretty low level. For instance, a hermit crab that goes out and grabs a tin can and takes it back to its lair, he's not sure he knows what he wants to do with it. It's part of instinct. Organisms who do it successfully are able to survive and ones who can't die and get eaten. That's why it's important for human beings to keep learning so their imaginations can keep them out of trouble. They think.

Do you think people take imagination with them when they die?

I don't believe our soul just disappears. I don't necessarily expect to go to heaven or hell. That may be too limiting of a concept. I'm [in] a Methodist kind of religion so I believe there may be such thing as a heaven, but I don't necessarily believe we have to go there right away. It might be an infinite journey. It might be some journey we don't get to right away. Maybe we have to bounce around the universe and experience different things—somewhat like Bill Murray did in *Groundhog Day*—before he became a more perfect human being.

Meaning, repetition will teach a person?

Right. Maybe next time I come back as Catherine, to be inside a female skin, experience some of what you've experienced and become a more perfect human being. Unless I learn to empathize with females, I'm not going to be a complete person because I've got X and Y chromosomes inside of me. Of course you, only have the Y. Maybe you do actually have a budding X inside of you somewhere. I don't know.

Well, I do hate to shop. So, there you go. We're talking about whether we take the imagination with us when we die. The reason I ask is because I'm wondering if there is any connection or correlation or even interplay between the person's soul and the person's imagination.

The soul that I got now, that I think I've got inside my body, I may have part of it somewhere else.

You're one step ahead of me the whole way because that's the next question. We might as well go there. Where is your soul? Where do you feel you are inside there?

I feel like I'm connected to all the members of my family and past, present. I feel like I'm going to be connected to any grandchildren that I might have. I feel a connection to a lot of my friends. I think I must get part of my soul from them because they were a good thing for my soul and I became a friend with him or her.

I think you can extrapolate your soul for different entities like an author transposes things they've read into different new things. Maybe some things that are written or spoken about appear to be new but they're really not. They're just transposed and maybe given a complexity or a meaning. Think of it as constantly re-editing your book, making it better and better. I guess you can do that to a fault, and you can get to the final draft that doesn't need any more editing, and you keep editing it and make it worse than it was two weeks ago. I guess you can try to do too much?

Maybe part of your soul comes from laying back on the grass and looking at the clouds and relaxing. Let some of the energy soak into you, the karma, whatever you call it.

People do yoga, they do stretching exercises and somehow it allows more free energy flow up through the spine. It relieves pain and stress. Here again, maybe it's realigning the crystals somehow so it can put into them the more positive aspects of the universe.

I know I was asleep on September the 11th, and I woke up with what I thought was a heart attack right when that building was hit, the first building, the south tower I think it was. I didn't know what it was, and I went back to bed and my wife came in and said one of the World Trade Center buildings got hit by a plane.

I said, "Oh, God Damn, that must have been a terrorist or something," and I kind of went back to sleep because my pain had gone away.

She came back in again and said terrorists had hit the building. I got up with a jolt and went in and started watching the replay of the events. I realized that I had that intense chest pain when that building was hit, or thereabouts somewhere.

Somewhere some soul was crying out in agony and I think I connected to it. Maybe, maybe not, but I don't have a heart problem. I'm sure some other people who were a lot closer to the location probably had the same feeling. One of the photographs of the building had smoke curling up and it almost looked like a cartoonish image from *Dante's Inferno* of the devil with horns and a beard with pointy ears, that sort of thing. You kind of wonder. I don't really think we know what the image of ultimate evil is, but that was sort of strange to see that photograph.

I think one reason people feel really good when they go to church is because there is a lot of other people going to church too. They are playing off each other's good vibrations I guess. In a more perverse way, people who go to practice some kind of devil worship, killing chickens or whatever they like to do at those things, probably get a thrill in a different way. They probably get a rush from going out and doing something bad to someone. I think it's nice that we realize, that [when] we put ourselves in circumstances where the vibrations might not be good, maybe we should not go to those places.

The last question then is what do you think the most important thing is? It sounds like a Miss America question, I know. But what do you think?

I don't have the body for that. The most important thing is, to me, family relationships. That's it to me. It's got to be different for somebody else. For them it might be achieving the pinnacle of success in their chosen occupation. For other people it's got to be spiritual greatness or nirvana at the top of a mountain. Writing a great book or a great poem or winning a great tennis or golf tournament. Perhaps becoming an astronaut and going into outer space. Someone like Steven Hawking who can manipulate his wheelchair with his mouth and come up with concepts that astound us all about the universe and how it's put together.

I suppose the most important thing for most people is mental enjoyment from the pursuit of something. It may be a financial or a spiritual goal or family goal or church goal or a society goal. In the case of the terrorist, it's a pursuit of murdering other people in the name of God. They are an operation but they want to believe in what they are doing. Hopefully, there won't be too many more of them in the years ahead. It does bother me that we have to waste our time dealing with people like that. Life is so short and you have these other people trying to cut it shorter. Americans are not going to allow that to happen. Maybe some other complacent societies around the world will allow that to happen, but we won't.

The most important thing other than my connection to my family, and that they all do well in life and do what they want to do and enjoy it, is to bring some of these other people a little closer to reality and normality.

I think it's also important that people work for themselves instead of having things given to them. I think we need to get away from the welfare state mentality. We need to get more productive, more achievement oriented, I think. You can be laid back at times, but at some point you have to do real work. People have to get serious at some point. People all around us here are not really serious about anything. They think that somehow somebody is going to come along and give them something. The true gift you get is when you earn or find out or discover something for yourself.

I also hope people don't get so connected to technology that they think that's the true meaning of life. Technology is useful, but have you ever noticed the amount of people walking down the street with a lot of other friendly people and they are all talking to somebody else, off in the distance, on their cell phone? That seems peculiar to me.

I think we've lost the art of conversation.

I think we need a society where you can walk up and say "hi" to someone without a complete element of distrust there. There is a university that has a policy called "Hey" day. Students are supposed to walk over to people they don't know and introduce themselves to the other student. Things like that are good and they help society function better. We wouldn't do very well without society would we?

Terminal Cancer Patient

This man was selected for the book not because of his occupation, but due to the fact that he is terminally ill with widespread cancer. It was obvious to me that a person in that stage of life would be thinking a great deal about spiritual matters and possible afterlife scenarios. As I searched for people from different backgrounds, I thought including someone facing their mortality would be a worthwhile contribution.

This is a very accomplished man, a MENSA member, an entrepreneur and business executive. He held many positions before his illness forced him into early retirement. He was in his late sixties at the time of the interview.

What are the purposes of imagination?

A God-given aspect of the intellect that allows one to explore and seek. As we are created in His image, we also have the ability to create through new ideas and concepts. The path to discovery is based upon imagination.

What is the origin of imagination?

God-given, to stimulate thinking and create a desire to seek Him.

Where is the imagination located?

In the brain. It is based upon all we have experienced and those events described to us. Stored in the brain, one can combine different events to reach another conclusion than the one experience tells us. For example, one can imagine beyond specific experiences the brain has stored. Space travel or flight in the air was imagined by the ancients probably based upon observing birds flying and wondering why man could not do the same. It is that ability to combine seemingly unrelated events into a new possibility that is the gift of the Creator.

Do you take it with you when you die?

Yes. More than any other point in our lives we will need the ability to learn and understand the mind of God and all His creation.

Where are you in your body?

The soul or the spirit of an individual likely resides in the brain, but it is not limited or confined to just one place as is a physical part of the body.

At the end of the day, what matters the most?

What was accomplished for the kingdom of God. Did my living this day contribute to that growth? Is someone closer to God's kingdom now than before the day started? Did I do all I could to live the way God has instructed?

At the end of a life, what matters most?

What was accomplished for the kingdom of God. Solomon, the wisest man to have ever lived on Earth, said that all was vanity if it did not honor and obey the Lord God Almighty. He encouraged all to remember the Lord and obey.

Life is not a dress rehearsal. It is important that we get it right as soon as possible and keep the faith for our entire life. God has given us all the tools we need to be successful in His sight. We must use all of the tools we have, including imagination, to be faithful. That does not mean, however, to use the imagination to make things up as some are prone to do. Telling the truth is complex enough for most of us. Becoming faithful to His Word is achievable. He even provided a "helper" to assist us in the task.

Imagination sets mankind apart from all other creatures. Only man is created in His image. Only man can reflect, (weakly), the attributes of God.

Perhaps the best example of imagination I can think of is this: How did God use His imagination? What existed before creation? Was it not dark and void and without form? It takes a good imagination to even try to comprehend how He spoke and all that was created came into existence. He made the light, the stars, the planets, everything on the Earth, everything that crawls upon the Earth or swims in its waters or lives below the surface. In short, He created life.

He created systems so complex that it could never be mistaken for an accident or occurring by chance or via evolution. How wondrous is our body made? After centuries of study, research and exploring we still cannot answer key questions about the functions of the body. We cannot create life. And certainly not from non-life elements as the evolutionists claim.

HOSPICE NURSE

"It is not death or pain that is to be dreaded, but the fear of pain and death."
Epictetus

"The young may die, but the old must."
Longfellow

Death is never a cheery topic and is often avoided. The inevitability of death is one of the main purposes for writing this book. People will go to great lengths to distract themselves from this reality.

When I was much younger I read some of Elisabeth Kubler-Ross' work and also an interesting book by Billy Graham. The common ground between the two authors was that they had witnessed numerous deaths. More important than the quantity was the similarities that they both witnessed at the deathbed. Quite often when the time of death neared, the dying patient would recognize a loved one who had already passed standing in the room. These apparitions were only perceptible to the patient. Mere moments before passing the patient would report what they saw or begin to converse with their deceased relative, sometimes they died smiling and waving.

That caused me to seek out someone who spent time with dying patients. Do not let the brevity of this hospice nurse's answers detract from what she has to teach us. She committed her life to a field that many of us know very little about. To be with dying people this often is very rare unless you are in the medical field. She is in attendance at a very significant, and for most, a very private moment.

What are the purposes of imagination?
    Be creative.

What is the origin of imagination?
    Your own mind, and a lot of it is from how you grew up.

What do you think the location of the imagination is?
In the mind.

Do you think you take imagination with you when you die?
I hope so.

I have one more question that doesn't have to do with imagination. What is the most important thing?
Life.

Before you go, can you think of anything in light of your line of work that would relate to how a person's imagination works?
A lot of people imagine what is coming after, so depending on what they imagine, that [determines] how well they accept what's going on in their life.

If they imagine that death is going to be a wonderful thing, then my work is easier. Because they imagine that it's something wonderful that they look forward to. But if they have a lot of fears and anxiety, they fight death and they are very hard to work with.

So if they already have something pictured in their mind that is pleasant, then they can imagine going on to the next realm and they look forward to it?
Yeah, but in my line of work you see people freaking out because they see people who no one else can see. I explain to them, that it's common when you're close to death—that they do see people. Usually people they know. It's not unusual. They will start to have conversations with people. When you see someone really close to death they talk, they reach out and have conversations with people.

You see this with almost every single patient so you know that happens. Sometimes it's people that they don't know. A patient the other day said they were having a conversation with Elijah, and they didn't know who Elijah was but Elijah came to see them. Some people say that it's an imaginary thing—that they imagine it. But almost every patient has this happen. One lady had someone coming to see her, and they knew each other but they didn't get along. So she would start screaming for her daughter that they were going to fight. It would totally freak her out. Or she would start seeing someone that wasn't there, and she would ask why we don't see them.

I tried to explain it to her and she said I was crazy. The daughter of this woman did not want to believe anyone could be there. I was just trying to tell her that it was normal to see this.

I think that we can agree that the fear of the unknown is probably really huge, right? So those who don't have a formulated plan or ideal or place they are heading, are they the most afraid?

They're the most afraid. And their families are also the most unaccepting—not willing to let them go.

How do they usually express their apprehension when they don't have something in their mind? Do they just simply tell you or do they cry?

Sometimes they tell you. Sometimes they just fight it. They are more uncomfortable. They are more agitated. They get upset easier. They are harder to deal with. They never find that peace. They struggle. No matter how much pain they are in, they will continue to struggle.

So that is their most important goal, above all else, even with pain?

They don't let go. They don't decide that it's okay to go, and they'll fight no matter what happens.

Can we put people into two groups then—those who have a pleasant expectation of what will happen after they die and those who don't?

There are four groups. Some that are not necessarily expecting something good, but they are at least accepting that they are ready to go. There are the ones who are looking forward to it and it's an end to suffering. There are the ones who are accepting that they are going to die, but they don't know where they are going. Then there are those who fight no matter what.

So the ones that have a good expectation are the most pleasant to get along with. Are they more apt to give up and get away from the pain?

Not usually. But they let go more easily when it is their time.

Rocket Scientist

"Dying is an integral part of life, as natural and predictable as being born. But whereas birth is cause for celebration, death has become a dreaded and unspeakable issue to be avoided by every means possible in our modern society."
Elisabeth Kubler-Ross

All kinds of different topics come up in this interview with a forty-eight-year-old senior technical writer who works in the aerospace industry. She is from Yankton, South Dakota, and she laughingly referred to herself as a "rocket scientist."

Her experiences and beliefs would shock many mainstream people, and yet a lot of what she speaks of has come into the common vernacular in our culture. An after-death experience, psychic healing, auras, and chakras—she touches on a lot of topics.

She spoke slowly and deliberately and with great detail and confidence, which reflects the technically precise way in which her mind functions.

What are the purposes of imagination?

Purposes of imagination, that's a good question. Imagination is your inner spirit and totally new ideas. I tend to call them bursts of energy, bursts of creativity. I think imagination is also an excellent outlet for writing, for art, for playing music or just lying out under a shady tree and imagining what could be possible.

What do you think the origin of imagination is?

The origin of imagination. Well I believe that each of us was born with what I like to think of as a spark, like a spark from a star. It's in our spirits when we are born and it only grows as we go through life, unless we block it with alcohol or drugs or just negative feelings. I think the origin is from God or a higher power, whatever you want to call the power that watches over each of us.

The third question, you already hit on a little bit, is what is the location of imagination?

Well, they say imagination is located in the brain, I believe that to be true to a point. I think the rest of it is tied in with our spirits, our intuition, those little voices we all hear telling us "go do this as soon as you can or don't do this." Like if you were going to fly on an airplane somewhere and you had that gut feeling, "Don't go! Don't get on the plane." I think it's all through us really.

I think it goes beyond the mind, but it's a whole person's gift. I think the way the person's personality is has a lot to do with it as well. If the person is negative all the time, I think it darkens the imagination. It suffocates it, keeps it from coming out.

Yes, I've noticed it can be used for evil as well as for good. Do you think people have varying amounts?

Oh yeah, definitely. I think they've estimated that as far as imagination goes and how much human beings use their brain, they've figured people use 10% of their mental or imaginative abilities in life. If they have some kind of intuition about something a lot of people tend to think of [them as a] "cracked pot." That can't be true, that only what we see in front of us is real.

I think it's much more than that, and it's much bigger than that. People only use 10% of their mental abilities and their imaginations. I think a lot of people are afraid to step outside that box for fear of ridicule. They feel they'll be ridiculed or maybe even harmed if they have an idea that is not accepted by society at that time. It's between the person's higher power and themselves, what they have inside, what they believe to be true. Whether or not they go with that idea, that intuition, or that gut feeling.

Whether they trust it or not?

Yes.

It's amazing how many people have brought up the topic of intuition during the interviews lately. Do you think there is a difference between imagination and intuition?

Oh yeah. I think intuition in some ways is a gift from your ancestors. My birth mother and her mother called it "second sight." My grandmother often times had dreams or visions of something happening to someone. In my family's case that's the way it seemed to be. This was always something that was going to harm someone.

For example, I had talked to my birth mother on July 23rd, 1995. At the end of the conversation she said she kept thinking my younger brother was involved in a car accident. I went to bed that evening, I'm usually a real sound sleeper, I woke up at 2:00 a.m. and I was totally awake. I even got up for a half hour and walked around wondering why I was so awake. I had total clarity. I went back to bed at 2:30 and at about 5:15 a.m. I got a phone call about my younger brother.

He had been living out in the country. About a sixteenth of a mile from his home there is a railroad crossing, unmarked, no gates. A two hundred car freight train was going through the crossing, and it was very foggy and humid. He couldn't stop, he was on a motorcycle but that wouldn't have mattered. He tried to stop. My mother's words just hit me.

I've had similar experiences throughout my life. About 3 to 4 months before September 11th happened, I went out in my yard. I was looking at the trees, watching the birds. The thought that kept coming to my head was, "Something big and something horrible is going to happen." I felt it was something that would affect the whole world, yet I didn't see a picture of what that was or where it was. It's intuition, but yet in some ways—because they are negative things, and because I don't usually get a real clear picture of what it is—that frustrates me. I know something is happening but I don't know what it is. I just have an overall sense that something is coming.

Do you think animals have imagination?

Yeah, I do, and I think they have stronger intuition than most human beings. It's a well-known fact that animals actually feel the electric pulses that go through the ground before an earthquake.

I had a sensation at work one time. The only way I can describe it is that the soles of my feet were like fluid. Again, I felt that something was coming, and two days later there was an earthquake. There was another beautiful, sunny morning and I have that thought come into my head quite a bit—that, "There's something coming" thought. I noticed later that most people were really edgy that day. I could call it scattered; their thoughts seemed jumbled up. Then a quake hit.

I had a direct experience with a German Shepherd. My partner and I were trying to get her to go out the front door. She wanted to go out, but as her muzzle reached the door frame, she stopped and she wouldn't go out. I jokingly said, "Maybe we had an earth quake." About five minutes later the news reported that we had just had one. It proved to me that, yes, they do have intuition. If we only listened to what they are trying to tell us and not try to say that they are just being stubborn or they are not feeling good. We should just stop and think and wonder what they might be trying to tell us. I know they have imagination.

I have a very curious one-year-old cat, and I can tell she is very intelligent. If I tell her to do something she'll actually go get the toy or go to the door. I know she understands, maybe not through my words but through something I'm thinking. I would say that animals have imagination but much more strongly they have intuition. That's because they are not restricted in the intuition. It's natural to them.

Do you think that you take imagination with you when you die?

I think imagination is part of your spirit. It's part of that essence that each one of us has inside of us. I do believe that when we die our bodies remain here, but I truly believe that our spirit leaves our body and goes elsewhere. I think we have imagination and intuition in that spirit. I had an experience when I was five years old, I had severe tonsillitis. I couldn't eat. I cried.

We went to the hospital. I remember being taken on the gurney to the operation room, the large light, the big black mask coming down to my face. The next sensation I noticed was I felt that I was spinning, and then I thought I was in the desert, I was very thirsty. The next thing I remember was being in a ward of the hospital with big windows and high ceilings. I was in a bed. There was a nurse, and I was vomiting blood—mass quantities of blood. I felt horrible. The next thing I remember was looking down. I was at the ceiling looking down on the bed where I lay.

I saw myself and my doctor and several nurses all around me. I wondered why they were all around me. Why are they so upset? I didn't see a light. I didn't hear voices, but my spirit was totally wrapped in something like a shield of tranquility. The only emotions I felt were love and just joy going through my spirit.

The next thing I remember was like the feeling of being in a swimming pool and walking up the steps to leave the pool. You feel gravity pulling at your body. It was stronger, more of a jolt. I was back in my body, looking at my left arm. The nurse was poking for a vein to give me a transfusion. It didn't hurt but I felt her poking repeatedly.

I've never forgotten that day; there is no way I could. It was from that point on that I don't fear death because I believe that death is inevitable, but our spirits go home. I'm not sure where that home is, but I know that our imaginations go along with us. I've often thought that home is somewhere way, way far out in the universe. Maybe it's another planet, maybe it's just out in the stars, but I'm not afraid to die. I may be afraid of physical pain if it was a violent death, but I'm not afraid to die.

I believe that people who have passed on before us are still here. Their spirits are here or at least they visit here. They do watch over us, probably for eternity. That's my own personal belief.

I had a dear friend who was operated on for colon cancer and they thought they had removed it all. They hadn't and it spread to her liver. I had a dream about her two years after her death. She wasn't one to hug a lot, and in the dream I knew she was gone. She gave me a big hug. I asked her how she was. She said she was very happy, "It's beautiful here. I love it and I've got to go. I'm very busy."

I woke up and I know it was her. It was her spirit coming back to me and telling me, "It's okay. I'm very happy, I'm not suffering, there's no more pain, there's no more fear."

I do believe in angels and perhaps some of us or all of us are angels. There's a saying about the little dip in our upper lips that we all have, that's from right before we are born. The angels put their finger on our lip and said, "Shhh, don't tell them about us." I believe we take our imagination and intuitions with us.

The spirit you spoke of, or soul, do you have any idea where this is inside of you?

I feel it closest to my heart, but I also feel it at the top of my head. I've taken classes about the aura and the different chakras in our body. I've always been open to new ideas. There were eight women in the class and there was a lot of deep meditation and "hands off" healing. You actually feel the person's energy field. Three of the eight were nurses, one of which was very ill and very skeptical. As we paired off to view one another's auras and what colors we saw, as I went over her chest area it was brown, almost black.

My hands were out but my eyes were closed and my hands felt like they were pulsating. She sat up suddenly and said, "Oh my god (her eyes had been closed). I saw your hands and they were surrounded by bright white light."

She actually started feeling better before the class was over, so I guess you could say she was a believer.

From skeptic to believer.

Right. I also have a picture that was taken with my stepbrother when I was three years old. There is a definite glow around me.

[She pulled out the picture she was speaking of. She showed me the picture and there was a glow.]

The glow reaches to my brother, he's holding my hand. My adoptive mother doesn't believe in anything that can't be proven to her. I showed her the picture and she thought that [the glow] was due to my dress. My step dad who is more open to ideas said, "It's your angel." Maybe it's just my energy, my essence, just shining out.

So your answer is a mixture of top of your head and heart area?

Yes. Sometimes I feel it my hands.

A woman with accurate premonition capabilities came up to me and said, "You have a very strong power and it's a very healing power. You should think about using it to help other people." That's all she said. She was in a trance state when she said this.

I would hope that people would use that gift that we've been given in a positive way and not in a negative way.

I think the reason we're all here is to let people know that there really is only one true emotion and that's love. Whether it's helping someone less fortunate than you...they say don't give money to people standing alongside the road. I say walk a mile in their shoes. We've all been in situations at one time in our lives where we had no money, no hope. We were frightened and there was always someone there to see me through those times.

I think the biggest power that helped me through was God. I definitely believe in God. God may be a woman. God may be neither, but that power does exist—it's all around us, if we take the time to notice.

PROLIFIC ARTIST

"A man paints with his brains and not with his hands."
Michelangelo

*"Some painters transform the sun into a yellow spot,
others transform a yellow spot into the sun."*
Pablo Picasso

People frequently counseled me to interview an artist for this book. The line of reasoning was that the person who would know the most about the imagination was a person who made their living from their art. I managed to locate a forty-one-year-old professional artist who is from Great Falls, Montana. He gave some very unique answers, as you will see.

What are the purposes of imagination?
For direction.

It probably works well with your line of work.
Yeah. It's often derived by mistake. All the tricks I do have all been derived by mistake. I leave myself open to imagination to help with creation. Creation goes on forever. So I don't have to worry about running out of imagination.

What do you think the origin of imagination is?
Origin. What does origin mean?

Origin is like where something comes from.
There's a beginning of everything.

Maybe we don't know the beginning. Where do you think imagination is located?
Within, and it's with others. I always try to be imaginative.

Do you think some people have more than other people?

Maybe not. Some people may just not choose to be imaginative. I bet everybody is though.

Do you think people take imagination with them when they die?

Oh sure, yes.

Do you believe you have a soul?

Yeah.

Do you know where your soul is?

Usually with me.

[Laughter] Do you sometimes wonder?

If I feel like I ain't got one, I have a feeling that it's not taking care of business.

What do you think is the most important thing?

For me, it's what I can do for all. Probably influence is a big drive behind what I do. I could go about what I do in much better ways, but I don't.

I started experimenting with art when I saw someone on television who was dropping cans of paint onto canvases and then letting airplane motors blow the paint around. He had a big splatter look. I thought about creating the world's biggest spin art. I started with a small motor and I started spinning art. It cost a lot of money. The idea always felt good. Everybody has a good idea but it doesn't always sound good forever. We all have ideas but we end up shelving them. This idea of art has always sounded good to me.

I listen to people. I've always gone in the direction of the feedback from people with my art. They always know more about me than I've known. They've known more about art than I've known, and I still have quite a bit to learn. I quit spinning art because I couldn't pay the bills anymore. I didn't have electricity anymore. I found new tricks and they take their own course. I've been strictly traveling and learning to challenge my ability to deal with it. It's still tough dealing with nature. The wind, the rain, the sun. It's getting a little easier.

Do you live outdoors mainly?

Anywhere I live, I'm never there. That's how busy I am. I prefer to be outdoors. The quality has always gone up in whatever I do. The art takes up all the time, and I've had to learn to be happy without money. I do make good money. I make as much I produce, but the quality comes first. With the quality being up so high right now, I'd just be trapped if I worked in a store, like a prison, or a studio. I'm more trapped outside living in the world.

I've painted over 12,000 paintings, probably more. There's a lot of work behind me and a paved road ahead of me.

Do you usually see something in your imagination and then produce what you see, or does the art wind up basically forming itself?

It always produces itself. There's two ways I go about it. One of them is spontaneous and one of them is meditative. Like when I drew pencil portraits, it's more meditative. I don't get that kind of time very often. Sundays and holidays I always feel like drawing. The other way would be the spontaneous way. As soon as just one line comes to mind, I scrape out a line and it takes off. It makes itself every time. I only use natural colors.

Do you have any philosophy of life that you'd like to leave people with?

Yeah, I used to be great at that. I wouldn't recommend anybody to live like I do. I wouldn't recommend it as a learning process anyway.

Professional Artist

"An artist is a dreamer consenting to dream of the actual world."
George Santayana

The other artist I interviewed was a man of few words, so I looked further. This artist was sixty years old at the time of our meeting. He is from South Beach, Florida.

He too was a man of few words. I think he was somewhat guarded and not sure if he could trust the process of being recorded, or perhaps he is always to the point. Or to hazard yet another guess, it could have been due to the mournful violin music playing in the background.

In his brevity, he reveals that he believes in a collective consciousness and an afterlife. Because he located imagination in his "love center," to take it with him when he dies provides a fairly logical set of answers.

What are the purposes of imagination?
Imagination...to bring forth my clarity and power in the universe. I can use it to be directed in what I want to do.

What do you think the origin of imagination is?
It comes from your creative center, your thoughts, your true god-self.

What do think the location of imagination is?
[Laugh] I think it's in my heart center, my love center.

Do you think animals have imagination?
Oh yes! They are living things. Maybe more so than we do.

Do you think people have different amounts of imagination?

I think we all have the same amount, but some people are more aware of it and it's more developed.

Do you use it in your work?

Sometimes, especially toward the inspirational part of it, when it comes together. Not all the time though.

Do you think you take imagination with you when you die?

I think it goes on. I don't really believe in death. Imagination is a part of life. Life goes on.

But when your body dies does your spirit, or whatever your word might be, continue to live?

Yes, I think so.

Just so I'm clear then, the imagination would probably still be alive with you in your spirit?

Sure, I think so.

Do you know where your spirit is inside of you?

No. It's probably not in my body. It's in the mind that's part of my body right now, but it's not really in my body. I think it can leave my body and be other places.

It can be in the body and other places too?

I think so. I think it's all one mind. So it's everywhere.

Everywhere? Do you believe in a collective consciousness then—meaning that everyone's mind is connected?

Yes. I believe in one mind.

Do you know what you are going to do after you die? Do you have an idea of where your spirit will go?

I think I'll just continue doing what I am doing now exactly where I am at...that's where I will take all that. Continue, so I don't think anything I am doing is wasted now because it's going to continue.

If you could pin it down to one thing, what do you think is the most important thing?

Probably love. Whatever that is. But we know what it is, we have to experience it.

So one definition would be treating people kindly?

Sure, being kind and creating beauty.

The opposite of pain and hatred.

Yeah, seeing their innocence and the guiltlessness.

Canadian Pharmacist

"Make me understand the way of Your precepts;
so shall I meditate on Your wonderful works."
Psalm 119

"In silence, we learn to make distinctions...a man who loves God necessarily loves
silence also...those who do not know there is another life after this one, or who
cannot bring themselves to live in time as if they were meant to spend their eternity
in God, resist the fruitful silence of their own being by continual noise."
Thomas Merton

This is a deep-thinking and pragmatic type of person, as pharmacists often are. She was sixty-two at the time of the interview and she is from Ontario, Canada.

Like many I interviewed, she surprised me with the topic of meditation. She combined scientific fact with metaphysical teachings, in a down-to-earth manner.

What are the purposes of imagination?
[Pause] I get to just make up what the reason or background is?

Yes, in this case the purposes; there will be about five questions. You can't really be right or wrong.
Okay. I think creativity is one of the basic defining factors of being a human being. Imagination is what lies behind that. I think it's just one of the basic functions of humans, to have and use an imagination for good or evil. It can be healthy or unhealthy.

What do you think is the origin of imagination?
I think it was probably when people started to have to plan—started to notice seasons, started to be aware of time passing. If they needed to plan, in order to plan they needed to imagine what possibilities would

happen in the future. Thinking about those possibilities opened up all the other artistic functions, planning functions, visualizing, things like that.

So you think it was a developmental milestone in human progression? We got to the point where it became a need?

I think it's part of why humans survived. I think it has always been there. I don't think it was developmental. I think it was like language. It's part of what it is to be a human being. Creatures without language are different. It's one of those things that makes a human being—like birds have feathers, humans have language, they have imagination. I don't really think of it as being developmental because babies have imagination. It isn't something you learn, it's something you have.

An innate, an inherent...

Yeah, a quality or characteristic.

Do you think it developed along the way, improved?

I don't think so. If you look at prehistoric caves, I think those people had just as good an imagination. I think it has always been the way it is for us. It's just a function of our being and how we express it has developed and changes all the time.

Like a built-in mechanism.

Yeah, like language, like babies starting to babble. Language changes and develops, but that inherent quality of babbling is always there.

Do you think people have different amounts? Like one person has more than another?

Well, it seems that way, but I'm not sure that's true. I think that individually it is a matter of development. I don't consider myself to have much imagination. At one time I may have had the potential for more imagination but the way my life went...I think with something like pharmacy where you have to pay attention to the details and the facts and memorize stuff, everything is out there, you just have to learn it. Imagination doesn't come into it at all. You kind of push that aspect of your being to one side.

In fact, in the last few years I have decided to make a concentrated effort to focus on that part by reading fiction, paying attention to art. I grew up in an artistic town. I paid attention to it then, but I haven't paid attention to it for years. Listening to different kinds of music and actually paying attention to it, listening to it critically, I don't do that well. I would like to develop. I would like to have more imagination. If I can't be creative at least appreciate other's creativity.

That makes sense. Where do you think is the location of imagination?
It feels like it's in the brain. I wouldn't bet my life on it. I think it's probably like a hormone and it floods your entire body in different ways. My body is always doing things that surprise me. [Laugh] I think it's quite possible that it comes from other parts of our brain. We may have been trained to think it's in our heads.

That may be because when we visualize something imaginative, we see it in our mind's eye.
Right.

That's the reason I sometimes ask people about the link with memory. For instance when you conjure up a memory, you can see it in your head and the same thing happens when you conjure up an imaginary event. I think we use the same visualization whether the memory is real or not. What do you think about memory and imagination being linked?
I think they can be interchangeable. I think people, myself included, can have heard something so often that we think it's happened or that we actually remember it. My mother tells stories about when we were kids, and they were so vivid that now I'm not sure whether I actually remember them or whether it's a case of having this story told over and over again. My sister and I remember very, very, different things about a single episode in our lives. She'll remember one thing that I'm totally blank on. I believe that false memories can be implanted, so I don't think there is that much difference between memory and imagination. I think it flows back and forth.

I do too.
Memories trigger imagination.

And imagination triggers memories. I know that you can create a false memory in your mind.

Or you can remember something when it's only been told to you. It may or may not be false. It's just that you don't really remember it.

Some of my earliest memories I've held onto all of my life, and the older the memory gets the more I question myself on whether it was real or if I just told myself this. I ask myself if I simply made it up.

The two things I remember about my early childhood I think are real memories because my mother didn't remember them. Nobody else remembered them except me.

There wasn't any input.

Yeah, it wasn't like a story that she told me.

Do you think animals have imagination?

Animals have memory...yeah I do. I've seen my dog grieve for another dog that died. I've seen this more in dogs than in cats [that] I've been around. I know that dogs have memory, and I believe they have imagination.

They look as though they dream.

They look like they dream, yeah.

Do you have to have an imagination to dream then?

Yeah, I think so. I think dreams are very complicated and so intertwined with imagination and actual events and projections and feelings, all of those things. I don't believe in dream books, the ones that say "if you dream this then this is what it means". I think it's much more complex than that. All of these different things come into play. I just wish I could remember more of my dreams. I always know that I'm dreaming while I am dreaming.

I nearly always know as well.

Sometimes I'll wake up and lie there half asleep and have a moment of incredible clarity about a situation that has been lying there below the surface, and all of a sudden I'll have an insight. It particularly happens if

I've been meditating. I love my moments of clarity, and so far they've been true and valid.

I think when I am in deep sleep and when I wake up and think about it, I find that those thoughts are every bit as valid and realistic as when I am awake. This seems to be a way to get insights for me. On very rare occasions I've awakened with a strong idea which is overwhelming. I've taken those few ideas and experienced life changing events because I've put the ideas into action.

Here is another question, do you think we take imagination with us when we die?

Well, what happens when we die is still very much an open question to me. [Laugh] I was raised to believe that when we die we are gone.

Oh really?

Yeah, dead. But I've been re-thinking that whole thing. I have not reached any interesting conclusions about it. I'm so unclear within myself. Sometimes I believe in reincarnation, sometimes I don't. I don't really believe in heaven. I don't really believe in heaven or hell as in you go "here" because you were bad. You get to go "here" because you were good. That doesn't resonate with me.

If there is indeed reincarnation, then I definitely think we would take imagination with you. I think you take your soul with you. I think your imagination is part of your soul, if there's a soul. [Laugh] Now, don't get into the soul thing.

That's coming up next.

Oh, is it? [Laugh]

Reincarnation aside, you don't have firm opinions...

No. Except I'm pretty damn sure about the heaven and hell thing. If there's a God, I don't see how God could have created such a complex thing as a human being, with an imagination, and then tell them, "You imagined the wrong thing." It doesn't make sense to me, and I don't think God is stupid. It doesn't make sense. It sounds like a trick to keep people in line.

Normally I would ask this question if the interviewee has said they believe they have a soul, but you're in your own group here because you're not firm on whether you have a soul or not. Would you like to elaborate?

My gut says that we have a soul because there are some things that can't be explained any other way. There are some parts of human beings that there is no other place to put it. Where does spirituality come from? We can say that emotions are too much serotonin in your body. You can sort of explain a lot.

Let me put it this way, right now there are a lot of things that we can't explain, but there is a possibility, a potential, that all we have to do is learn a little more and we'll be able to explain it. There are some things that I cannot visualize ever being able to explain and that is spirituality and love. I don't mean sexual love. I mean non-sexual, open...where you just love somebody.

Do you mean unconditional love?

Yeah, unconditional—where does that come from? It doesn't sound like too much serotonin, fear does. Those kinds of emotions do. But love? That's what makes me think that there may be a soul.

However, having these last few years read more about Buddhism...I was mostly reading about it to learn how to meditate better, but you sort of pick these things up as you go along. They say, at least my interpretation, is that we are all...that there is no separation. That could be. There could be something broader than just being that I have a soul. It may not be that defined. We are all the same. Everything is the same.

The "oneness" teaching.

Yeah, that the molecules are interchangeable. They are just sort of clumped together. We perceive things as being solid because of how our brains are structured, but they are really not. It's just a bunch of molecules and that's a possibility too.

I've read a lot about that too. I've read that when you break down the molecules to their final degree, that there is a lot of space there. Some books I've read state that your body seems dense, but it's actually filled with space.

Yeah. It's the only way that our brains can perceive it. It has to be solid because we can't perceive all of these molecules because it's too confusing.

The point then is that in a finite body, a finite three-dimensional world, we need to make sense of it, so objects appear to be firm. But we do know scientifically that there are molecules in the air and it doesn't appear to be firm?

Yes, there are as many molecules in the air as in a solid object. We can't see it, just like we can't hear a dog whistle.

The dog whistle is beyond our hearing, but that does not mean that it does not exist. It does exist. We just can't perceive it.
Our brains aren't set up that way.

I have considered some of these concepts and compared them to Christianity. Some of these are not at all compatible with Christianity, but I have seen some correlations. There are things that Buddhism has in common with Christianity. Meditation can be one example. Has it aided you? Isn't that a good state of mind to ask yourself if you are simply a biological unit or whether you are something else inside of your body besides your molecules and your blood stream?
I don't think I am that good at meditation. I meditate because it seems to make things better. Things go better when I meditate. I don't meditate well. My mind...I have to constantly pull my mind back. It's a struggle. I don't feel like I'm getting anywhere. It just sort of makes me ask why am I doing this? It's a constant battle. But things go better when I fight that battle.

Things go better in your waking life?
And, I think that when I'm meditating that's when I wake up and have those moments of clarity. It seems as though I have traded my old way of obsessing about something and trying to figure something out. I can spend hours trying to work something out, thinking about it, figuring it out. I gave that up, and I think that with meditation comes an awareness of compassion and loving kindness and equanimity and all those things. Being aware that those things exist.
That's the soul thing that I can't sort out. Where do those come from? I don't think that equanimity comes from serotonin either. I think that I am able to substitute that "not knowing" through meditation for the "having to know" and having to figure it out. I have no idea where I am going to as to your question.

[Laugh] We are establishing how firm you are on whether you have a soul before I ask you this: Where is your soul?

It's like imagination. It doesn't have a location. It certainly has much less location in your brain because...that's the one thing that makes me think about the "oneness" because where is the soul? It's not a brain. It's absolutely not a brain thing. That has opened the door to this whole "oneness" thing. If we are only what we think we are because of our limited perceptions, then maybe those things that I consider to be soul issues, like compassion, those don't have that much of a location. It could be somewhere out there.

Do you mean linked with other consciousnesses?

Yes.

When you are meditating, or even when you're not, but in context with meditation...if we didn't use the word soul, if we used the word "awareness" or a sense of I am, I exist...

Awareness is more how I think of it.

When you think about that awareness, have you ever had a sense of where it feels like it is?

I actually try to locate it.

Do you?

It moves around.

Really?

Yeah. When they talk about the breathing meditation you try to find where the energy is in the breath and sometimes it's in my belly and sometimes it's in my throat and sometimes in my nose. I think that moves around. They talk about going through your body and looking for what hurts.

That is one meaning for the word "awareness"—becoming aware.

That's what I'm looking for when I meditate. An awareness of me as a part of everything else. And get away from the "me" that is those little thoughts racing around in my brain. A phrase, a slogan that I use is, "Feel the energy, drop the story line." That's what I try to do when I meditate.

There are so many forms of meditation. There is visualization and guided imagery, and whether each person knows it or not, what they are ultimately heading for is "no thought," according to many but not all teachers and theories. There are many methods such as staring at a candle, and some insist you must be seated or lying down, and so many other styles of meditation are based on imaginative scenario. They imagine a desert island or their happy pasture.

I've done that.

The guided imagery?

Yes, I've visualized myself in a specific spot. It's okay, but it only works once. The next time I try to do it I get bored and I go back to...

Thinking?

Yes.

Another common method is using repetitive words. What America has come to call the "mantra" does not have to come from a holy person or a monk. We don't have to be given some secret words in another language. It can be any words. I think this is proven by scoping brain waves. Repeating the same words helps to crowd out the other random thoughts. When they come they are easier to get rid of because of the repetition.

I've wondered whether I should go to a retreat where you sit there for a weekend.

Silent retreats provide more opportunity to rest and it will be completely quiet. It makes me wonder what would happen if someone tried to meditate in a sensory deprivation tank. However, there are those who teach that thoughts and distractions are okay during meditation. In fact this is getting very popular. They teach that those thoughts are coming to your brain for a reason.

My favorite example is that one day I was meditating, and somehow in forty-five seconds I was wondering how George Harrison could remain friends with Eric Clapton after Eric stole his wife. [Laugh]

My life is consumed with useless trivia. In several books that I've read it says to just stay, just stay, don't get mad, just come back.

Another question that I have is: At the end of your life, or more simplistically, at the end of a day, what is the most important thing?

215

[Long pause] Competence, not excellence, competence. If I have finished my day being competent I get a sense of satisfaction. That isn't just job competence; it's if I have been a competent human being. If I have not done anything harmful to myself, or to anybody else. I don't expect to do anybody any good, but as long as I've not done anybody any harm, that's competence. If for any reason somebody thinks I did something good, that's a bonus. If I've not done unhealthy things. If I have taken care of myself and honored myself and other people. Respected them, offered them justice, that's the sort of thing that I'm looking for.

I used to think that it was wisdom, but that's too much. I used to think it was being a spiritual person, you know, having exercised spirituality. I don't think that's it either. That's not where it's at for me. Being spiritual, being aware of that, being aware of my spirit, that's part of being competent, of being a healthy human being. I'm starting to look at being a spiritual person...what does that mean? It doesn't mean anything. It could be that I don't understand it that well. [Laugh] Having behaved in a decent manner, using the tools that I have as well as I can, I think that's it.

I've always been a fairly pragmatic person. If something isn't useful, that doesn't necessarily mean that it isn't good, but useful in a very broad sense. I guess that I don't put much stock in things that I don't understand. If it's not practical [or doesn't] have a useful outcome. I don't know what people mean when they say they want to be a spiritual person. Do they want to act in a good way? Do they want to love God? Do they mean that they want to go door to door passing out pamphlets? What does that mean? Do they want to sit in a small room and pray all day? That's not something that I worry about very much. I think it's being the best person I can be, but that sounds corny.

How about the word "optimal?"

Yeah, maybe. That's better, that's better. Competent means that I can be in the middle there. I don't have to be wonderful. I don't have to be the best just so long as I struggle along, not harming.

That reminds me of the Hippocratic oath, first do no harm.

That's my background, so it's very possible that all of that comes from that. That's quite a goal. Half the time we don't know what will be harmful.

We don't. And, sometimes we have silly goals that we think are important. As if people are going to gather around my casket and say, "She had the best credit score. She sure could write a timely check. She paid everything on time."

I could say, yes, that was one of my life goals. What a strange goal. When I'm dying I won't care about my credit rating. It might affect me while I'm alive but that's it. Part of the reason I ask this question is for the sake of the people reading this. I would want each reader to think about their own goals.

I think that as I get older, I discard a lot of stuff that I cherished when I was younger. Like I said about wisdom, yeah right, that one is not going to happen because I don't have enough time. Maybe if I came to that realization earlier then I would have had enough time, but maybe not. Maybe I don't have it. Maybe wisdom is not in the mix. Love has become much more important. Loving everybody, not just people that I know in my family or my close friends. To be as loving as I can to everybody, the customers that I serve [in the inner city]. Smelly people. People who shoplift. People who I see selling crack, being loving to them. Treating them fairly. Not letting them shoplift from me. [Laugh] I think that's part of it. Making them responsible for themselves, that's a loving thing to do. That's become much more important to me.

BUDDHIST MONK

"Do not dwell in the past, do not dream of the future,
concentrate the mind on the present moment."
The Buddha

"I am a simple Buddhist monk."
The Dalai Lama

At the airport I could not help but notice a group of people surrounding a man wearing long orange robes. I had my recording device with me, and I asked for an interview.

He spoke in English. However, he had many assistants nearby to interpret for him. They were also very protective of him and his time. Evidently, he had just landed. I was not able to get his exact age, but I assume he was between thirty and forty-five years old. He revealed immediately that he is from Thailand and that he is a Buddhist Monk.

I have known countless American Buddhists. That is why I jumped at the chance to interview a monk. I was curious to see how his answers would differ from other Buddhists interviewed. You will notice the monk insists that our memories are not deleted, as the Vietnamese Buddhist asserted.

He seemed familiar with the interview process and acted as though he expected this to be a regular occurrence. He began without any questions from me.

I am Buddhist Monk. I come here from Thailand to help people from my country. Also, after the Vietnam War there is many immigrants here who need my help. I have a temple to help people who are lonely here. They come to study. They help each other.

Some people pass away and it is lonely for them. They need a temple. They wrote to my master and after that they formed group, Buddhist Association. I came to run small place, small temple with Monks. My teacher come first. I speak Thai, Lao, Cambodian and English.

That's a big accomplishment. You were born in Thailand?

Yes and I grew up with four language. Every family member and friend spoke a different language, so I learn their native language.

I teach Buddhist way, meditation, try to be clear of mind, exercise mind, let them know about philosophy of life. If they feel lonely, they can come any time. I'm doing now this work. That's the story of myself.

Let me ask you a question about imagination. What do you think are the purposes of imagination?

Imagination, everybody have imagination but all imagination not true. So the same way, you can have too much, like a dream. You can dream, you can imagine it is true.

Do you use it when you meditate yourself?

I meditate in the true. Meditation must be in the true of life. Cause of suffering comes from thought.

Like attachment?

All that, human beings all suffering. Do I want to get sick? No way. Do I want to die? No. In the Buddhist way just practice your mind to understand reality. Prepare the mind when it's all coming. Accept it. Imagination is not the true of life. Your part is true. Everything will be accept.

Where do you think imagination is located at?

Everything is like a dream. If we wish something like a power to send you to a destination. When you leave something, you must have some dream. Everything you dream, you wish not everything. So you started something, you let it go through. You have to try hard. That mean imagination is the first start. So that you cause something to be.

Do you think that you would take imagination with you when die?

If you imagine too much, then you lost control. Imagination in Buddhist faith, you must imagine in the truth. Then you have the truth coming, the law of reaction. The law of karma. It's my body, my speak, my mind. If you beat somebody they are going to beat you back. Reaction. If you talk nice to somebody, somebody talk nice back to you. If you say the things bad to somebody, you are suffering. If you make somebody happy, you'll be happy. Everything must be that way. The law of reaction.

Cause and effect.
Yes.

Karma.
Yes.

Do you believe you have a spirit?
Oh sure! Man has a spirit.

Do you know where your spirit is?
Yes, that is my job. Your feelings are your spirit, your memories, good or bad, they go with you forever.

Memories go with you forever?
You can't get rid of it. Long time ago, you should remember. My recycle, you take it with you. The Buddhist must believe in the law of karma, the law of reaction. You cannot delete the memory.

You can't delete it?
You can practice your mind, have power, be enlightened.

You get the enlightenment then you can stop the cause and effect, right?
Because the contract is completed, there is no point to continue.

Do you think you have reached enlightenment?
I tried.

You tried?
I tried.

Did you get there? [Laughter]
I try. Like a billionaire, difficult to achieve it, but we try to get there.

MEXICAN PSYCHOLOGIST

"Without this playing with fantasy no creative work has ever yet come to birth.
The debt we owe to the play of the imagination is incalculable."
Carl Jung

Here we get another chance to sit down with a psychologist. She is a thirty-one-year-old woman who had earned her first university degree in psychology and was, at the time, working toward her masters, also in psychology. You might be expecting scientific answers—I know I was. However, we once again get a series of answers that are completely unpredictable.

As I said in a previous chapter, I think of psychologists as brain experts, and that is the reason I pursued two of them for this book. I wanted to hear from professionals about brain anatomy and about how the mind functions. This is not what we get with this pleasant woman from Mexico City. You will see that her answers are out of the ordinary, not so much in a mystical sense, but they do lean toward a Jungian philosophy and then beyond that to an unusual spirituality.

The first interview question is, what are the purposes of imagination?
The purposes of imagination. Wow, what a question. [Laugh] It's a great question. I think that it is to create or to make sense in life.

What do you think is the origin of imagination?
The origin. I think that it comes from feelings. Of course from the brain. I don't know the original part of the brain that creates imagination. I think that it's more related to feelings than with thoughts.

The third question is; what is the location of imagination? From what you are saying so far, you're saying the brain, but that our emotions are connected.

221

Do you think our emotions come out of our brain too then?

Yes and no. What I learned in a school with a great teacher, she used to say that imagination or the creation of everything comes with us from a spirit, but the spirit is between minds. It doesn't come from mind or brains, it's between them.

Between two different people's minds? Is it a type of communication?

Communication, yes. I think the location comes from a spirit between minds. It's something we do with other people.

Do you think some people have more and some people have less?

Maybe some people are born with more abilities than other people. Maybe that's related with parts of the body. I think it's almost the same. It's just that some people can increase their ability. It depends on the situation they are in—their friends, their school, the family, the work, everything.

Do you think we take imagination with us when we die?

I don't know. [Laugh] I hope so. I can believe that, but I cannot answer that.

Imagination plays a big part in dreaming.

When you asked about taking imagination with us when we die, I remember now that sometimes we have dreams with colors and we think we see things that we've never seen before. There's a psychologist, Carl Jung, he talks about the collective consciousness.

The collective consciousness? We can draw from other people's consciousness, especially when we are asleep?

Yes, we remember all the other epochs, eras, times.

Do you believe you have a soul then, a spirit that is communicating with other people?

Yes. I don't call it a soul, I call it intuition. Like something we can see before we know that, at the same time. The scientific theories are created this way. [First] comes intuition, then comes the theory.

Right. Scientists use a thing called an intuitive leap. They have all the facts they can collect, but they claim to make a leap of intuition into the next set of ideas that will make something new. Scientists recognize that.

Yes. We have intuition and we have rational thoughts. Sometimes it's difficult to have some perception about our intuition because of our rational thoughts.

Have you ever asked yourself where your spirit is inside of you?

No. I mean, I learned in school that emotions come from a little part, like a nut, I don't know how to say it in English.

Amygdala? The emotions are in the amygdala.

Yes, that's the word. I think emotions are more related with the spirit, yes.

Do you have any idea at all, even though you haven't thought about it before, where your awareness is?

Awareness? No.

What do you think is the most important thing? Say you were at the end of your life and you were looking back over your whole life, what would have the deepest meaning?

It sounds weird, but I think that it is to have found this soul that you're talking about. Because, what I feel sometimes, that's more related with the scars of my emotional life, my personal life. Because I had a difficult situation with my family. I grew almost alone by myself. Of course I have some emotional problems when I relate with people. I have like a mask; I think Carl Jung talked about masks. I think that it's something more than that.

So, are you saying that the problems that you had in your family inhibited your ability to...

Relate to people. Those kind of things repress your feelings and your feelings cannot create anything.

Are things more repaired now?

No, no it's the same.

You've learned to overcome?

Yes, with time and a lot of work. I was in psychoanalysis, for years.

For yourself?

Yes. My analyst showed me the way to analyze dreams. That's part of myself that I can reach, I want to reach that part. At the same time I can see the other parts.

Like the more problematic parts?

The problems, yes. Now, I can see the difference. The one that I want to reach and the one that I want to destroy or take away. To be happy, because it's very hard, very painful.

Sometimes painful childhoods actually improve the person. Not always, but sometimes the person is happy to be who they are after it's all over, and they feel like they are a better person at the end of it all.

Yes.

It's funny how that works. Do you know the word resilient?

No.

It's a nice word. It means being able to weather a storm, to withstand. Sometimes that withstanding seems to make people stronger in a good way. Some people develop really nice personalities from adversity. They become some of the world's most remarkable people. Maybe that will be that way for you. It seems like already you are a wonderful person.

Yes.

PROPERTY MANAGER

"We were like those who dream. Then our mouth was filled with laughter, and our tongue with singing."
126th Psalm

"...he who hears My word and believes in Him who sent Me has everlasting life, and shall not come into judgment, but has passed from death into life."
Jesus Christ

This thirty-two-year-old woman certainly enjoyed the questions and laughed merrily throughout our time together. She is a property manager from Nevada and may well be the jolliest person I interviewed.

What are the purposes of imagination?

Wow, to make life's experiences and make them grand, make them fun. Take a book and make it what you want it to be.

What do you think the origin of imagination is?

Wow. My goodness. Interesting questions. [Laugh] Obviously, I think that everything is created by God and that is part of who He is too. I think it's shaped by our childhood and the encouragement of the adults in our lives as we're growing up. Also the books that are read to us, and the freedom that our parents and our influences give us to be creative.

Do you think everybody has the same amount of imagination, or do some people have different amounts?

I think that we all have a potential amount that is similar; I don't think it's always used equally.

Like a body builder? We all have a bicep but one person can develop their...

Right, exactly. Sometimes it's stifled by ourselves. Sometimes it's stifled by outside influences.

What do you think the location of imagination is?

Hmm. I think it has to come from our heart and our head. I think they have to work together. I think the picture is drawn in our head, but a lot of it comes from who we are and what we believe, and how we love and experience life.

Do you think animals have imagination?

No. I don't. [Laugh] I think they can enjoy what's in front of them, but I think they live too much in the moment and what's right in front of them.

Do you think we take imagination with us when we die?

[Pause] Interesting. I've never thought of this. I love these kinds of questions. [Laugh] I don't think we do because I think God has something so much more grand in store for us that we can't imagine it in our own selves. I think He is going to paint the pictures in heaven. It will be so grand that we won't need our imaginations.

I think that the Bible says that it is beyond anything that we can imagine in heaven. Would that change if we were there? I don't know.

What do you think is the most important thing?

I think the most important thing is a relationship with Christ. That gives me eternity. A living eternity with Christ instead of eternal damnation. I don't think that anything is more important than that. Everything comes from that. It cascades down from that.

So you think it affects you here and not just later when you die?

Right. It affects everything you do here, relationships and everything.

ASPIRING ACTOR

"No one is so accursed by fate,
no one so utterly desolate,
but some heart, though unknown,
responds unto his own."
Longfellow

"O thoughtless mortals! Ever blind to fate, Too soon dejected, and too soon elate!"
Alexander Pope, *Essay on Man*

This interview is with a thirty-seven-year-old aspiring actor. He was born in Orlando, Florida, and currently works as a courier in a large city. I witnessed a certain level of hesitancy in his answers, and I cannot know why some people have an immediate sense of freedom with a recording device present and some people do not.

I can tell you that when the recorder was turned off, this person felt the freedom to explain his beliefs, which are an unusual combination of materialism and a lack of free will. In an attempt to recap, he does not believe in a soul, deity, heaven or an afterlife. He does, however, believe that human beings have absolutely no free will whatsoever. They cannot control their thoughts because they are programmed in the actual brain, much like a computer. There are no random thoughts, desires, or actions ever. He demonstrated the lack of randomness, otherwise known as free will, by pretending to throw his cell phone into the street. He said that even if that appeared to be a random "out of nowhere" action, it was still without free will. All thoughts are circular, one sprouts another and it can't be stopped. Murderers are actually innocent because their thoughts are programmed and out of their control as much as the rest of humanity's thoughts and actions.

He may be the only person I have ever met that disregards both God and Free Will. Personally, I cannot fathom who or what would be controlling the thoughts and actions, thereby removing the ability for free will, if there were no God or deity or higher being than mankind. I can only imagine the existence of predetermination if there is indeed a higher power than the one who is being controlled.

What are the purposes of imagination?

The purposes of imagination. I would say that in the context of living you'd have to say that imagination is part of the process of coming to new ideas, working through problems, problem solving. It's a part of the process of dealing with life.

What do you think the origin of imagination is?

I think it's rooted pretty much in emotions along with our thoughts. It's kind of like a higher level of thinking. Emotions bring the "maybes," the "ifs," the ability to create stories so you can create an analogy for things. Then you have the ability to compare one aspect of life to another. That helps you get through. It also can be a detriment, something that bogs a person down in their thinking. They can fantasize too much. Basically, it's a part of the thinking process.

When you talk about the negatives of it, do you think some people have too much of it?

Oh yeah, definitely. You'd have the people who use their imagination to create stories, whether they're an author or musician, and that is a plus. But then you have the people who get deluded. I mean what's going on inside their mind is as real to them as what's going on in real life. You have some people who lose touch with reality in a sense because of imagination.

They forget the difference between reality and the unreal.

Right.

Where do you think imagination is located?

Since I'm not very familiar with anatomy and physiology of the brain, that's kind of a hard question for me to answer. I don't have a concise answer for that. In fact, I don't even have a vague answer for that.

What role do you think imagination plays with memories?

Memories are what help us to create fantasies, to create analogies. In the process of imagination we are able to draw on our memories to create some ideal situation or some possible situation.

Has it ever occurred to you that it feels like the same part of yourself when you're remembering? For instance, we have a memory of dragging the chairs out here a little while ago. That's because we really lived it. But if we imagined that the waitress brought the chairs out and we had watched her, you can probably see that in your head right? When you compare the real way the chairs got here with the imagined way the chairs got here, does it feel like it's in the same spot?

It's not too different really. I would say it's slightly more dream-like to see the waitress bringing them out. It's not quite as solid of a memory. I can get a stronger sensation of my actually bringing them out here. It's interesting. It's not too different.

Where do you think the real you, your real essence is located inside your body?

Yeah, I can't honestly say that I've thought about that. It's somewhere in that mixture of brain and the continuation of the brain, the sensory organs. Where that all meets and creates the mind I can't really say exactly. I don't know where the seat of "me" is. I would tend to say it's in my brain.

Do you think that you or people in general can or would take imagination with them when they die?

It's hard for me to imagine not living, so I don't believe in an afterlife. The feeling would be that yeah, it would go with me, but I can't say that I believe that.

If you had to pin it down between imagination being a part of your personality or a part of your brain structure, which one do you think you would choose?

That's tough...because I don't know if I can separate the two. I'd probably have to say that it's part of my brain structure. I don't like that. I'd like to say there's some essence of me outside of that in a sense, but I don't think that's true. So yeah, it's probably in my brain.

What is the most important thing?

The most important thing. To me the fact of "being" or "existing" is what probably occupies my mind the most. What is most important to me about existing is what I think and feel. I would say predominately, what I feel. I don't mean that in a simplistic way. I don't mean just going with my gut feeling and living by your heart. I mean what is so ingrained in a person, how they feel in general, the deepest emotions that a person has. I would say that is the most important.

Love is very important and I know that to a lot of people that it's not. I can't speak for those individuals because they obviously feel different than I do. I'm not going to side with them. If somebody has more of an affinity with hatred or evil I can't judge that to be an inaccurate way to feel to that particular person. That's why again it comes down to feelings, why they are the most important. Even beyond thinking. Thinking is part of it to me. Feelings and thinking are part of higher emotions. I don't think you have higher emotions if you don't have that mixture of thought and feeling.

It's like the whole idea of artificial intelligence where a machine is thinking. Can it have thought on its own? Does that necessarily mean that there's going to be intelligence? I don't believe that there would be. I think that emotions, brains, there's that intuition that can be misguiding, but it is also what brings the leaps of imagination. It brings the creativity, and I don't think without feeling that thought would really be all that spectacular. I don't think we would have intelligence without it.

Is there anything else you think the world needs to know, that would be important for them to contemplate?

I think feelings are misunderstood and kind of underplayed. We get so caught up on this "I think, therefore I am." I think that's misguided. We need to put more emphasis on the feelings of people. If you sit and try to take away or eliminate the distractions and all that comes in through the senses, what you're left with is more of a feeling or sense of just being.

What would happen in a sensory deprivation tank? Would it just be raw feeling?

I think so, yes. Obviously, in day-to-day living we have more of a sense of fear or pain. If you're in a deprivation chamber, you're going to eliminate a lot of conflicts and pain that we generally perceive in our day-to-day life. You would be left more with just that sense of being. Which is why it's interesting. When we live, we don't tend to think about the fact that we're alive so much. It's only in those moments that we're meditative or contemplative.

FRENCH CANADIAN NOVELIST

"Where did it come from, this imagination that peopled
Middle-earth with elves, orcs, and hobbits?"
Humphrey Carpenter, of Tolkien

Here I have selected a novelist to interview as I thought this occupation might provide all of us a glimpse into a mind whose profession is dependent upon a strong imagination. As you know, the goal of the questions is not really to learn all we can about imagination, but I could not resist making the effort to find a person who would be reputed to have an active one. For example, it would have been great fun to interview Tolkien, the author of *The Lord of the Rings,* or any other fiction writer who had invented a rich fantasy land full of imaginative characters and scenery.

This fifty-eight-year-old French Canadian describes herself as a "three times divorced woman, two times grandmother [and] a naturalized Jamaican, born to an Irish mother." As if that were not enough variety, she taught Eskimos, and earlier in her life she earned a degree in Theology. Her main occupation was translator of official directives as she is fluent in both French and English, and her birthplace was Quebec City, Quebec.

She is a very gracious woman with a lovely accent. There is a great deal of femininity about her and a strong intellect as well, always an interesting combination.

What are the purposes of imagination?
To me it is creativity, that's all I can come up with. I'm a writer now so that's all I do is tap into that function of my brain and try to get it on paper. It can produce some very satisfactory results at times, sometimes frustrating too.

Is it pretty easy to take your imagination and get it...

It's like a muscle that you exercise, the more you do it the better you get at it. The better in tune you get with yourself with whatever external powers are at play here. It's a matter of practice, I've been doing it for ten years, not on a consistent basis, but now much, much more, and I realize that is indeed the key.

I spent six weeks away from home very recently, all by myself in a cottage out in the wilderness, and that was the purpose—to see how my writing would work out there, if the muses would visit or not. They did, now I know that isolation is a major element in order to tap into those forces. Otherwise, I think that everyday life, especially, in our environment, with the noises, the interruptions, it's just really counterproductive. That's my belief.

Do you think some people have more imagination than other people?

Yes, I think so. Everybody's got it to some extent and then it's only a matter of tapping it, of listening or finding the ways to listen. I think we are also programmed, very much, in this society not to listen to those voices very often because they can be scary. So, we can choose to look in other directions.

What's the origin of imagination?

[Pause] I think your imagination probably stems from your culture as a child, your experiences as a child. How they're given to thrive or not. How you've been encouraged to read or even to write. I realized I was good at writing only later.

I was thinking about [this] the other day. I was about maybe fifteen when I realized I was good at writing, at putting the structures together. I wasn't necessarily good at producing the ideas, but I got steered into the translation process because I could come up with a very correct form of the French language starting from the English.

Now, I'm not translating my ideas or my thoughts or anything here. I'm just using somebody else's ideas and putting them into French words. Gradually, my husband at the time, who is a writer, encouraged me to do some writing because he knew I was [familiar] with the language, it was part of my work. That's how I got into it.

Back to your question, where does it originate? I would say a whole lot in your environment, growing up. Your cultural environment, your parents, brothers and sisters, interactions. If you were read stories before you went to bed, if you were encouraged to go to the library, visit museums—which I thought was such a boring thing when I was a child, I didn't relate to that at all—so I think there is something that may sit within us for a long while. Then for whatever reason, then you will start to bloom, to thrive, through a variety of circumstances. But some never do, I'm sure about that. Some never actualize that. It just sits there and it doesn't get anywhere because they don't have the right motivation, they don't have the right spark, I don't know. But, there's got to be some of it in all of us, unless we've had a very dull and unstimulating childhood. I couldn't say about that because I have had a very good childhood. But I can't say I was a creative child. That came way into my thirties and beyond. Does that answer the question at all?

Yes, what do think the location of it is?
Oh my God. I'm not a scientist, it's got to be somewhere in the brain.

So somewhere there in the gray matter?
Oh yeah, somewhere on that left side, for sure. I don't know what color it is or what size it is in each of us. I read somewhere that people with Alzheimer's—I am concerned there because my mother died of Alzheimer's—they say the left side of the brain, the creative, the imaginary side of the brain is the last one to go. That's why people with Alzheimer's, it is believed, would lose their reasoning powers before they lose their ability to appreciate beauty for instance.

I remember very vividly, it was days before she died, my mother would be out there sitting on a chaise lounge on the verandah and it was the middle of summer and it was very pretty. The trees, the birds, the nature and she obviously appreciated that and she would comment on it. She didn't know her own name, mind you, but she certainly related to that. I think it is something that stays, that is very powerful in us.

Do you think people would take imagination with them when they die?
Well, there's an underlying question here. Wherever they go, wherever this takes us, it would be the first element to carry us as baggage, I think so. Because it's our ability to marvel, it's our ability to relate to anything else in a loving way. I don't think the reasoning part of the brain

is very much a part of that, I don't think so, I wouldn't be here today. I wouldn't be speaking to you now. I would be sitting right at home where I was if I had used my right side of my brain and all of my reasoning powers. I would have stayed [in my home country]. Using strictly my logic, that wouldn't have taken me here. But the other part of me, no restrictions, so here I am and I'm a very happy person too.

Do you think the imagination is linked with the personality?

With the type of personality in the standard category that we know, passionate, somatic and active, I think so. It would have an impact. If you were more pragmatic you would not realize that component in the same way, but if you were angry, passionate or active, then imagination would kick in big time. Might get you into trouble, mind you, but it would have a major impact on your life whether it was something you had to learn to control at times.

Do you think you could have too much imagination? Do you think some people have more than others?

Yes. One of my daughters has a wild imagination and it's gotten her into some trouble here and there. She was at times unable to balance; I think we need to learn to balance. That only comes with age, I think, and experience.

The answer is yes. They can have too much for their own good.

Do you think it plays a role in insanity in any possible way?

You know it may. Because if it goes uncontrolled you may just eventually lose touch with reality. I think so. Great artists have been known to become neurotic and I'm sure their imagination had a good part of that. Oh yes. I think it's something that needs to be mastered, controlled to a point. If you don't have too much it's not a problem. Too much of anything...how do you say in English, too much of a good thing? Then if you don't have it, that would make for a terribly boring life.

So too little imagination would equal boredom.

Well, that's my perception, that's a subjective concept. I would say it this way, their lifestyle is more flat. I can envision a civil servant going to work for twenty-five years with his satchel under his arm and his lunch box, that kind of routine. I knew a person like that in my childhood and it was just absolutely amazing. It would have killed me, after three weeks I would have been in an asylum probably. He did it for all that time and didn't seem to be in pain or anything. Personality kicks in a lot.

Seems to be linked a little bit. That brings up a sub-question that somebody else spoke of the other night about intelligence. The opinion expressed was that the less intelligent a person is the happier they are. What do you think about that?

Ah, that's interesting, we might have to have a definition of intelligence to begin with because I've changed a whole lot on that concept, the definition proper, of intelligence. I used to think it was the ability to reason, to put concepts together and to draw conclusions, which I think is the standard definition. I have learned a whole lot in the past ten years or so about the intelligence of the heart, which is another kind of mode of reasoning within the brain.

My old definition of intelligence would be the one to use and that means a very rational intelligence, a very academic kind of intelligence, and it's pretty wonderful. I was very slow in learning this but it doesn't do very much for nurturing relationships. It really doesn't. Then when I found out about this intelligence of the heart, I realized that it is the one that matters most if you are going to relate to people.

If you have a person with an average intelligence who will relate to emotions and feelings, be able to express them, communicate them, be able to want to know about other's feelings and not only their own. I think they win very big over the standard intelligence.

This question is hard to phrase but where do you think you, the real you, where do you think you are?

In my process?

Where is your awareness? For example, you probably don't feel like you are in your left foot.

I'm very much in my guts, my mind, in my imagination and I shall call it my loving heart. I wish I had learned that much longer ago than I did, but I think we all have a process in life and that is how it is meant to be.

I've become a very different person in the last five years. I would have told you that everything is happening in my mind and my brain for the longest time, but I feel very differently now. I was able to let go of a lot things that went on, expectations toward myself and toward others, that helps. It helps to take down all the barriers and look at yourself in a different place. To concentrate, to establish priorities in a different way.

People tend to answer that they are in their head or in their heart. That's the two places...

That's what they think? I think that makes a lot of sense and I've moved considerably away from the head into the heart, and it's a much more comfortable place.

Do you think you have a soul?

Yes, I do. I have an immortal soul, of course I'm coming from a very Catholic background. Further, which helps or doesn't help, I have a Bachelor of Theology. It's kind of colored my perception, but I think I'm able to distance myself now twenty years later. That concept of a soul is not gone, it's very much there. I relate to my higher power in a very different way now. My higher power is very present in my life, very strong, very positive. Nowhere near the higher power that I knew growing up a Catholic. It's a totally different being. God, the higher power, my Lord is another entity compared to what I used to know.

Actually, I'm writing a novel about a friend in a fictional [style] where I'm expanding on something that happened to her, as a young woman, which she reacted to in a very traditional, Catholic way. That's the only way that she knew. It's a very interesting process for me to analyze how she went about this. Because, if it happened to me or my daughters now, they would react differently.

That Catholic [faith] had such a stringent effect on people's lives. It would dictate their every breath. That generation, my grandmother for sure, they definitely had a rapport with a different kind of God than what I know now. A very staunch, judgmental God. I think it made for some pretty miserable lives.

So where do you think your soul is?

I don't know that it has somewhere to be. I just know that it's part of my whole definition, I don't see it sitting anywhere within me, it's just me. It's as much me as my name is me, it's not a physical concept, it's just me.

It is you.
It's me, yeah.

In some ways it's your personality?
It's my personality, it's my name, yes, it's who I am. If you had to dissect me there would be the heart, the experience, the genetics and somewhere there would be my soul. I can't tell you if mine is like everybody else's or if it is totally, absolutely identical for everyone. I just don't have the answer.

So do you see any links between the soul and the imagination?
I see a link between my faith and my imagination because I think it brings in a whole lot of light. It just sheds light on what my imagination is able to produce.

I don't know that soul connects with the imagination, I can't see it, maybe it does but I can't see it. I will call the spin-off of my soul that causes me to be a believing person in that higher power that has an impact on my creativity. It's an added quality. I would say it's mostly good, it's mostly positive. I can't say that it's not good, I can't.

If I told you to name one thing that really, really mattered, of all the things there are, what do you think is really important?
It would certainly be linked to some form of love, of giving it or learning to give it, or spreading it, be it on the planetary level or in your immediate family or even your Lord, your significant other. Yourself first. I think if you don't love yourself first and can't give anything else beyond. In other words, you can't preach what you don't have and you can't love others in a productive way, in a satisfactory way, if you don't love yourself. That's what my novel is about. If you don't do that your life is just a struggle. Is that an answer?

That's a good answer.
[I am] 58 years old, three times divorced woman, two times grandmother. I am a naturalized Jamaican, born to an Irish mother. That added up to an interesting mix, the values and how I grew up, how I perceived the world growing up. My mother was a driving force. She encouraged me to do everything that I wanted to do, and that was pretty wonderful. I tried to do the same thing with my children when their turn came. I came to the [United States] to answer a calling.

What was the calling?

The calling was my partner. We connected very strongly on the internet. We decided to trust each other and eventually visit. We're talking about 4,000 kilometers away. It was a little scary. It was like jumping off the Eiffel Tower, coming here for the first time.

My daughters were petrified. They thought they were going to find my body in a ditch or at best he's going to be a no-show at the airport and I would have to visit museums for three days and catch a flight back. Well, it didn't happen that way. I trusted my instincts, and I was right. It turned out to be extraordinary. It's still an adventure. That is my nature. I'm an adventurous person.

Someone I know thinks people divide naturally into two camps, one that are risk takers and others that aren't. You seem to have categorized yourself.

Oh, I agree wholeheartedly with that distinction.

Are there any other distinctions, like hers, that are your own, that you see people tend to follow naturally, not that you go about judging other people.

That is a very big one in my life because I've been separated from a lot of people because of this quality in me. A lot of my friends, parents and acquaintances are very much on the other side of that fence. They either think I'm a little off, crazy, or they think I'm leading a very dangerous life. Or they admire me, they envy me.

I was the first woman to have a Bachelor's of Theology at the University [I attended]. That was a big thing then, back in 1972. I was proud of it because I had broken a barrier. Before me, women were not acknowledged or accepted into the program.

I went up north to teach the Eskimos for three summers, none of my friends did that. Can you imagine? Of course I learned a whole lot more from them about their culture.

Many years later, I decided to go to Jamaica and teach—a lot of people were really scared when they saw me leave. There were some scary things happening there too.

I've noticed traveling changes people's outlooks.

I'm terribly grateful to my mom for encouraging me. When I go home, I get the feeling of safety, but I don't know if that is good for me.

When I moved to [the States] that was big. I was 50 years old. You sell everything you've got—this is my Saint Francis exercise, this is my calling—I left everything behind and I did it gladly. It was not torturing or hurting in any way. It was actually liberating.

STUDENT DISHWASHER

"Speak properly, and in as few words as you can, but always plainly;
for the end of speech is not ostentations, but to be understood."
William Penn

This interview was given by a sixteen-year-old dishwasher who was, at the time, working for his university funds. He is originally from Texas and has an interest in science, mathematics, and computers.

What are the purposes of imagination?
    Purposes for imagination...I guess for me, since I write fairly often, it's...a person with a strong imagination, in my opinion, gets a lot more out of life. They aren't really confined in a box of ideas or behaviors. They see things constantly new and fresh. That's what it is for me, and I feel that I'm fairly imaginative. It spices up your life.

Do you think that some people have more than others have?
    I think some people have more than others in terms of personalities. Some of us are just more easy going and joking and imaginative. It all comes down to personalities and also where you live. What happens in your life, that dictates it a lot too.

What do you think the origin of imagination is?
    I've never been asked that before. I've been asked if I have a big imagination, and those are easy questions. But back to your question, the origin of imagination. I don't think I can name a place or time, but it's probably developed about the time of first sentient thought. Sentient is: You're not thinking fully. You're thinking only of your food or for where you're going to live. It's the basic building blocks for humans. It's what makes us fundamentally human—that higher level of thought. That's my best guess.

That the origin came from that time while we were developing?
Yes.

Where do you think imagination is located?
I don't have the foggiest idea. I haven't studied my brain thoroughly or brains in general, so I can't really answer that question.

Do you think it would be in the brain somewhere?
Probably. I've heard about where the reasoning centers are in the brain so it seems to make sense that it would be somewhere in the brain.

Do you think animals have imagination?
It's difficult to make that decision because we first have to define what imagination is. And we also need to read the animal's minds or at least thoroughly study their behaviors over the course of time. They might or they might not.

Do you think you take imagination with you when you die?
I guess it's kind of like saying, "Will you take your brain with you when you die?" I don't really know what is in the next life or if there is one at this point in time. I can't really answer that one either.

Do you believe that you have a soul?
I do believe that we have something that sets us apart from other beings in this world, and if that's what you're asking, then yes.

There is something that makes you different than every other creature? So we might have something like a spirit and maybe the animals don't? Is that another way to say that?
Not that either. For me it's very hard because I haven't heard of a concrete example of what a soul is or a definition. I personally believe that we do [have one]. But for "why" or "where" it came from, I don't really know.

Honestly, I don't think about it that much. It's enough to get through the day.

If I asked you if you take your soul with you when you die you would say...?

I would like to. It's a very nice thing to have. But again, there is so much that we don't know about it that I'm not really sure.

You don't sound completely clear on whether you have or soul or not, so you may not know what to say to this question, but do you know where your soul is at?

Biologically? No. Physically I feel something in my heart, like whenever I really feel emotional. As far as location, it certainly provides a reaction in my heart. That's the best answer I can give.

What do you think is the most important thing?

Most important thing? Can you be any more specific?

No, because then I would lead you.

The most important thing...a very difficult answer to say. Probably, if you were talking about my life, I really value other people, so maybe it's other people. That's probably my best answer because you certainly won't get far by yourself. Without more clarification I can't answer that very well.

It sounds like the alternative is loneliness.

Yes.

Other people are important, there's no doubt.

I haven't been interviewed. It's kind of like stage fright only through a recorder. I hope I helped.

You have.

Retired Executive

"The power of imagination, a blind but indispensable function of the soul, without which we should have no knowledge whatsoever, but of which we are scarcely ever conscious."
Immanuel Kant

In this brief interview we have a sixty-year-old, happily retired business executive. He is originally from Glendale, California. He is the type of person who socializes easily with other people. His friendliness affords him many opportunities to be in conversation with people from all walks of life.

He, without hesitation, places the location of the imagination in the soul rather than in the brain. His answers conclude logically, as you will see, when he confidently states his hope that we will take imagination with us when we die.

This is an older, established man, with ample gray hair from whom we might expect more mainstream answers. I am certain you will be surprised by his answers as he proves that, just like you can't judge a book by its cover, you never know what people are truly thinking based on their outward appearance.

What are the purposes of imagination?

Of imagination? Creativity, learning how to take an idea that's somewhere in the back of your head or from an idea that will change something, and imagining a way for it to really happen. To bring [an idea] to fruition.

What do you think the origin of imagination is?

The origin. [Long pause] As a child it's one of the ways, when you're alone, of not feeling alone. You create a friend or a situation which you're comfortable with so that you can learn to cope with your aloneness with a lot of respects. It's where you develop ideas for stories and concepts and it's probably the most important aspect of keeping your youth. Because your youth is really who you are.

It's interesting. I'm sixty and I feel like a thirty-year-old in a sixty-year-old body, and there's still a part of me that's a small child, that's still dealing with events based on how I dealt with them when I was little. I may have modified them to deal with things today based on being an adult. But much of the adaptation was created in my imagination on how to do that.

Some of it was healthy and some of it wasn't, because my imagination can be destructive as well as creative. If I imagine that something can hurt me but it really can't, then I can create a fear. That fear can keep me from experiencing something I need to experience. It's really important to know that imagination is imagination and that reality is reality.

Where do you think imagination is located?

In the soul. That's the easiest answer I can think of. It comes from...I believe we are all in contact with guides. Some of them are human, some of them are people we encounter which send us in certain directions. They just have a natural ability to influence us. Other guides are instinctual and part of intuition. Part of that area of the unexplained that tells us this is good or this is bad. That is all a part of our soul.

I really believe that one of the reasons, [is that] we're given certain reasons for living, and one of those is to learn to share. I honestly believe that the people who are given the gift of life are given an opportunity to work together. Many people don't try to do that. They try to pull away from everyone and do it by themselves. The real successful people are the ones who not only can do it with others, but also can bring others into doing it with them. Sometimes that takes tremendous imagination. That has to come from someplace and that's not just something from up here [pointing at head] in the mind. It's not just something that's taught to us by our parents.

I've seen little kids who just take over a situation and lead other children, and they didn't come from parents who were leaders. That had to be something from within them and brought into their life from outside. I believe those guides are always talking to us. Some of us are more receptive than others, some would call them angels. It depends on what you want to call them. There is something beyond what we see that gives us the guidance to become who we are.

It isn't all just about day-to-day encounters. Some people live beyond the five senses, and some only live within the five senses. They don't see, hear, feel, touch or taste something that is not real, and people with imagination, those are just a few of the elements that they depend on. They go far beyond those elements and so they become multi-sensory and they're able to feel and touch a lot of things without seeing or feeling or touching them.

One of my favorite things I came up with one time was that you can hear the flowers, but you don't have to see them to hear them. A lot of times nature is talking to us and all we see is what we're seeing. We don't feel what it is really giving us. It's kind of like a spectacular sunset. It can send chills up and down the spine for some people. Other people can turn around and say, "Wasn't that nice?" There's more to it than that. Then the people with imagination see that there's more to everything than what is just available to the five senses.

What part do you think imagination plays with memory?

Well, if you're imagining something it's got to be pulled from some experience from the past. So it's a tremendous part of memory. I think the most interesting people I've ever known were the ones who could tell a story and have a room dead silent while they told the story. Not everyone can do that.

Those people can bring up stories and myths and ways of saying it that just captivates you. I remember there was a guy on television. I couldn't turn off his show. It was just a man sitting there telling a story, but the way he told it, and the words, and the feeling he put into it was unlike anybody I'd ever heard tell a story. It was just a fascinating thing to hear. Some people are able to pull up all that information from back in their memory, and they have to be able to pull it up from experience, because really, imagination is based on experience. If you haven't experienced something then you can't create an imaginary thing about that subject.

Do you think you take imagination with you when you die?

I hope so. I don't know. Either you do take imagination with you or you don't. I would imagine, I can't imagine, after death not having imagination because I believe that's how we will communicate when we are gone. It's how we will be the guides for others too. Because I believe that's what we're really trained for. That's what life is really training us is to be able to give to others, and the only way to give to others is to learn how to deal with life before you die.

Do you know where your soul is?

My soul? Yes, it's right down here in the pit of my stomach. It's where my heart is and where my emotions are. They are not intellectually a part of me, they are a part of my physical being and they are caused as a part of the process. The soul is the fire in me, in life, it's the spark. Without that spark the rest of me wouldn't work. When you take away the soul the fire goes out.

What is the most important thing?

[No hesitation] Love. It's the most important thing. Love is the only thing we really have to give each other. That's it. Loving myself is just as important. If I can't love myself how can I love others? I've had to learn to love myself, and in loving myself I've learned how important loving others is. Giving love is more important than receiving it. It's interesting. It's like how I approached work. I never gave 100 percent to a job, I always gave 110 percent. That's the same way I love. I love [others] 110 percent and it doesn't matter what I get back, because that's how I love "me" is 110 percent.

MIDWESTERN LAWYER

*"In law it is a good policy to never plead what you need not,
lest you oblige yourself to prove what you cannot."*
Abraham Lincoln

Perhaps typical of a lawyer, this thirty-year-old was brief and concise with his answers. He followed Lincoln's words above well by not going any further than what he could prove if forced. He was cautious and therefore not ensnared by answers that could not be reconciled logically.

He is from Topeka, Kansas, and he is the only one to ever bring up that he loves his imagination.

The first question is, what are the purposes of imagination?

The purposes of imagination are to...free your mind, give you hope. To put yourself in a place that you would not normally be. Kind of a way to live outside yourself. Do things, maybe that you just want to do. Think about people that you'd want to be, that's different from your life. In a way, you could use your imagination to be somebody that you wanted to be but you're not.

What do you think the origin of imagination is?

The origin of imagination. To me it's a very personal thing to each individual. I'm sure some people don't have a healthy dream world, imaginative world, so I think the origin of it is probably created by one's own experiences. Outside of the origin being the human brain, I guess. Your own experiences, your own travels, what you see, what you do, your biggest joys and most horrific times, that makes us who we are. Kind of like the nurture issue about how you are formed by your experiences.

Do you think, generally speaking, that we all have the same amount or have varying amounts?

Varying amounts, very much so. Some people have very healthy ones and some people don't. I think it depends, but I'd say varying amounts.

So you might be saying, in other words, that it could be used in a negative way?
Yeah, it's negative or positive. I think it's positive to give you a release, if you use it to be somebody that you wanted to be. If you weren't happy with your life, you could use your imagination to make yourself happier. Likewise, you can use your imagination to [pretend to] be things that are not exactly healthy for you. And if you buy into that too much and think that you can truly become someone that you are not, and it's for the wrong reasons, I think it could become deleterious to your own personal life than reality.

What do you think, in your opinion, is the location of imagination?
[Pause] Literally speaking I guess your brain. It all comes from inside. That's the physical part. But if you're talking about, if I'm understanding the question fully, [pause] I would just go back to the location of your imagination is based on your experiences and it forms from what you imagine about. What you dream about, what you strive for. I think it's nurture.

Do you think you take imagination with you when you die?
That depends on what you believe happens to you when you die.

Yes.
That's a true lawyer answer. It always starts with, "it depends."

That's what makes it your own personal...
Yeah, I know. It's subject to whether you think you are reincarnated or you're off to heaven or do you just poof to dust? It depends on whether you continue on. I think I'll continue on as some sort of being. Whether I'll have my imagination, I don't know. Maybe I'll be in a perfect state and I won't need to imagine.

Would you want to if it were up to you?
I would. I love my imagination.

I would want to as well, if it were up to me. The last question is, what do you think is the most important thing at the end of the day or at the end of a life?

It's happiness. Doing things that make you happy. Being happy with what you are or where you are or who you are with. Because that's the stuff that you'll remember. You won't remember the things that you didn't enjoy. You might remember them for perhaps that very reason, but you wouldn't have a fond memory of them.

So at the end of the day when you look back, you want to smile at what you see. You hope you did things that were worth it. That just depends on where you put stock. Some people put it in their family and their friendships. Some people put it in their career. Some people put it in how much money they have, how big their car is. It's a very "to each his own" question. It's wherever you put your worth.

I put my worth on being happy with what I do. I figure if I'm happy with what I'm doing then I'm doing something right.

VIETNAMESE BOAT PERSON

"The true meaning of religion is thus not simply morality,
but morality touched by emotion."
Matthew Arnold

This interview was conducted in a noisy, crowded restaurant. Our interviewee here is a thirty-seven-year-old pharmacist. She was very nervous, yet kind and considerate. She emigrated from Vietnam at sixteen years old.

You have lived in the United States more than half your life, right?
Right. I came here, and I start with high school, sophomore. First year I did pretty much English as a second language and then second year I catch up with whatever people are taking their junior year. That's what I did. By the time I reach my senior year I take all advance courses. I graduated from the University in 1991, from the school of Pharmacy.

You enjoyed it?
Very much, very much.

What are the purposes of imagination?
That would give the vision of what you want to accomplish in your life, if you see the whole picture of what it's supposed to be or what you want. It would give the encouragement of how to get there.

What do you think the origin of imagination is? Where did it come from?
I would say the origins of imagination is what you associate with, like who you are around, what you have seen, what you have read. It's mainly within you, what you have seen or what you want to see. So it's mainly within you, the origin comes from you, from within your mind.

Where do you think it's located?
Within you. In their own mind. It is a matter of mind.

Do some people have more than other people?
I would say more is...each person has their own way of how they think, what they imagine, it doesn't [mean that] more is better and less is meaning not good enough. It's more what it can do for that person, what good it can do for that person. That's more important than more or less.

Do you think a person could ever have way too much? Like it might cause them problems?
I would say a person, if they have too much, that could cause problems, it could possibly if they have way too much and they cannot accomplish and they look at things in a negative way, then it can be. But if they are thinking in a more positive way of how good imagination can do for their life then it's okay to have as much as they desire to have.

Again, I cannot say too much about other people, how they think or their mind would work. [If] too much would harm them or if not enough would harm them. I can speak for myself, imagination is a good thing.

What part does it play in memory? Imagination and memory, can you see any connections?
[long pause] I think it's a different part of memories.

A different part?
I would say it's different parts. I would say that we don't recall things back that we would because memory is something factual that you see and you can recall those memories back. Imagination is something that we have so vast, big pictures, you can imagine different things and those usually imagination for a short period of time then it's gone. It can be brought back but not that often, unless you're obsessed with something in your mind all the time.

Do you think you take imagination with you when you die?
No. When I die it's done. Imagination is just a way of how people are trying to escape or how they are trying to think what could possibly be better than what they have. When you die you don't need to think about that kind of a thing.

So it's no longer necessary?

No.

No need to escape any longer, do you think?

I don't think so. I believe there is no need. When you are done, then you go on with the next stage of the circle. You move on.

Do you know where you are in your body? Like the "real" you.

I haven't thought about that. Let me think about that a little bit first. The real me, who I am? When I heard that question I think between my head and my heart. So which one would I want to pick? Or can I have both?

[Laughter] You can have both if you want to.

I would say heart and head.

What do you think really matters the most?

In life? That you can serve and help other people. Helping whoever. [Crying] You do whatever you can do. I would say to be the best you can be. To help yourself and other people. Helping yourself enough that you can help other people. So that you can earn...be worthwhile while you're in this stage of life. To be willing to work, willing to help, to see other people's needs.

I'm sorry that you cried.

I'm pretty emotional, very sensitive. My family knows I can be very touchy, not touchy, but I have a good strong feeling for what we're talking about.

So it is important to you?

It is important to me. Yeah. I attract to people who are good, to people who do good things. I admire people being good. I have wonderful parents. My mom is really super mom, I feel really blessed that I have her.

Does she live here in this country?

Yeah. We came over at separate times. I came over by boat, I'm a "boat people." My mother saved money to buy our way out, she let us go on the boat that she paid gold for. My adventure was very fortunate that I was on the boat for a day and a night and I got rescued by the Germany ship. I don't have any horrible event or story. I was really well blessed and protected.

I came to Philippines for a few months. Then I got to U. S. A. My brother was here before I was here. That's how he sponsored us. After we came here we did paperwork to sponsor our parents over. We came here all working hard.

What kind of jobs did you find?

We have a Vietnamese restaurant. We do really well. We are all working really hard for it. We have a business for our family.

The need to leave Vietnam was due to violence there or oppression?

No, actually our parents did not see any future for us back home. They wanted to give us a chance to be in the best place in the whole world, you know how parents are. They say this is one of the ways to have an education and have a chance to be the best person I can be. At home you cannot really have too much options. Here you have lots of different opportunities as long as you are a hard working person and you stick with what you are doing. You can pretty much do whatever you want to do.

You must have been from South Vietnam.

Yes.

I suppose if you were from North Vietnam you wouldn't have been able to leave?

No. Interesting story is that my parents come from the North.

Oh really? They made it out and came south?

They migrated from the north to the south in 1945 or 1950 and then to here.

What about your Catholic faith? Are you Catholic now?

I've always been a Catholic, I was born a Catholic.

Were there a lot of Catholic churches there?

Oh yes. We went to Catholic Church every Sunday back in Vietnam. My mom is a very religious lady, she strongly believes in God, and she raised us to be that way. That's one reason I have a great appreciation for my mom because she is helping me, guiding me so I have a good faith. I think God is helping me a lot, giving me strength to go through with my life with my daughters and their disability.

At first I had a tough time accepting the fact of why would I, a smart, intelligent lady, have disabled kids. Why would I, with my intelligence, a good ordinary person have disabled kids, it doesn't really match with me. At first that was my perception. As time went on, with lots of prayers, I realized that I'm actually a special person, that God would give me not only one but two special kids. It gives me an opportunity, a chance, to work.

Like earlier, when I talked about serving other people, here they are here at my hands. It's an opportunity to help and serve. It's working out for good. I think it's a joy to raise them to see how they develop. To see them change from when they were just born and now they're growing and learning the skills they would need. It's a good thing to be a part of their life and for me to contribute to make a difference in their life. They're looking better and better each day.

It has the potential to change and to change for the better?

Yes. I would say so, yeah. I see the change, I experience the change. I can confer with myself that what I say is the truth, the fact, I see with my own eyes that things change.

WILDLIFE NATURALIST

"Opposites are not contradictory but complementary."
Neils Bohrfrom

"Come forth into the light of things, let nature be your teacher."
William Wordsworth

This was another beautiful setting in which to have a good conversation. I was in a National Wildlife Refuge that is over 4,000 acres. The director at this refuge is a thirty-six-year-old naturalist who spends his life among the wildlife. He has taught biological and ecologic science for fifteen years. He has a long list of educational accomplishments and duties as director and as he detailed these he said, "I spend many hours looking out the window and just observing what is out here because it's great to watch what's happening outside. Being a naturalist for so long, I like to observe wildlife and what it does." I had the same issue with the window. The quantity of wild birds was startling and it was amazingly gorgeous.

Another element that made this interview enjoyable was how much this man from Dayton, Ohio, enjoyed the interview itself. Some people are very guarded and cautious, while some people truly enjoy the process and answering the questions. He was one of the latter and that makes it fun for me as well as fun for you to read.

Another factor made this interview unique. This man is considerably steeped in science. He teaches at the college level, and yet he has left room for spiritual matters and has not followed many of his fellow scientists in disposing of a possible afterlife.

What are the purposes of imagination?
Ah...that's a tough question, the purpose of imagination, or purposes? Imagination is something that can take you wherever you want to go. There's no limit. In fact, a lot of time in educational programming

with students we try to have students use their imagination to be creative and take analyzing science to another level.

Science is not just numbers on a page and graphs. It's also the art of being able to draw an animal. I believe you should not try to stifle your imagination; you shouldn't let it run wild either. Obviously, you have to ground yourself in reality.

Imagination gives you the ability to solve problems. A lot of scientists use their imagination to be creative in problem solving. It's not just scientists. I think it's just about everybody. They have an imagination to work through problems. Imagination is a great thing.

What do you think the origin of imagination is?
That's an interesting question, too. The origin of imagination? That question is broad. I would just have to say the origin is wonder. It's difficult to define. Where does imagination come from? Obviously, I might be able to analyze the brain function and say that our brains operate in this type of fashion. There's probably an area in your brain that causes you to be able to use your imagination. It helps to figure out or create realities for yourself. That would be very complicated. I'd probably have to study a little to get all of the ins and outs.

Where does it come from? Once again it comes from an inquisitive nature, people being curious about things. People use their imagination to find their place. There are some big questions you might be asking about life, what is our purpose here? Philosophy, in some cases, can be a part of imagination, of creating a place.

Do you think that imagination is more of a by-product of natural curiosity? Perhaps a necessity to the thinking process?
I would definitely think yes. I would say imagination is a necessity. I think that the healthy mind should have imagination. Being able to create ideas and places in their mind and utilize that information. To tell you the truth, I can't imagine life without imagination. [Laugh] It would be a hard life.

It would be dull, to say the least.
It would be very dull.

I like what you said before about scientists. Formerly, I thought that many people held to the belief that scientists and imagination are opposites. The more people I talk to, the more I see that people are linking the two together. People do invent new inventions and new cures, and scientists appear to be very imaginative people. You being in the natural science branch probably see imaginative things with birds and animals.

Being able to look at any natural process and get an idea of what is happening you have to be able to study and research, but then there are all of these questions that come up. Is this bird nesting here because it likes that tree? You go through a series of steps. Imagination is creating the resources to get to the end product, to find out what behavior means.

It's being able to reach out, begin to study something, setting up different parameters. Each study is a little bit different. It depends on what you want to get out of it. Imagination is going to give you the ability to see what has been done before and then decide to do something new.

The third question is: Where do you think is the location of imagination?

Where does imagination come from? That question was asked earlier. The brain is a very complex thing. We still don't understand how it operates. I don't think we ever will. I hate to put absolutes on anything because creativity will give us the ability to go anywhere we want. Imagination, who knows? Maybe someday we'll map the entire brain.

We are learning more about it and there might be a distinct area where people are being creative. When the solution is not clear then they have to use their imagination. They might be able to pinpoint that to a certain place in the brain. Then you can actually ask if it's something outside of the brain?

You could get into spiritualism if you wanted. Is imagination connected to the spirit? You could have a huge philosophical conversation about that. Through science, I would say that the brain probably has a process. There's another side of me that says we really don't know for sure. I don't have to know where everything is especially something as cool as imagination. My answers are not straight-forward in a lot of ways because imagination is a different thing for everybody. I think it's kind of a personal thing. It's your connection with your surroundings. You can use your imagination to create your vision of self. Interesting topic by the way.

Thank you.

Trying to answer these questions, these are tough, they are personal. They have to do with how you view things. But it's cool.

It's very much a matter of opinion. It really is. It is personal and people do have very individual answers. It's like thinking out loud because they are questions you might not have been thinking of earlier in the day.

Oh yeah, I wasn't thinking about those questions earlier.

Here comes the reason I sought you out. The fourth question is, do you think animals or birds, non-human life forms, have imagination? Of course it's your opinion in case you cannot know scientifically.

Once again, it would be really hard to set up a test to find out if an animal would have imagination. They've done many experiments in the past, and in my research studying natural science I know that animals can problem solve. Humans can problem solve. How do we problem solve? We use our imagination.

So in that sense you could probably say, trying to quantify it, in science we can't really do that...unless you want to put some more solid definitions that I don't have privy to right now on what exactly imagination is. What exactly is it? Obviously, I could look it up in the dictionary that would be an interesting thing to do, I'm not exactly sure what it would say.

Years into this project and I still haven't looked it up in a dictionary.

It would be handy, you know. What's the standardized definition of imagination?

Do you have a dictionary handy?

Yeah, I do. [Reading from the *American Heritage Dictionary:*] "The power of the mind to form mental image or concept, something that is not real or present. Such power of the mind to be used creatively. The ability to confront and deal with reality by the creative power of the mind. Resourcefulness. An unrealistic idea or notion or fancy. A plan or scheme. A traditional or widely held belief or opinion."

They used the word "creative" and the word "image" which of course is in the word "imagination." Do they use the word visualization anywhere there?

I think this goes to the whole problem-solving thing. If you don't know the answer to something you have to think of what it might be, even if the solution is not in front of you. You have to be creative, visualize it in your head and then try it out to see if it works.

Do you think the animals are doing that? Other people who I talked with have had a lot of input about the common animals we have in our lives, cats and dogs. But you are living your life surrounded by animals that the average person is not spending any time with.

Actually, they are imagining in some ways. That's part of the definition. We don't know but we can theorize. I think in some cases theories are using your imagination to create what might be. If you can quantify it and prove it, that's going into a scientific realm and asking if an animal has imagination. I would have to say that in a problem-solving way they would have imagination. They have a brain; it operates, maybe on a more simple level than ours might. But imagination, in some cases, I think is a simple primal thing.

If you study natural science, one of the things that animals do, they adapt [but] how do they adapt? Some people can say it's genetic selection. Others might say it's a problem-solving thing.

Okay, there's no food here. I should leave. They'll make a choice to do that. Are they using their imagination to do that or are they forced by the food to leave? That's a tough thing. It's adapt or die in nature. If something is affecting your habitat you can change the way you live or die. That's the cycle of nature. Tough question, once again. Animals are really different. Does a worm have imagination? It's an animal. Part of me thinks, it's a worm; it doesn't really do much; it just goes through the mud.

Hmm. [Pause] Does a zooplankton have an imagination? Tiny little things swimming around in the water that you can only see with a microscope? Do skin mites have imagination?

Wow. I have a cat named Steve. Does the cat have an imagination? It would be kind of interesting to think of a cat having little dreams. You know what? I've seen animals dream. Pets, they jiggle in their sleep so I'm imagining they are having some kind of mind thing going on. Something they are remembering is making them think they are running in the woods, happy, food everywhere. But what about that worm? That's a tough one.

I was reading that someone did some studies on lizards and birds and they had documented these life forms in REM sleep. The theory then or the question became, are these lizards and birds dreaming? It appears that dogs are dreaming when they bark and move in their sleep, and that causes us humans to think that they are dreaming. Do you have to have imagination in order to dream?

I would think so. This is just me totally hypothetically thinking this, because imagination gives you the ability to visualize something that's not really there. Obviously, if you are asleep you're not really doing it. Your mind is creating it, therefore, that would be the greatest example of imagination that we can have. Dreams, because you're not doing it, your mind is just thinking. You're just lying there on the ground. All of a sudden your mind is out there in the woods.

Just think about your own dreams. Dreams are a really good way to see in somebody's imagination. I think dreams have to be total imagination. You create it, they come right out of the mind and you're not doing it. It's really cool.

Then again, I always have to look back at the little organisms. Animals—there are a lot of animals out there. Does a sea sponge dream? I don't know. It's alive. Does a bacteria dream? I don't know, but it's alive.

Does a bacteria sleep?

Does it sleep? I don't know. Does it go dormant? I think some small creatures have dormant periods. There are so many different classifications of animals.

Yes, there are. Some people have decided that it's the higher order animals, such as chimpanzees and apes because they have theorized that you would need a frontal lobe. I have seen a diagram of a cat's brain. It's small to begin with and allegedly a large portion of it is dedicated to vision. With vision you are back to imagination again, but if that's all you are doing all day is surviving and eating and you don't have a lot of frontal lobe action...that's the reason some other people have answered that the higher order animals with bigger brains would be able to imagine or at least dream, or both.

You could just stick with mammals.

Okay, let's stay with mammals and not birds or fish.

Right. Because structurally those animals are pretty different in a lot of ways. Do all mammals have imagination? I would say yes. If they have the ability, whether it's an anteater, your cat, the fox, Orca whale, a pig—those animals share a lot [of aspects]. They sleep. I would say yes they have imagination, but in science it's going to be hard to prove. It's just total opinion. For some reason I just don't think worms have imagination.

I know.

I don't think the sponge and the zooplankton, sea stars have an imagination. I think very simple order of life things, the more simplified they are, I think they just sort of exist. As you go up the hierarchy you start getting higher brain function, therefore being able to use imagination and problem-solving skills.

I think we are the prime example of it. We are beings that evolved to the point where we can really use our imagination to create buildings, cars, factories, sustainable agriculture. We can make choices; we don't have to do things. Imagination gives us the ability to be who we are. I think we are the top echelon of animals that have the ability to do this.

We are the only ones that can study the brain. Whales and dolphins might be pretty smart, but they don't have the ability to dissect the human brain or any other brain in order to study it. We are the only ones who can take apart a brain or hook electrodes up to it. Dolphins do not have that capability.

Studying sections like which part is responsible for what actions. The only way we've been able to accomplish these things is with active imagination. Wonder. It's connecting that wonder—why and how do these things work? To find out we'll have to be creative. To be creative you have to use imagination.

I think in a lot of ways, if you step down from human beings, you go to our closest relatives, monkeys and apes. I think they use imagination, but their brain is not quite as developed as ours. Therefore, I don't think they have as much imagination as we do. I would have to say people have more. Maybe that's an evolutionary trait. Perhaps at some point when we were evolving we had an adaptation that is what really brought us apart from these other species. Something developed in the brain and it gave us a better imagination. That gave us the ability to start to modify our environment and create what we have now, for better or worse.

We're very much animalistic in our behavior still. I've studied a lot of natural history and our cycles, if you look at the history of humans and what we do, we are still sort of territorial. Instead of using muscle might, we equate might with money and power. We still flex these same things back and forth. There is a hierarchy of who has and who has not. A lot of times in nature it's the same way. You'll see dominant animals go forward and the lesser ones either adapt or fall underneath some of the leads of their particular genre of animal. We still kill each other, we do all these things. We have reasoning power, we've got imagination. Has it really fixed things for us? I'm not quite sure about that. Hopefully, someday we'll be able to use our imagination in better ways to improve our quality of life.

Speaking of future uses, there is another question. Do you think you take imagination with you when you die?

I think it goes on when you die. Who you are, what you are goes on when you die. Where it goes...I don't know. I think energy is not created or destroyed. I think imagination is a part of your energy. It's a law of physics. Your energy just keeps going. Where it goes—I've got a whole lot of theories on this, but I guess I won't know until that time comes.

What is your favorite theory today?

Once again, my theory is that it just goes on. I think one of the ways your imagination, your spirit goes on is by who you were when you were alive. Who you talked to, who you influenced, making choices that people were able to see. When you die, what are people going to remember about you? I think that energy passes on. Everybody that I've talked to in my life, if they've made some sort of decision based on something that I might have said to them, then a little piece of me went with them. It keeps spreading out. We are all connected in one way or another.

Conservation of energy. Do you exist in a conscious form after you die, you yourself?

I really can't answer that. Haven't been there yet.

Haven't been dead yet? [Laugh]

Yeah, haven't been there yet. The science part of me says, I just don't know. I was raised Christian. I still believe in God, but I quantify it because there have been so many bad things done in the name of God that really upset me. Religion has been the seed of a lot...I think in many cases religion actually stifles imagination.

My imagination says that I think there is something that happens but I'm not sure what it is. I can dream about it a lot. I've got energy in my body right now, and even though my physical body might stop, I have to say that the energy of who I am probably goes on to something. Some people would say it goes on to heaven and other people would say it just gets transformed.

In a far Eastern religion you are re-born into another vessel that you carry on. I kind of blend a lot of those together. My religious beliefs go into multi-category. It's a really interesting thing too, if you want to talk about God, well, God is kind of a product of imagination, of having faith. It's being able to say, I don't know the answer to that but I'll believe it anyway. I'll believe this because it's written. Belief—your mind creates it.

I think religion can do a lot of good for people. There was a pastor back home who recently passed away, I was really sad about that. He was a really brilliant man, a good communicator. I kept going to church for his benefit because I really liked what he had to say. I haven't found somebody else that is as wise as him. What happens to you when you die? You go on, somewhere. Where, I'm not sure. It would be interesting.

I have a question about that part of you that goes on. You are calling it energy, somebody else might call it a spirit or a soul or whatever word makes people comfortable...
Synonymous, I think.

Okay, synonymous. Then do you know where that is inside of you? Do you have an awareness of where that energy thing is? Do you have a feeling of where you are inside your body?
I would probably say it's a product of...I think it surrounds you, it's the aura of it...it is you.

So it could be a little bigger than the physical body?
It could be a little bit bigger. Dealing with this type of energy, I have to use a lot of imagination to even think of what it is. It's a very

personal thing. For myself it's the energy that surrounds me. It is me. It's my everyday actions. It's my fingernail. It's my hair. It's the color of my eyes. It's not something you can touch. It's small, but it's large. I've read in different books that cover where energies in the body are kept.

Like Chakras?

Chakras and meridians. I think there's some reality in that. But I think the energy they are talking about isn't necessarily that part of the body. I think there are fulcrums on your body that center energy, but is that where the soul is? I don't know. I guess that depends on how you want to define it.

I'd have to go back to energy. It's you. It's who you are and you can't touch it. You never will be able to touch it, and you'll never be able to define it. I never say "never," but I really don't think we will be able to find it. I don't think we'll be able to say, "That's the soul, that's where it lies." If we were able to do that I think we would transcend into a whole other being or people. If we got advanced enough to say we can put our finger on the soul, then that's it. Perhaps we can. I don't know. It's interesting though.

A relative of mine did pinpoint his soul and that's why I ask.

But how could he find it?

He said he spent a lot of time on it. He knew where his soul was, and he said if any given person spent time on it, they too, could know.

What I'm thinking is that it is not a pinpointed thing. My analytical side of my brain always wants to give an exact answer like it's here in my toe, but the answer is, it is everywhere. It's your essence, it's who you are. It's wrong for me to say that I can define what somebody's path to knowing their soul is. That's a personal choice. There are probably ten billion different ways to do it, but the most important way is the way that you know. I think that being a good person is letting everyone do that for themselves and realizing that everyone is different. Being okay with that is a pretty important thing.

Coincidentally, the last question is, what is the most important thing? For example, at the end of a life, is that the most important thing? Letting people get to this stage you are talking about?

Yeah, just personally I think we spend a lot time trying to tell people how to live their lives. Being an educator and being into science, education really goes hand in hand with this. If you want somebody to really learn something, you're not going to tell them how to do it. You're going to have them find out themselves. If somebody finds out something for themselves they'll walk away with a sense of getting it. I might be able to tell you something, and you might be able to recite it, especially if you record it [points at tape recorder].

[Laugh] Or if you're somewhat intelligent or have a strong memory.
Education is giving people the tools to learn themselves. Ask those critical questions. Find out how it works and go forward. I think that is very important. When you die, hmmm, I think the most important thing...what is the question again?

What is the most important thing when you look back over your life?
Okay, the most important if you try to look back. Being yourself, knowing yourself, being kind to others. That goes hand in hand. If you're kind to yourself, and you know yourself, then you are kind to others. I think that's synonymous. But if you don't know yourself and you deny yourself truths because you are afraid of them, not good. I think a lot of people deny themselves truths because they don't want to know it. It's hard. Sometimes the truth is hurtful, and you don't want to know it so you delude yourself completely. You can live a long, nice, healthy life, but in the end you'll always be like an empty hole. Maybe that's a part of your energy or your soul. Denying yourself instead of truly living. You're not quite there.

BLIND MAN

"The best and most beautiful things in the world cannot be seen or even touched.
They must be felt with the heart."
Helen Keller

This is an exceedingly kind man who granted me a wonderful interview with a very touching conclusion. When he said, "It's easy to get caught up in the day-to-day, and we never take time for the important things," he managed to sum up my entire book in one concise sentence.

He was fifty-five years old at the time of our meeting. Originally from Idaho, he has made his vocation helping young people transition as blind students.

The first question is, what are the purposes of imagination?
Hmmm, interesting question. I think there are multiple purposes. I think that part one is entertainment. I think another is that it sparks you to creativity. If you can't imagine something new and different, then it would be pretty hard to create something new and different.

Sometimes, I look at my children and I think that children don't use their imagination enough. It's almost like it has to be literal. When I was a kid I would grab a couple of toy cars or a couple of toy airplanes and create all kinds of little events, anything from aerial dog fights to car crashes to parking a car. Nowadays it's almost like kids have to have a DVD to entertain them. I sometimes think this generation does not have the ability to create something out of nothing.

That's an interesting point and I think you're right. We would sit and make believe when we were young. I was doing that with a child a few days ago. We had a lot of fun. We didn't have a computer game with us. We just had one little toy to play with.

Do you think some people have more imagination than other people have?

Obviously. Some people have more intelligence than others. Some are stronger verbally than others. I certainly think that some people have a more inventive mind.

What do you think the origin of imagination is?

To shape our world in some way. You were talking about make believe. There is fantasy. We all to some degree or another want to shape our world the way we would like it to be, and maybe that is beyond our abilities to do in the real world around us, but we can certainly do that in our mind.

Where do you think imagination is located?

Obviously, it's in our consciousness. I suppose if you look deeper than that, it's probably in our subconscious because I'm sure we dredge up things—look at our dreams—we dredge up things that sometimes we haven't experienced in years or maybe we never have. We can dream about these things easily, so I think probably it originates in our conscious and our subconscious mind.

That's interesting. Do you think that imagination plays a part in memory?

Hmmm.

For people who can see, for instance when you walked into the room, I can still remember that. When I remember it, I see it. For me it's visually connected—meaning my memory and my imagination—because I can imagine you coming in like you did in reality, or I can imagine you coming into the room and doing a somersault. I can see that either way.

[Laugh] Not at my age.

That is what I mean when I ask if you think it correlates with memory or plays a role in memory.

I think it can. If you are looking back on memories, we can often times recover our memories and what we remember. I think we sometimes screen it through imagination or, if you will, the world we create within us.

267

For sighted people we can see a memory. Do you see a memory, or how is it that you process one?

I would think of it in the terms that I relate to—touch, sound, taste, smell. For example the primary memories I would have of you at this moment, if I think back in a while, is your handshake. The touch of your hand, your voice, those are the things I relate to. Obviously, I have no visual concept of you but I would certainly think of you in terms of those senses that I've employed in dealing with you.

Your seeing-eye dog reminds me of one of the questions, do you think animals have imagination?

I think so. I know that might be a strange concept, but I've seen her and the way she reacts to things around her. Yeah, I think they do. I don't think they can express it the way that we do. They obviously have, the closest term I can think of, wishful thinking. That's certainly a form of imagination.

True, you can tell when they want something. Some people have mentioned that they look like they are dreaming.

Oh, she does. When you watch a dog you'll see that their feet will move. Obviously, they are thinking of doing something like running down the path.

You think they have imagination?

I think they do.

Do you think that you take imagination with you when you die?

Yeah, I obviously believe that we have a soul, and I think that soul is part of our conscious—for lack of a better word. Maybe it inhabits this body we carry around. If that's the case, then yeah.

When I asked you about the location of imagination, you answered in the consciousness and that means that you will take that consciousness with you when you die?

I think so.

Even though you would leave your cranium and your brain here and it would decay.

Yeah, I think so.

Do you like the word "soul"? Does that word work for you?
Yes.

Do you happen to have any idea in the world, maybe you've never been asked this before, do you know where this soul is located?
No.

No. [Laugh] Have you spent any time wondering?
No. I guess I would say that it's literally within us somewhere. I've studied a lot of different religions over the years. I've been a member of various religions over the years. You'll hear various descriptions of what the soul is and where it is and how it works. But I haven't given it a lot of thought in terms of me or those around me.

You're fairly confident that you have one though?
Yeah.

And that it goes on after death.
Very much so.

If you wouldn't mind my directly asking, what religion is it that you are?
I'm a Lutheran.

The only other question I have is, if you had to think of just one thing that matters the most, the most important thing, what do you think that is?
I can best illustrate that with a story. I used to live in a really small town in North Idaho. There were about 1,200 people in the mountains. I spent a lot of time with the Baptist preacher for the town. We all kind of think of the Baptists as really strict, and a lot of things are a sin that a lot of us enjoy, so to speak. He came to my house when I was in my very early twenties. There wasn't a whole lot to do in a little town, so a lot of the time I would have a beer opened and I'd be smoking a cigarette. He used to drive me crazy because he wouldn't say anything. He wouldn't be critical of me.

[Laugh] And you wanted him to be?

One time I actually said to him, "I don't understand. Here you are a pastor of a very strict sect and yet you never criticize me. You never try to tell me my evil ways."

He said to never tell his congregation I said this because he would deny it, but he said, "I think that when the final day comes, whatever you think that day is going to be, you can call it judgment or whatever, I don't think they are going to sit there with a little book and tell you that on December 21, 1976, you drank three beers and smoked a pack of cigarettes."

He also said, "What I *really* think you are going to look at is this. Did you treat those around you with respect, with honor, with kindness, with generosity?"

I agree with him. I think that is the bottom line. When I walk out of this world, or however I leave it, I'd really like people to say, "I'm glad that he was my friend. When he gave his word you could count on it. He was good to people. He was generous. He was kind." I think that's the ultimate important thing. It's how we treat those around us.

The pursuit of income is such a big priority that you would think, looking at human behavior, that money is the most important thing. If you were to watch somebody for a day or a week I mean. I'm not saying you are like that.

You're right.

You wouldn't really know (if you only went by people's behaviors) that these attributes that you are talking about are something of importance. I think that the way you make people feel is really important too. You can't always control that [laugh].

You can do your best to avoid things that would hurt.

Exactly.

My daughter got married last Friday. Her husband was home from the army for one week. He flew back to Germany and then he will go on to Afghanistan. I've had kind of a rough relationship with him over the years, but this morning I hugged him and told him goodbye and jokingly told him, well not jokingly, to keep his ammo dry and his helmet on. It struck me to the point that I had tears in my eyes after he left. I've said goodbye to people in a lot of different instances over the years, whether they are going to work or I was visiting them and I'm going back home. I've never said goodbye to someone who is walking right into hell, so to speak. That is walking into harm's way on purpose. It really struck me. It really moved me. This could be the last time I hug him and tell him that I'm glad he married my daughter. It really brought home how short life can be.

That's a good perspective.

I wanted him to go away knowing we were with him and we support him and we care and that we'll pray for him. If he gets hurt and killed, I want him to remember that we cared.

Interesting that you would say that. Truthfully that is the purpose of my book. To remind people that life is finite and that there are important issues. To try to not get caught up in the hustle-bustle of day-to-day busyness. You were able to think about that deeply due to this recent event. I'm trying to remind the readers of this.

It's easy to get caught up in the day-to-day and we never take time for the important things. I know a lot of couples whose children have grown up, and now they know it would have been nice if they had taken the time for each other. My wife and I always make sure that we take time for each other despite everything, and I'm really glad that we have. There are only two of us in the house now and we are still best friends. A lot of people miss out on that.

I think it's important too for all marriages. I think it's great marriage advice to have a relationship with each other. I've raised five children, and my husband and I had date night every Friday. We never miss that. We made sure that we had something going on there, so that when the children are finally grown, we will have that relationship with each other. I agree with what you are saying...to keep in mind what people are feeling, what you can do to not hurt them, what you can do to help them and have a relationship with them.

It takes a while to get there. I certainly wasn't that way at twenty.

It comes with maturity or with a simple awareness in place of this constant forgetfulness that this life is a temporary situation. Thank you for being interviewed.

My pleasure Catherine.

CONCLUSION

Summarization

When I began this project, one of my goals was to include people from every walk of life. I expected unpredictability and I hoped to be surprised by people with typical markers for success, such as doctorate degrees, to be stumped by the simple yet difficult nature of the questions. From the opposite stance, I hoped to show that those with little education and financial success could answer with great intelligence.

Because I conducted these interviews in person, I witnessed the reactions and was able to observe the working of the mind. A few of the people interviewed were able to hide behind the use of large vocabularies, but overall everyone was surprisingly honest and sincere.

I was not surprised to find that some had conflicts in their beliefs or a lack of firm beliefs. It was clear that many had not thought previously about these topics. Many people revealed an eclectic combination of ideas gathered over a lifetime.

I knew that no two interviews would be alike, but I found it surprising how many wanted to give very correct and complex answers on brain structure, for example, as if they were taking a college examination.

You were able to see that some answered very logically with consistent and sequential answers and some did not. At first glance those who answered that imagination is located in the human brain and at the same time believe that it follows us after death appear to be illogical. Quite a high percentage answered in that manner. The zoologist, you might recall, explained how this could possibly work. When one stops to think about it, there are a lot of unanswered questions in regard to human behavior and characteristics that we clearly exhibit here and take for granted we will have at our disposal after we die. Of course, that only applies to those who believe in an afterlife.

The question about animals and whether they have imagination contained another potential to reveal inconsistencies or raise interesting subtopics. I found it intriguing when a person firmly believed that animals have imagination and at the same time believed that human imagination resides in the soul. Doesn't that bring up the topic of whether animals have souls? If so, do they take it with them when they die?

Other issues surfaced that took me by surprise. One was the quantity of people who have been influenced by Buddhism. People I would never have guessed would have any leanings in that direction quoted Buddhist teachings. I want you to know this was a surprise and I did not intentionally seek out as many Buddhists as I could find. The only Buddhist I knowingly interviewed was the monk. I did not expect the college administrator to call Jesus a "good Jewish, Buddhist mystic." There are nearly forty mentions of the word Buddha and Buddhist in this book.

Similarly, meditation is mentioned over forty times, and I was again very surprised by this. There was no prior agenda or desire to focus on topics like these. The goal was to present as diverse a spectrum of people from all over the world as I could.

When dealing with the topic of religion, it is difficult to appease everyone. I anticipate that some readers will find the book and myself to not be Christian enough. Others may find us both to be far too Christian. I proceeded with this project with the intent of learning more about the people I interviewed and to show their unique reactions. While I did not agree with many of the opinions expressed, I made an effort to contain my own beliefs for the sake of the project. I tried not to lead the train of thought, and I used empathy whenever possible to bring out the best in the person who was exposing themselves both intellectually and spiritually. I also transcribed the interviews as accurately as possible to convey their ideas rather than mine.

This, like most published books on the market, has undergone some editing. Edits were made to present the interviews in a more cohesive and readable fashion, however none of the interviews were altered for the sake of false representation. The intent in editing was to bring the actual words to you exactly as they were said. Edits do exist here in the final version, but they have been kept to a minimum in order to keep the integrity of what was spoken and not to make anyone look better or worse than they were at the time. For ease of reading there are some areas that were smoothed out and that was only done to facilitate comprehension, not to alter the meaning of what was shared.

Results of my self-interview

Because I created the questions, I thought it only right to answer them myself. I did this before I asked anyone what they thought. I wrote my first answer over twelve years ago and I will share it with you here:

What are the purposes of imagination? It is necessary to avoid insanity. For example, it can be a tool. It can be used for escapism during trauma and from the toil of a tedious work day. It can distract from chronic and acute pain, even the agony of the dentist's chair.

As a coping mechanism it can be used to entertain the mind. If I were a bored farmer sitting on a tractor for an entire day then I could use my imagination to escape. I have used my imagination on long car rides and during other tedious situations.

Imagination is also necessary to create, invent, problem solve, make decisions, empathize, paint, write, and design. It aids in memory and sometimes interferes and even substitutes for memory. I think it is wrapped up in the uniqueness of each person. It is clear that each individual imagination is unique, and what we have in common is the capacity to use it. The material point is not whether we use our imagination. It is how we each put it to work that varies greatly.

As to its location, that could be in our personality or for that matter in our soul. Our personalities impact imagination and we know it can be used in a good way or in a bad way. Obviously its potential can be directed toward aberrant fantasies and evil desires or the exact opposite.

I believe the origin is from God who appears to have an imagination when creating such strange animals like the platypus. God's imagination may be reflected in His creation of the flowers, fish, and clouds. We are created in His image, and imagination seems to be an attribute we share with God. If this is true then I think it must be both excellent and benevolent.

Imagination is used in some forms of meditation, such as guided imagery. It can be instrumental in helping people reach various levels of brain activity such as the Alpha and Theta state as proven by brainwave technology. Another way of regarding this is simply recognizing that the use of imagination can be calming and relaxing.

Imagination is used during sleep as the act of dreaming seems to prove. To some degree we seem to use it for problem solving during dreaming.

Imagination is integral with thinking itself. For example, our minds can imagine two or more outcomes. Imagination also has the negative potential to drive the mind into greater and greater states of worry. Our minds are capable of imagining events that are very unlikely to occur. One other negative use could be involved with envying others and their successes. Imagination is probably a factor in greed and discontentment.

Imagination is tied to ideas, and ideas have remarkable potential to become tangible. From ideas come events, cures for disease, even books.

Another purpose for imagination is motivation. An example of this could be a medical student who might use imagination as a motivation to continue under all of the demands of studying and testing.

I also think that if a person has too much imagination or allows it too much free reign, it could be one precipitator to insanity. On the other hand, I feel that too little use could result in a lack of creativity. Or worse yet, some might use it so sparingly that they suffer boredom.

Imagination is very obviously used by scientists and philosophers, sometimes very speculatively.

Based on this lengthy response, you might be able to see why I was inspired to ask other people these questions and I fully expected long answers with lengthy lists full of purposes. I was surprised at how brief some people were when they answered. I knew from my own answers that the questions were a springboard into many other topics.

I became very curious to know where other people thought imagination was located and where it came from. I was surprised when people struggled to answer or when they did not comprehend the question.

What did not surprise me was the variety of answers on the location because I knew this was another very open-ended question with wide potential to reveal someone's spiritual orientation.

That was one of the main objectives in addition to promoting deeper conversations, which is becoming a lost art. My opinion is that our current society too often hides from reality and meaningful pursuits through busyness, substance abuse, and various other distractions.

Personally, I believe meaningful conversations involve interesting questions. I am curious about other people. I like to find myself in conversation with someone who enjoys thinking and discussing things they think about; they are willing to "test" their thinking in discussion with someone else. I enjoy it even more when I discover that the person is a "good" thinker. That does not always mean "logical" because some brilliant thinkers seem to have random insights and sudden brainstorms. This type of conversation gives me far more insight into a person than we usually are privileged with.

Meaningful conversation itself is not as important as the main reason for the questions. I really designed these questions around the topic of imagination to use as a vehicle to get to the subject of the afterlife. I have had the strongest urge to pursue that topic since my earliest memories, and as the topic is so volatile I was happy to find a way to discuss it with the most ease possible. During my lifespan I have gone from curiosity to absolute assurance on the afterlife. I have lived nearly thirty years without any fear of death.

You also know by this point that I am fascinated by other people's thoughts on whether they have a spirit or a soul and if so, where is it? During the twelve years it took to go from idea to finished book, I changed my opinion on this question a lot. You have read some of my input on this during the interviews. At this point I am far more aware of my spirit "body" for lack of a better word. While my awareness may be in my head due to the thought process itself, my spirit is much larger than that and is not only contained above the neck. I am aware that it is in my torso, arms, and hands as well as my head.

The question about taking imagination with us when we die is both a gateway question and truly a question in itself. My personal answer before I interviewed anyone and currently is this: I hope so. I think it would be fantastic.

As to how I would answer the last question on what matters most, that can range from one sentence to a book-length dissertation.

Truth is vital. The cornerstone of my personal faith claims to be the way, the truth, and the life. I find that Jesus Christ's claim that He is the Truth draws me like no other religion or philosophy can. Promises need to be true to have any value. I have a need to place my soul in the care of an honest God, a God who does not lie and does not mislead.

Being a virtuous person, generosity, compassion, and love are important and are worth pursuing, but they are not the most important thing to me. This is what matters most: God's truth. On a personal level what matters most is my reaction to all of that truth. That very reaction is my faith and even that is a gift from God. What I have learned from contemplation, prayer, meditation and Bible study is to surrender to God. As I learn to stop resisting God, what I would share with others is this: Stop running away from the truth.

Allow me to remind you that the purpose of the book is not to foist my views on my interviewees or my readers. I may at some point write a book that further details my beliefs, but for now I am still full of questions for other people. I have curiosity about what others are thinking. At this point I might want to ask people this: "Who was the wisest person you ever knew personally?" Or I might want to delve into fate and destiny and ask this: "Is everything in your life exactly as it was meant to be? Do you have free will? Have you ever almost *not* gone some place but you changed your mind, you turned around, you went somewhere at the last minute and something or someone was there that changed your life?"

I have questions for you even now. I would want to ask each and every reader this: Of all the questions asked during the interviews, which will you think about the most later?

I would also love to follow up with the people who granted me these interviews. From the man who camps in his driveway to get away from his house to the man who thinks that alien beings are beaming imagination from faraway places, I would like an opportunity to ask them more questions and to find out even more about what they think. I do hope that one day all of my curiosity will be quenched, that all of my questions will be answered in the afterlife.

ACKNOWLEDGEMENTS

My most sincere gratitude goes to my friend who greatly inspired me through her initial enthusiasm for this project. Without her ongoing encouragement this book would not have been completed.

I also want to thank my family for allowing me the time necessary to conduct interviews and other needed work. I thank my friends who devoted themselves to reading the unabridged version of the manuscript.

I am grateful to the publisher for their confidence in this book. May all authors have the kind of support I received.

I also thank and acknowledge every person who consented to an interview. Without your time this book would not exist.

Catherine Levison's bicoastal education at over thirteen schools expanded her appreciation for different cultures and belief systems. As a proponent of self-education, Catherine continues to research and seek out inspiring conversations.

Catherine's writing career began in 1996 with a highly successful series of books on education. Her titles include, *A Literary Education, A Charlotte Mason Education,* and *More Charlotte Mason Education.* She is the contributing author in other works and a long-term newspaper columnist. Many of her articles and interviews have been published in major magazines and she has been featured on ABC's World News.

Catherine's international public speaking appearances number in the hundreds and include numerous keynote addresses. She resides with her family in the Puget Sound region of Washington.

CatherineLevison.com

Made in the USA
Charleston, SC
05 February 2015